AIRCRAFT
OF THE
U.S.A.F.
sixty years in pictures

AIRCRAFT
OF THE
U.S.A.F.
sixty years in pictures

Paul Ellis

JANE'S
LONDON · NEW YORK · SYDNEY

Copyright © Jane's Publishing Company Limited 1980

First published in the United Kingdom in 1980 by
Jane's Publishing Company Limited
238 City Road
London EC1V 2PU

ISBN 0 7106 0016 X cased
 0 7106 0022 4 limp

Published in the United States of America in 1980 by
Jane's Publishing Incorporated
730 Fifth Avenue
New York
N.Y. 10019

ISBN 0 531 03701 0 cased
 0 531 03726 6 limp

Designed by Peter Matthews

Printed in Great Britain by
Netherwood Dalton and Co. Ltd.

For Rupert

Introduction

The history of the United States Air Force spans more than seventy years, and it is as much a story of men as it is of machines. To visualise the evolution of this mighty organisation as no more than the piecemeal introduction into service of a succession of aircraft types would thus be to do less than justice both to one of the largest armed forces in the world and to the industry whose energy and ingenuity continue to feed it. However, *Aircraft of the USAF* is not intended as a history, but as a pictorial record of the Air Force's stock in trade over the past sixty years.

Armed with this definition, I have riffled through the catalogue of all the hundreds of aircraft which have carried Air Force serials over the years, picking out those which merit inclusion either for operational or technological reasons. One or two have an appeal which is somewhat harder to define, evoking as they do an earlier time when aircraft engineering still favoured human intuition over electronic data-processing.

Each of the 158 types described in this book is treated more or less in isolation, like an individual scene in a historical tapestry. It seemed logical to arrange them chronologically by date of introduction into service (or by date of first flight in the case of those aircraft which never made it into quantity production). The pattern which emerged reflects the changing fortunes and philosophies of the Air Force during the course of its life. Thus in times of severe financial stringency, as in the mid to late 1920s, procurement of new models is cut, technical development is starved of investment and seriously arrested, and aircraft already in the inventory have their service lives stretched beyond prudent limits in an effort to bridge the fiscal gap. During the boom years, however, production of existing models and the proliferation of new designs reaches unbelievable levels, as typified by the middle years of the Second World War, when the total number of aircraft in the USAF's inventory approached 80,000.

Other peaks coincide with such isolated technological breakthroughs as the introduction of cantilever monoplane wings and monocoque construction, jet propulsion and area rule, all of which resulted in a welter of new designs from manufacturers eager to convert expensive research and development into lucrative government contracts.

Most of these causes and their effects can be detected in the following pages, in the progression from the unsophisticated but highly successful Curtiss JN series of the First World War, through the austere Curtiss and Keystone fighters and bombers of the inter-war years and the burgeoning developments of such staple Second World War fighters as the P-47 Thunderbolt, to the awesomely effective McDonnell Douglas F-15 Eagle and the General Dynamics F-16.

The aircraft described in this book are all drawn from the period between the creation of the United States Air Service in 1918 and the present day, and include almost every major production model adopted by the Air Force during that time. To keep this book to an economical length, the variety of one-off Signal Corps aircraft acquired between 1907 and 1917 have not been included; neither have those Army aircraft introduced after the formation of the USAF as a separate arm in 1947. In a book of this type it is inevitable that some aircraft will have to be omitted, but in most cases these are minor types whose service life was short or otherwise unremarkable. In any case the final choice was entirely mine and I apologise in advance for any hint of prejudice which might have barred any reader's particular favourite.

Since this is primarily a book about aircraft and not a chronicle of Air Force exploits the photographs have been selected more for their clarity and visual appeal (while at the

same time attempting to depict as many variants as possible) than for drama or operational information. Likewise, the text which accompanies them is intended as a production rather than a service history. Finally, in the interests of a less cluttered text all of the data tables have been collected at the end of the book. Arranged in the same order as the main entries, they include a limited number of important subvariants whenever dimensions or performance of these models varied significantly.

Acknowledgements
The compiler of a book like this relies on a great many sources, not only for basic information but also when attempting to unravel the many anomalous and misleading threads that so often obscure a particular aircraft's history. These sources are as diverse as the subject itself and it would be impractical to list them all. I must however acknowledge my very great debt to the excellent Putnams series of books and to the annual *Jane's All The World's Aircraft,* without which my task would have been much harder. Much contemporary information was gleaned from the news pages of the monthly *Air International,* and the occasional historical nugget was mined from *Aeroplane Monthly.*

US airframe manufacturers were without exception generous and prompt with both information and photographs. Other photographs were provided by Gordon Swanborough of *Air International* and by Michael Taylor, to whom special thanks are due.

No less a debt is owed to my editor, Brendan Gallagher, and Jane's managing editor Christy Campbell, who have been instrumental in steering this series through to fruition.

PAUL ELLIS
APRIL 1980

Curtiss JN series

The immortal Curtiss JN series of tractor biplanes nicknamed the "Jennies" were evolved from two distinct prototypes, the Type J and the Type N. The J was designed for Curtiss in 1914 by Sopwith's B. D. Thomas and was flown for the first time on May 10, 1914; the N was designed by Glenn Curtiss himself. By combining the best features of each aircraft Curtiss produced the JN-1.

By far the most popular version was the JN-4D, which first appeared in June 1917. This had ailerons on both sets of wings, stick as opposed to wheel-type controls, and was powered by the relatively reliable 90 hp OX-5 engine. Some 2,765 JN-4Ds were built and the type became the principal Army trainer during the short time that the United States was involved in the First World War.

The JN-4D was followed by the -4H, modified to take the more powerful 150 hp or 180 hp Wright-built Hispano-Suiza engine. A total of 929 were built and the type was used for training in a variety of specialised roles, including bombing, gunnery and reconnaissance.

Final production model was the JN-6H, some 1,035 of which were built. These and many Hispano-engined JN-4s lasted until well after the end of the war, and the last Army Jennies were withdrawn from Air National Guard service in 1927. In all, some 8,000 Jennies were built, and the type served in Canada and Britain as well as with the US Army and Navy.

Curtiss JN-4D

Nieuport 17 of the type used by the AEF

Thomas-Morse S-4 series

The first of the Thomas S-4 series was designed by B. Douglas Thomas (no relation to the founding Thomas brothers) in late 1916 and flew for the first time in June 1917. Originally conceived as a fighter, the Gnome-engined S-4 did not meet the combat requirements of the US Army, which showed more interest in European designs such as the SPADs and Nieuports.

At the end of January 1917 the Thomas brothers had merged with the Morse Chain Works of Ithaca, New York, to form the Thomas-Morse Aircraft Corporation, the resulting company having more capacity for aircraft production.

Following America's entry into the First World War in April the S-4 was re-evaluated and the Army Signal Corps ordered 100 S-4Bs with shortened fuselages for advanced training. It was generally liked, having pleasant handling characteristics and a sound structure suitable for vigorous aerobatics by student pilots, but the 100 hp Gnome Monosoupape rotary engine had a number of shortcomings, including a tendency to leak oil. Thus when the Army ordered 400 improved S-4Cs in January 1918 it was decided to use the 80 hp Le Rhône rotary, although the first 50 S-4Cs were completed with the Gnome engine installed. Armament was

a single 0.30 in Marlin machine gun mounted in front of the cockpit on the starboard side and synchronised to fire through the propeller arc. In training the machine gun was often replaced by a camera gun.

Further orders for the S-4C were placed in 1918: 150 in August and 500 in October. But with the signing of the Armistice in November the latter order was immediately cancelled and only 97 of the August order were delivered.

Thomas-Morse designed a further variant, the tapered-wing S-4E, but this went no further than the prototype stage.

Nieuport 17

The Nieuport 17 was one of the most famous fighter aircraft of the First World War, and deservedly so. A development of Gustav Delage's diminutive Nieuport 11 *(Bébé),* it was less fragile than the earlier sesquiplanes and combined outstanding manoeuvrability with a respectable top speed and rate of climb..

The type made its debut on the Western Front in early May 1916 with the French 57th *Escadrille* and, together with the contemporary British D.H.2, set about putting an end to the so-called "Fokker scourge". Nieuport 17s were later to equip units of both the British Royal Flying Corps and Royal Naval Air Service as well as the air forces of the Netherlands, Belgium, Russia, Italy and the United States.

The American Expeditionary Force (AEF) bought some 76 Nieuport 17s from France in 1917 for use as fighter trainers, but even before the USA entered the war in April 1917 American pilots had been flying the earlier Nieuport 11 in combat with the Lafayette *Escadrille.* AEF Nieuport 17s were later supplemented by large numbers of two-seat Ni 21s, and by Ni 23s, 24s and 27s. All were used as trainers by the AEF, which bought a grand total of 870 from the French.

Thomas-Morse S-4E

SPAD VII and XIII

In 1910 financier Armand Deperdussin teamed up with engineer Louis Bêchéreau to form the Société pour les Appareils Deperdussin (SPAD) and to manufacture a remarkable series of Gordon Bennett Trophy racing aircraft. In 1913 Deperdussin was arrested for fraud and the company, starved of financial backing, was bought for almost nothing by cross-Channel pioneer Louis Blériot and renamed Société Anonyme pour l'Aviation et ses Derivées, thus retaining the acronym SPAD.

Bêchéreau was kept on as chief designer (as was chief carpenter André Herbemont) and was responsible for designing the immortal SPAD fighters of the First World War. After a false start with the well intentioned but absurd SPAD A.4, with its gunner's nacelle perched in front of the propeller, the company produced (via the SPAD V) the SPAD VII, a conventional wood-and-fabric tractor biplane which first flew in April 1916. Powered by Marc Birkigt's superlative Hispano-Suiza engine, the early SPADs were formidable in performance and began replacing the diminutive Nieuport 11 in front-line service from September of that year.

AEF squadrons began to equip with the VII from December 1917 and a total of 189 of the French-built fighters were eventually acquired. Because of the imminent appearance of the improved SPAD XIII, few VIIs of the United States Air Service (as the Airplane Division of the Signal Corps was known from mid-1918) were used as fighters, the majority being employed on training duties.

The SPAD XIII, armed with twin Vickers machine guns located above the 220 hp Hispano-Suiza 8Be, was a direct development of the single-gun VII and first flew in prototype form in April 1917. It was one of the designs selected by the Bolling Commission for mass production in the US, but orders for several thousand to be manufactured by Curtiss were cancelled and all of the 893 acquired by the AEF were purchased from France.

SPAD VII at Seattle, March 1919

The type was popular with American pilots and was used with great success by such aces as Rickenbacker and Luke. In all, 15 of the AEF's 16 pursuit squadrons were equipped with XIIIs (13th, 17th, 22nd, 27th, 28th, 49th, 93rd, 94th, 95th, 103rd, 139th, 141st, 147th, 185th and 213th Aero Squadrons) and some 328 were in USAS service in France at the time of the Armistice. After the war about 435 were shipped to the United States and many were re-engined with the less troublesome ungeared Wright-Hispano engine.

Eddie Rickenbacker with SPAD XIII

Standard E-1

The Standard Aircraft
Corporation of Elizabeth, New
Jersey, was responsible for the
construction under licence of an
assortment of aircraft during the
latter part of the First World War,
including D.H.4s, Caproni and
Handley Page bombers and a
quantity of Standard-designed
two-seat SJ trainers. The E-1,
designed in 1917 by Charles E.
Day, was a single-seat home
defence fighter which originally
carried the designation
"M-Defense".

No two published histories of
this attractive little
rotary-engined aircraft agree on
the initial quantity ordered, but
two prototypes of the fighter
were certainly delivered for
evaluation during January 1918.
It was soon found that the 100 hp
Gnome 9-B was insufficiently
powerful for a fighter and
subsequent aircraft,
redesignated E-1, were
delivered as advanced trainers.

After some 93 E-1s had been
delivered it was found that the
American-built Gnome engines
were unacceptably troublesome
and the final batch of 75 aircraft
were re-engined with the 80 hp
Le Rhône, built by the Union
Switch and Signal Company.

After the war Sperry
converted three E-1s into
radio-controlled flying bombs
by lengthening the fuselage and
making other modifications.
This programme was covered
by a contract for the similar
conversion of a number of
Sperry Messengers under the
designation MAT (Messenger
Aerial Torpedo).

Nieuport 28 of the AEF

Nieuport 24 in highly individual personal markings

Nieuport 28

The Nieuport 28 was markedly different in appearance from Gustav Delage's earlier V-strut sesquiplanes in that it featured equal-span wings and a new, streamlined fuselage of circular cross-section. It was not as good a fighting machine as it looked, however, being rather underpowered and structurally weak.

Because of these shortcomings the type was not adopted in quantity by the French, although it had entered series production, and the American Expeditionary Force (AEF) was able to buy 297 aircraft "off the shelf" for the pursuit squadrons arriving in France in the early months of 1918. The two-gun Nieuport 28

was thus the first AEF fighter to see combat, and the first enemy Albatros fell to the type on April 14, 1918.

First units to be equipped were the 94th and 95th Pursuit Squadrons, joined later by the 27th, 103rd and 147th. Leading AEF pilots who flew the type included Lt Douglas Campbell, America's first "ace" (ace status

was awarded to pilots with five or more victories), top-scoring Capt Eddie Rickenbacker, and Raoul Lufbery and Quentin Roosevelt, both of whom were killed in the 28.

At the end of the war a number of 28s were taken back to the US, where some were transferred to the United States Navy for shipboard use.

de Havilland DH-4
"Liberty Plane"

The DH-4 made an outstanding contribution to Allied air power during the First World War, and so adaptable was the airframe that versions continued in service with the US armed forces until as late as 1929.

The first British-built airframe arrived at McCook Field, Dayton, in August 1917 and flew for the first time on October 29 powered by the American 400 hp Liberty engine. Although it proved less potent than the Army had hoped, the type was nevertheless put into quantity production. By the time of the Armistice in November 1918 more than 3,400 had been built, 1,213 of which were shipped to France, and by the end of the year three plants —Standard Aircraft, Dayton-Wright and the Fisher Body Division of General Motors—had turned out a grand total of 4,846 "Liberty Planes". During the war the type equipped five bombing and seven observations squadrons of the AEF and first flew operationally on August 2, 1918.

Armament was two forward-firing Vickers or Marlin machine guns mounted on the nose, two Lewis guns in the rear cockpit and up to 220 lb of bombs on underwing racks. Placement of the fuel tank between the pilot and observer helped to generate a popular myth in the US that the DH-4 was a "flying coffin," following reports of a number of fiery descents, although the loss rate

was in fact no worse than those of other two-seaters.

The aircraft initially had many operational shortcomings caused by design deficiencies. Several of these were rectified in the DH-4B, which featured relocated undercarriage and a revised cockpit arrangement, with the pilot behind the fuel tank and closer to the observer, as in the D.H.9. Powerplant was a 416 hp Liberty 12A engine. Tests in October 1918 revealed the aircraft to be a success and the Army arranged for up to 1,500 DH-4s in the US to be converted to the new standard.

A large number of sub-variants — including ambulance versions, trainers and photographic survey aircraft — were built in the early post-war years.

The first major update of the type, after the DH-4B, was the 1923 DH-4M (for Modified), which had a steel-tube fuselage and new equipment. Boeing obtained an Army contract to build 150 of the new aircraft, 53 of which were designated DH-4M and the remainder DH-4M-1; the difference in designation related to the proportion of original DH-4B incorporated in the rebuild.

In 1924 Atlantic Aircraft was awarded a production contract for a further 135 aircraft designated DH-4M-2.

de Havilland DH-4B refuelling aircraft from Rockwell Field, 1924

Breguet 14A

Packard-Le Pere LUSAC-11

Breguet 14

The big two-seat Breguet 14 first appeared early in 1917, the prototype (designated Breguet AV) having flown for the first time at Villacoublay on November 21, 1916, just six months after Louis Breguet's assistant designer, Vuillierme, had begun work on the project. By 1926, when production finally ended, no fewer than 8,370 had been built by a total of eight manufacturers, some 5,500 of them during the war. The type's remarkable longevity was due in part to the basic soundness of the design but also to the many technical and material innovations in its structure, including the extensive use of the new light alloy Duralumin.

Two basic versions of this substantial biplane were developed: the Br.14A.2 for reconnaissance, 508 of which were ordered in early 1917, and the Br.14B.2 bomber, 2,000 of which had been ordered by the end of the year. Both versions were externally similar, although the bomber had lower wings of greater span and transparent panels in the observer's section.

The French *Aviation Militaire* took to the Breguet with enthusiasm and within a year of its introduction some 93 units were equipped with the type, 71 of them on the Western Front and the remainder in Greece, Serbia, Macedonia and Morocco.

Having no combat aircraft of their own when they entered the war, the Americans adopted the Breguet 14 for two of their light bomber squadrons, 47 aircraft having been supplied by France in March 1918. Together with the Salmson 2A.2, the Breguet 14 was the AEF's main two-seater until the arrival of the DH-4 in August 1918.

Packard-Le Pere LUSAC-11

This handsome two-bay biplane was designed in 1918 for the US Army Engineering Division by Captain G. Le Pere, a member of the French aviation mission to the United States during the First World War. Of the several American two-seat fighters developed in 1918, it was the only one to go into series production. It was also the only American-designed and manufactured model other than the US Navy's Curtiss flying boats to reach France before the Armistice, although it did not see combat.

The LUSAC-11 was designed around the 400 hp Liberty engine and was built by the Packard Motor Car Co, the prototype flying for the first time in September 1918. Orders totalled about 4,500 but only 27 were completed: two prototypes and 25 production examples. The LUSAC-11 (for Le Pere **US A**rmy **C**ombat) would have been a useful combat aircraft, displaying strength, speed and manoeuvrability. Armament was two fixed Marlin machine guns in the nose and two Lewis guns mounted on Scarff rings in the rear cockpit.

Never used in combat, the type achieved some measure of fame for the series of high-altitude flights from McCook Field by Capt Rudolph Schroeder and later by Lt John Macready which culminated in an absolute height record of 34,508 ft on September 18, 1921.

Three examples of the 420 hp Bugatti 16-powered LUSAC-21 were built, but they were inferior in performance to the LUSAC-11 and were not proceeded with. Neither were other variations on the LUSAC theme, such as the LUSAGH-11 and -21.

Sopwith A.2 and B.1
1½-Strutter

The Sopwith 1½-Strutter, the first true tractor-engined two-seat fighter to see operational service during the First World War, was designed and built for the Admiralty in 1915. The name 1½-Strutter—derived from the then unusual arrangement of wing struts—was one of those unofficial appellations which through frequent use eventually become a type's official designation.

French interest in the type started early in its career and the 1½-Strutter was flying under French colours by the summer of 1916. The French used a different designation system for their aircraft, reconnaissance variants becoming the 1A.2 and the bombers 1B.1. Production in France, totalling some 4,500 units, was almost three times the British output, and it was to France that the desperately underequipped American Expeditionary Force turned in the early months of 1918 for its training and combat aircraft. Between February and May the AEF bought from the French Government a total of 514 1½-Strutters, consisting of 384 two-seat 1A.2s and 130 single-seat 1B.1s. Most of these were used for training, although the 88th, 90th and 99th Aero Squadrons used the type operationally for a short time during 1918.

Martin MB-2

20

Martin MB-1 and MB-2

Glenn Martin re-established his own aviation company, Glenn Martin Co of Cleveland, Ohio, in late 1917 after a short spell as the Wright-Martin Company. In January 1918 he was awarded a contract to build ten examples of a bomber that would outperform the Handley Page O/400, which was being built under licence in the US by the Standard Aircraft Corporation of Elizabeth, New Jersey.

Powered by two Liberty engines, the prototype MB-1 (also known as the GMB, for Glenn Martin Bomber) flew for the first time just six months later, on August 17, 1918. It carried a crew of three or four and was equipped with three gun stations: in the nose, aft of the pilot's cockpit and under the fuselage.

Four of the first machines were completed as observation aircraft, four as bombers, one for long-range flights and one as a passenger transport. This last aircraft had accommodation for twelve passengers and was designated T-1.

The MB-1 did not enter squadron service, but in June 1920 the Army issued a specification for an improved version, the MB-2. A direct development of the MB-1, it incorporated essentially the same fuselage mated to larger, foldable wings, more powerful engines and revised landing gear. Bomb load was also increased, from 1,040lb to 1,790lb.

The Army ordered 20 MB-2s in

1920, five under the original designation and 15 as the NBS-1 (Night Bomber, Short-Range) under the new Army designation system. Further production contracts for the type went to other companies in the industry: Lowe, Willard and Fowler (LWF) built 35, Curtiss 50 and Aeromarine the final 25.

First deliveries went to General Billy Mitchell's 1st Provisional Air Brigade at Langley Field, Virginia, which used the bomber in the controversial experimental attacks on the "unsinkable" ex-German battleship *Ostfriesland* in July 1921. MB-2s and NBS-1s formed the bulk of the Air Service's bomber force until the arrival of the Keystones during the mid-1920s.

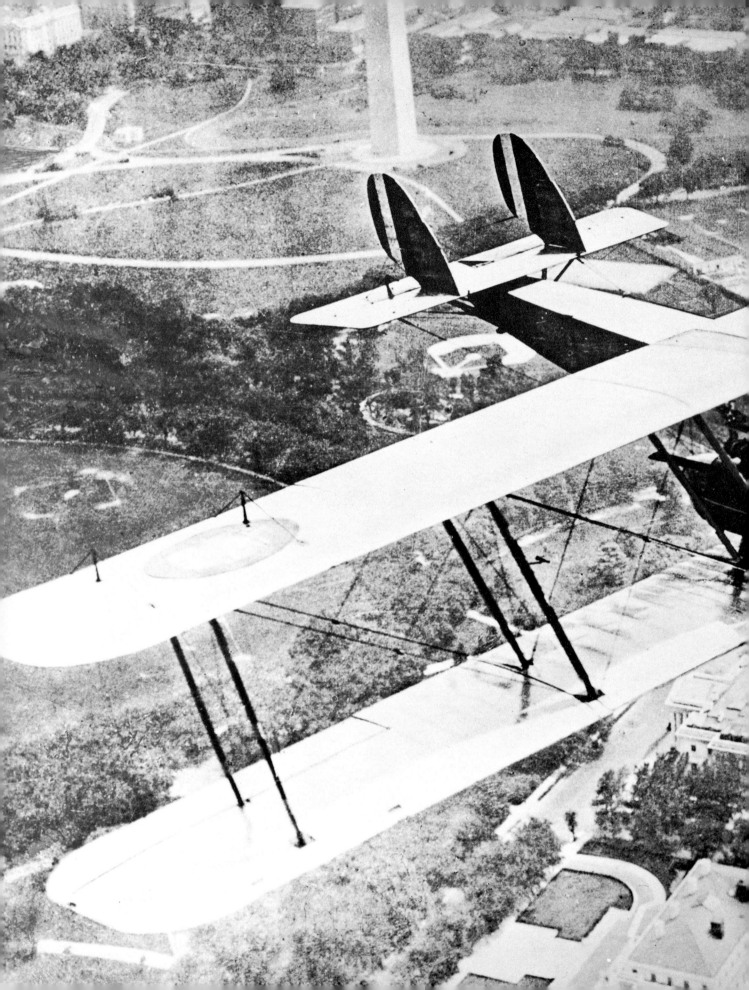

Martin MB-1

Orenco/Curtiss D

A cumbersome and ill-informed bureaucracy at home was largely responsible for robbing the United States of the chance to bring to Europe a fighter or bomber of indigenous design and manufacture during the First World War, forcing the AEF to equip itself mostly with French and British combat aircraft.

First of the post-war American fighters was the Orenco Model D. Four all-wood prototypes were built by the Ordnance Engineering Corporation (Orenco) to an Army Engineering Division specification centred on the 300 hp Hispano-Suiza H engine. The first was completed in January 1919. The production contract was put up for industry-wide bidding, as was the procedure at that time, and Curtiss was awarded an Army order for 50 machines, the first of which was delivered in August 1921. The Curtiss-built aircraft were heavier than the prototypes and performance suffered as a result. Powerplant was the 330 hp Wright-built Hispano H and the aircraft was armed with one 0.30in and one 0.50in machine gun.

Little information on the type's operational history survives, but it was not a success and was largely overshadowed by the contemporary Thomas-Morse MB-3A.

Orenco/Curtiss D

Production MB-3A

Thomas-Morse MB-3

In the spring of 1918 the Thomas-Morse Aviation Corporation was invited by the US Army to develop a single-seat fighter around the licence-produced 300 hp Wright-Hispano H engine. Heart of the requirement was a performance superior to that of the SPAD fighters then in use with front-line squadrons of the AEF, and the resulting MB-3 showed SPAD influence in its lines and general robustness.

Development was unusually protracted and the first of four prototypes did not fly until February 21, 1919. Thomas-Morse was contracted to build a further 50 production aircraft even though the war in Europe had ended by then, but a further bulk order for 200 improved MB-3As was won by Boeing with a bid of $1,448,000. This order, placed in February 1922, was the largest by the US Army since the end of the war and was instrumental in establishing Boeing as a major force in fighter production.

The MB-3A differed from the MB-3 mainly in the revised engine cooling system and the addition of several small structural refinements; the final 50 aircraft delivered also had a changed tail profile. It was to be the standard single-seat pursuit in the early 1920s until superseded by the Curtiss Hawk and the Boeing PW-9. As MB-3As were retired from fighter duties they were redesignated MB-3M and transferred to training units at Kelley Field, Texas, where they served until 1928.

Billy Mitchell's special Thomas-Morse MB-3A

Consolidated PT-1

Consolidated PT-1, PT-3 and PT-11

The long line of Consolidated primary trainers originated in the side-by-side Dayton-Wright TW-3, a simple aircraft powered by a 180 hp Wright E engine. After the absorption of Dayton-Wright into the Consolidated Aircraft Corporation of Buffalo, New York, in 1923 the type was delivered as the Consolidated TW-3.

The PT-1 was a refined TW-3 with tandem seating and revised tail surfaces. A total of 171 of these unsophisticated trainers were built, followed by 130 production PT-3s. The PT-3 was the production version of the 220 hp Wright R-790-powered XPT-3. Further detailed improvements resulted in the PT-3A, of which 120 were built.

A parallel development of the PT-3 trainer series was the O-17, a reconnaissance type which incorporated minimal improvements to fit it for its operational role, such as wheel brakes, oleo shock-absorbers and increased fuel capacity. Some 29 O-17s were built, mostly for the National Guard.

The PT-11 was a further refinement of the PT-3A with a more streamlined shape. The four service-test YPT-11s were powered by the 165 hp Continental R-545-1 radial engine, the last in the series later being fitted with a Curtiss R-600 and re-designated PT-11A; this was subsequently changed to PT-11C when the type was fitted with a 220 hp Lycoming YR-680-1 radial. The production variant was the PT-11D with the Lycoming engine.

The ten PT-12s built were virtually identical to the PT-11 except for their 300 hp Pratt & Whitney engines.

Consolidated PT-3A

Barling NBL-1

Barling NBL-1

After the First World War the Army looked at a number of designs to supplement the Martin bombers that were entering service in the early 1920s. Amongst these projects was the giant six-engined Barling XNBL-1 triplane, two prototypes of which were ordered in June 1920. Intended as a night bomber, the NBL-1 was to take up to 5,000lb of bombs internally and carry a crew of six. Four of the six Liberty engines were arranged as tractors and the remaining two as pushers.

Designed by Walter Barling, designer of the British Tarrant Tabor bomber, the XNBL-1 was built by Witteman-Lewis of Teterboro, New Jersey, and first flew on August 22, 1923. Marginally less ill-conceived than the Tabor, Barling's behemoth was however no more successful. Although General Billy Mitchell is quoted as having said that it was "entirely successful from an experimental standpoint", it was elsewhere described as "Mitchell's Folly".

Because of multiplying costs the original contract was cut back to one aircraft. Little flying was done after the first flight and the $350,000 monster was scrapped in 1928.

27

Curtiss PW-8

In the early 1920s the name Curtiss began increasingly to be associated with high-speed aircraft. The mating of an exceptionally clean airframe with the developing 420 hp D-12 engine led to an outright win for the Curtiss R-6 in the 1922 Pulitzer race, in which it was flown by Army Lt Russell L. Maughan at an average speed of more than 205 mph. Curtiss aircraft also took the next three places in that race.

When Curtiss began development of a single-seat fighter based on the R-6 racer an enthusiastic Air Service showed interest even before the prototype was complete. The first XPW-8 was flown in January 1923 and, together with two others, was sold to the Army in April that year.

The second prototype, more streamlined and heavier, became the production version and 25 PW-8s were built, all featuring the novel if vulnerable wing-skin radiator first tried out on the racers. The PW-8 and the Boeing PW-9 were the mainstay of Air Corps pursuit squadrons in the mid-1920s until superseded by the P-1 Hawk.

PW-8s lined up for the John L. Mitchell Trophy race at the 1924 National Air Races

Loening OA-1A

Loening OA-1

Grover Loening's Liberty-engined Army amphibians were among the most distinctive aircraft of the 1920s. The unique feature of their design was the central float faired into the deep fuselage. First of the line was the XCOA-1, the first prototype of which was tested in July 1924. This was followed by a second prototype and then by nine service-test COA-1s. Three of the COA-1s were later turned over to the US Navy.

The "C" was dropped from the designation of the 15 production aircraft, which became simply OA-1As. Five were used on an extensive goodwill flight around South America which left San Antonio, Texas, on December 21, 1926. Named after American cities—*New York, San Antonio, San Francisco, Detroit* and *St Louis*—the aircraft covered

more than 22,000 miles, visiting Mexico, Central and South America and the West Indies. Sadly, two of the Loenings—*Detroit* and *New York*—were involved in a fatal accident in Buenos Aires.

The OA-1As were followed into service by nine OA-1Bs with minor refinements, and by 10 OA-1Cs with new vertical tails which remained standard for all subsequent Loening amphibians of that class. The eight OA-2s built in 1929 were fitted with the 480 hp Wright V-1460-1 in place of the 400 hp Liberty.

Douglas DWC and O-5

When in 1923 the Army Air Service decided to attempt a round-the-world flight it chose an aircraft based on the Navy's DT-2 (Douglas Torpedo). The Army aircraft was a two-seater with the imposing name of Douglas World Cruiser (DWC), and the prototype was delivered just 45 days after the order was placed in July. Four more production aircraft were delivered in March 1924. These all had the same airframe and Liberty engine of the prototype but fuel capacity was increased to 500 gallons (373 gallons in the seaplane version).

Named *Seattle, Chicago,* *Boston* and *New Orleans,* the four World Cruisers set off from Seattle on April 6, 1924, on their record-breaking attempt. Only two completed the 27,500-mile flight, however, *Seattle* having crashed in Alaska and *Boston* ditching in the North Atlantic.

Five other DWCs were ordered after the flight; they were designated DOS (Douglas Observation Seaplane), changed to O-5 under the new system adopted in May 1924. They were substantially the same as the earlier aircraft but carried standard military equipment and a reduced fuel capacity of 110 gallons.

Douglas DWC *Chicago*

Douglas Observation Biplanes

The Douglas observation biplanes were one of the longest-running series of the inter-war years, starting with the O-2 of 1924 and finishing in 1936 with the last of the O-38s. Some of the last O-38Es were still in service at the time of the Japanese attack on Pearl Harbor in December 1941.

Two XO-2s were built in response to an Air Service contract for the design and development of an observation aircraft to replace the ageing DH-4B and DH-4M, one powered by a 420 hp Liberty V-1650-1 and the second by a 510 hp Packard 1A-1500.

The Liberty-engined version was completed in the autumn of 1924 and test-flown by Eric Springer before delivery to McCook Field for evaluation. A contract for 75 aircraft was awarded in February 1925. The Packard-powered XO-2 was not adopted, losing to the Curtiss XO-1 in the competition.

The O-2 was the first production version, 45 of which were built. They were followed by 18 O-2As, identical to the O-2 but for the inclusion of night-flying equipment. The O-2B (six built) was an unarmed training version with dual controls, while the O-2C was an improved O-2A with revised armament and a new nose with the radiator mounted above instead of below the propeller shaft. Of 46 built, 19 went to the Air Corps and the other 27 were delivered to the Militia Bureau for use by National Guard units.

The next major production variant was the O-2H, 71 of which were built. This was virtually a new design, with revised fuselage construction, new tail surfaces, streamlined undercarriage and staggered wings. Last of the O-2 variants was the O-2K, an improved version of the late-production O-2H. Some 37 were built for the Air Corps and 20 for the National Guard.

Three O-7s were built under the original 1925 contract; all had O-2 airframes but were powered by direct-drive 510 hp Packard 1A-1500 engines. They were later converted to O-2 standard.

Following the O-8, O-9, XO-14 (one built of each) and O-22 (two built) came the production O-25A, powered by the 600 hp

Douglas O-38S

Curtiss V-1570-27 Conqueror engine. A total of 50 were built for the Air Corps, followed by 30 O-25Cs with minor changes to the engine cooling system. The O-25C was the last Douglas Observation Biplane to be fitted with a liquid-cooled engine.

First of the production radial-engined aircraft was the O-32A, powered by a 450 hp Pratt & Whitney R-1340-3; a total of 30 were built for the Air Corps. The O-32 was succeeded by the last of the Douglas Observation biplanes, the O-38 series. This

line of Pratt & Whitney-engined aircraft comprised 45 O-38s for the National Guard, one unarmed O-38A for the National Guard, 30 O-38Bs for the Air Corps and a further 33 for the ANG, 37 O-38Es and eight National Guard O-39Fs.

Boeing PW-9

Spurred on by its success in bidding for the Thomas-Morse MB-3A contract, Boeing pressed ahead with a private-venture single-seat fighter, the Model 15. First flown by Frank Tyndall on April 29, 1923, and powered by the 435 hp Curtiss D-12, it was evaluated at McCook Field, Ohio, by the Army, which at that time had already approved the competing private-venture Curtiss XPW-8 for series production. Although it was similar in many ways to the Curtiss fighter, the Army bought the prototype Boeing aircraft and two additional machines in September 1923, assigning them the designation XPW-9 (the PW stood for Pursuit, Water-cooled).

Following comparative tests a production order for 12 PW-9s was placed in September 1924; this was increased to 30 aircraft in December of that year. Deliveries to the Army began in October 1925, a follow-on contract for 25 PW-9As being placed at the same time.

In 1926 Boeing received contracts for a total of 39 PW-9Cs, and a final contract in August 1927 covered a further 16 PW-9Ds, the last of which was delivered in May 1928. Differences in this model included a redesigned radiator, revised cowling contours and a new rudder profile incorporating aerodynamic balancing. All production PW-9s were powered by the 440 hp Curtiss V-1150. Although later versions of the fighter suffered from reduced performance as a result of steadily increasing weight, the Boeing aircraft were still regarded as marginally more manoeuvrable than their Curtiss counterparts.

The PW-9 structure owed a great deal to the German Fokker D.VII of the First World War, having a welded steel-tube fuselage and double box spars for each wing; the centre-section struts were also almost identical to those of the D.VII. Armament was a pair of 0.30in machine guns and a Single 0.50in machine gun.

Boeing PW-9, November 1925

Curtiss Hawk series

Sturdy, reliable and quite fast for their day, the first generation of Curtiss Hawks were the dominant Army fighter types for nearly ten years before finally being ousted by the Boeing P-26 monoplane.

The P-1 was a direct development of the single-seat PW-8, and in fact the tapered-wing XPW-8B was essentially the prototype P-1. Powerplant was the liquid-cooled 435 hp Curtiss V-1150-1.

Although the type was criticised as being little improvement on Boeing's PW-9, 15 production aircraft were ordered in March 1925. The first P-1s were delivered to the Engineering Division at McCook Field in August and reports show that the aircraft was found to be more manoeuvrable than the PW-8 and required less servicing. Some changes were recommended, however, including new wheels with larger tyres and a longer radiator.

On September 9, 1925, the Army ordered a further production batch of 25 similar P-1As, with a 3in-longer fuselage, changed cowling lines and additional equipment. They were delivered during the following year. In August 1926 the Army ordered 25 P-1Bs incorporating the Curtiss V-1150-3, wheels of larger diameter and more equipment changes. Deliveries to the Air Corps began in late October.

The P-1C, 33 of which were ordered in October 1928, was an improved P-1B with wheel brakes. Weight was increasing with each successive variant, however, and performance was falling off as a result.

The P-2 designation was given to five P-1s ordered under the original contract but fitted with the 505 hp Curtiss V-1400. The first was also equipped with an experimental turbo-supercharger; three others were later reconverted to P-1A standard, while the fifth became the XP-6 racer powered by a 600 hp V-1570-1.

Following delivery of the

Curtiss P-1C on skis

Curtiss P-1D

P-1Cs in April 1929, the Army set about acquiring a further 71 Hawks by converting two batches of Curtiss AT-4 and AT-5 advanced trainers. By 1937 the Army had taken delivery of 35 AT-4s powered by the 180 hp Wright V-720, five AT-5s with 220 hp Wright R-790 radials, and 31 similar AT-5As. All were re-engined with the 435 hp Curtiss V-1150-3 and redesignated P-1D, P-1E and P-1F respectively.

Two radial-engined Hawk fighter variants were built: a single P-3 powered by a 410 hp Pratt & Whitney R-1340-9, and the R-1340-3-powered P-3A, five of which were built.

The P-5 "Superhawk" was generally similar to the P-1C but was powered by a turbo-supercharged Curtiss V-1150-4. Five were ordered by the Air Corps in May 1927, the first being delivered in January 1928.

Most famous of the biplane Hawks were probably the P-6 series. The XP-6 was a P-2 with 600 hp V-1570-1 engine, while the XP-6A was a complete hybrid with a P-1A fuselage, XPW-8A wings with wing radiators, and a high-compression Curtiss Conqueror engine. Built specially for the 1927 National Air Races, the XP-6A and XP-6 took first and second places at 201 mph and 189 mph respectively.

Impressed by their performance, the Army ordered a batch of service-test YP-6s in October 1928; the nine aircraft were delivered between October 1929 and December 1930. Nine P-6As ordered at the same time had V-1570-23 engines cooled by ethylene glycol. During 1932 the surviving P-6s and P-6As were converted to P-6D standard by the installation of turbo-superchargers and three-bladed propellers.

Major production version was the P-6E, 46 of which were ordered in July 1931 at a unit cost of $12,211. Delivery was all but complete by the end of 1932. Powered by the Curtiss V-1570-23, this the sleekest of the biplane Hawks had a top speed of almost 200 mph.

Radial-engined Curtiss P-3A

Curtiss O-1E, March 1931

Curtiss O-1 and A-3 Falcon

Winner of the US Army's 1925 competition for Packard-engined observation aircraft was the Curtiss XO-1, which had lost to the Liberty-engined Douglas XO-2 in the previous year's competition. Ironically, however, the specified Packard A-1500 engine was not a success and the ten production O-1s, ordered in 1925, were powered by the 435 hp Curtiss V-1150. This became standard on all O-1s apart from the single O-1A

conversion, which had a 420 hp Liberty V-1650-3.

During 1927 a total of 25 O-1Bs were built; four of these aircraft were later converted to O-1C VIP transports. There was no O-1D, but 37 O-1Es with refinements to the engine cowling profile and the control surfaces were built. This variant was followed by the one-off O-1F and YO-1G, both modified O-1Es. Production of the next variant, the O-1G, totalled 30.

First of the production

Liberty-engined Falcons was the O-11, some 66 of which were built from 1927. Several one-off variants with different powerplants were evolved from the basic O-11. Final production Falcon was the O-39, a V-1570-engined variant similar to the O-1G; ten were built during 1932.

The A-3 attack version of the O-1B was initially thought of as an interim aircraft when the first production contract was awarded in February 1927. A

total of 76 A-3s were ultimately built, however; they were armed with a 0.30in machine gun in each lower wing, supplementing two nose-mounted 0.30in guns. A pair of flexible Lewis guns were installed in the rear cockpit.

Five A-3As were built as dual-control trainers, while the 78 A-3Bs incorporated the improvements applied to the O-1E. First tested in April 1930, the A-3B had a unit cost of about $11,200.

Curtiss A-3

Huff-Daland LB-1

Though the single-engined Huff-Daland LB-1 was not a particularly successful aircraft, the twin-engined Keystone bombers which were developed from it were extremely valuable. In fact they dominated the US Army's bomber force for the best part of a decade, from the mid-1920s to the mid-1930s.

The XLB-1 was an uncomplicated three-seat bomber powered by a single 800 hp Packard 1A-2540 engine. It was designed to carry its 1,500lb bomb load at 114 mph for nearly 1,000 miles, almost 300 miles more than the Martin NBS-1. The prototype flew for the first time in the summer of 1925 and was followed by ten

production machines, which were delivered during the latter part of 1926. These aircraft were powered by the improved 787 hp Packard 2A.2540.

By the time that deliveries of the production aircraft had begun, however, the Army had decided to discontinue further development of single-engined bombers and Huff-Daland had abandoned its prototype XHB-1 four-man bomber. Meanwhile, the company was beginning development of a twin-engined series, and a move to Bristol, Pennsylvania, from Ogdensburg, New York, resulted in the revitalised company changing its name to Keystone.

Huff-Daland LB-1

Keystone Bombers

The failure of the single-engined Huff-Daland LB-1 and XHB-1 designs led an Army Board to declare in April 1926 that single-engined aircraft were unsatisfactory for bombing. As a result, attention was directed towards development of a series of twin-engined aircraft. This configuration was preferred for its greater safety and the fact that it left the nose vacant for a gunner or bomb-aimer. First project was the XLB-3, virtually a twin-engined LB-1 with two inverted Liberty engines.

The prototype XLB-5 flew in late 1926, and an Army evaluation resulted in an order for 10 production LB-5s. Powered by war-surplus Liberty engines, these triple-finned aircraft were succeeded by 25 twin-tailed LB-5As during 1928.

Next came the XLB-6, powered by two 525 hp Wright R-1750 radials. There followed orders for 16 LB-6s and 18 LB-7s powered by Pratt & Whitney R-1690-3 Hornets, all delivered during 1929.

A flurry of Keystone LB designations, from the LB-8 to the LB-14, then amounted to some 79 aircraft. All were basically the same airframe fitted with different engines. An element of confusion was introduced into the designation system during 1929, however, when the 63 LB-10As were completed as single-rudder B-3As, while the seven LB-13s became service-test Y1B-4s and Y1B-6s and the three LB-14s were completed as Y1B-5s.

The last production Keystone bombers were delivered during 1931 and 1932, by which time they were already obsolescent. Deliveries comprised 25 Hornet-powered B-4As (converted from B-3As) and 39 B-6As powered by two 575 hp Wright R-1820-1s.

Keystone B-3A

Keystone B-6A

Thomas-Morse O-19

The Thomas-Morse O-19 was an all-metal observation biplane carrying a crew of two in tandem open cockpits. Built by the Thomas-Morse Aircraft Corporation of Ithaca, New York, it was a development of the private-venture XO-6B. The XO-6B was a one-off design based on the Douglas O-2 observation biplane, which Thomas-Morse had built under licence under the designation O-6. This explains the strong family resemblance between the sturdy O-19 and the earlier Douglas aircraft.

Between 1928 and 1931 the US Army ordered 180 O-19s and variants. The initial order was for four aircraft: one XO-19, a Wasp-engined O-19 and two other identical airframes for use as engine testbeds. Three other service-test aircraft were subsequently ordered: an O-19 and an O-19A, both with Pratt & Whitney Wasps, and an O-23 with the water-cooled Curtiss Conqueror.

Production orders covered 70 O-19Bs, which had new cockpits with more modern gun mounts, and 71 O-19Cs with minor refinements and a Townend ring around the engine. Final production variant was the O-19E, of which 30 were built.

Boeing P-12D

Thomas-Morse O-19B

Ira Eaker with Boeing P-12, February 1929

Boeing P-12 series

Boeing's P-12 series of Army fighters originated in mid-1928 with the Model 83 and Model 89 private-venture biplanes powered by the 450 hp Pratt & Whitney R-1340C Wasp. First flown on June 25 and August 7, 1928, respectively, both prototypes were tested by the US Navy, which later bought the aircraft as F4B-1s.

Enthusiastic Navy reports led the Army to evaluate the Model 89 at Bolling Field, and in November 1928 nine P-12s and one XP-12A were ordered. The first P-12 flew for the first time at Seattle on April 11, 1929, and differed from the Navy F4B-1s only in lacking the arrester hook and other naval equipment. Power was provided by a 450 hp Pratt & Whitney R-1340-7, and armament was a pair of 0.30in machine guns. The XP-12A, with Frise ailerons and 525 hp R-1340-9 engine beneath a long-chord NACA cowl, was destroyed on May 18, 1929, in a mid-air collision.

First major production version was the P-12B, some 90 of which were ordered in June 1929. This variant had no cowling ring but retained the Frise ailerons of the XP-12A; a short-chord cowl was added later. Deliveries to squadrons began in the first part of 1930 and in June that year Boeing received a follow-on order for 131 improved P-12Bs, designated P-12C and powered by the R-1340-9. The last 35 aircraft of this order were delivered as P-12Ds and were powered by the 525 hp R-1340-17.

The P-12E, first flown on September 29, 1930, as the private-venture Model 218, introduced a number of new features to the design, including a redesigned monocoque fuselage with pilot's headrest and a larger, rounded fin and rudder. The Army ordered 135 P-12Es in March 1931, the first production aircraft flying on October 15. The first 110 of these were similar to the Model 218 and were powered by the R-1340-17. The final 25, powered by the 600 hp R-1340-19 and offering significantly improved performance, were redesignated P-12F. The first examples of this version were delivered to the Air Corps in March 1932.

Boeing P-12F

Formation of Boeing P-12Fs

Curtiss B-2 Condor

Curtiss B-2 Condor

Curtiss broke into bomber design and manufacture through its 1920 contract to build 50 Martin MB-2 (NBS-1) bombers for the Air Corps. The prototype XB-2 shared many of the Martin bomber's features, differing principally in having a steel-tube fuselage in place of the Martin's wooden structure and in being powered by two 600 hp Curtiss GV-1570 Conquerors instead of Liberties.

First flown in September 1927, the XB-2 had a useful performance: a bomb load of 4,000lb at a maximum speed of 130 mph. The most unusual feature of the aircraft was the location of the gunners in the rear of the engine nacelles, each gunner being provided with two Lewis guns, with two more guns mounted in the nose.

The XB-2 crashed and was destroyed on December 8, 1927, though this did not influence the Army board which met in February 1928 to decide on a new bomber for production. Of the five contenders, Keystone's XB-1B, the Atlantic-Fokker XLB-2 and the Sikorsky S-37B were dismissed, but the board was split between the Keystone XLB-6 and the Curtiss XB-2. Although the Curtiss had significantly better performance than the XLB-6, critics complained of its high cost and inability to fit existing hangars. Keystone won on a four-to-three majority and was awarded the important production contract. In June, however, Curtiss was awarded a consolation prize of a $1.05 million contract to build 12 B-2s, which were delivered between May 1929 and January 1930.

The B-2 served initially with the 96th Bomb Squadron at Langley Field before being assigned to the West Coast for service with the 11th BS from March and Rockwell Fields. The Condor was progressively withdrawn during the 1930s, the last flight being completed in May 1936.

Berliner-Joyce P-16/PB-1

The Army held a design competition for two-seat fighters in April 1929, some four years after the last aircraft of that species had been built for the Air Corps. Boeing, Curtiss and Berliner-Joyce each submitted proposals, and in June Berliner-Joyce was declared the winner and awarded a prototype contract for the XP-16, the first military aircraft to be designed by that company.

This gull-winged biplane had tandem open cockpits and was powered by a supercharged 600 hp Curtiss V-1570-25 Conqueror. Armament included two forward-firing machine guns, a flexible 0.30in rear gun and up to 244lb of bombs.

The prototype was completed in October 1929 and, following trials, 25 service-test Y1P-16s were ordered in March 1931. Testing of the P-16, later changed to PB-1 (for Pursuit, Biplace), started in 1932. Production aircraft differed from the prototype in having three-bladed propellers and unsupercharged engines.

The type was attached to the 1st Pursuit Group at Selfridge Field, Michigan, equipping the 94th Pursuit Squadron, while a number served with the 27th Pursuit Squadron during 1932 and 1933. The PB-1 suffered from a number of defects, including inferior manoeuvrability, poor visibility and a tendency to nose over on landing, and was withdrawn from Air Corps service at the end of January 1934.

Berliner-Joyce PB-1 in wargames camouflage

Douglas O-31 series

The Douglas XO-31, the company's first monoplane, first appeared in 1930. An all-metal two-seater with distinctive gull wings, it was powered by the ubiquitous Curtiss V-1570 Conqueror.

Five service-test Y1O-31As were ordered in 1931. Later designated O-31A, they were quite different from the prototype, incorporating revised wing and tail profiles. The fuselage structure was also changed, from wrap-around corrugated duralumin sheet to a built-up semi-monocoque of flat sheets. Powerplant was a 675 hp Curtiss GIV-1570-FM engine and armament consisted of one fixed and one flexible 0.30in Browning machine gun.

The five Y1O-31Cs built differed from the -A only in their single-strut undercarriage. Later fitted with revised tail surfaces and parasol wings, the type became the O-43A, of which 24 production examples were built.

Last production variant was the O-46A, some 90 of which were ordered during 1935. Powered by the 725 hp twin-row Pratt & Whitney R-1535-7, it had a cockpit faired into the rear fuselage top decking, in the manner of the O-31A.

Douglas YO-31A, December 1931

Douglas XO-46

Curtiss A-8

Seeking an improvement in performance over that of its old Curtiss A-3s, the Army turned to the monoplane for its new generation of attack aircraft for the 1930s. Prototypes were built by the Atlantic-Fokker Company and by Curtiss. Both the Fokker XA-7 and the Curtiss XA-8 were powered by the Curtiss V-1570 Conqueror in-line liquid-cooled engine and both were armed with four forward-firing 0.30in Browning machine guns, with a fifth Browning for the rear gunner. Up to 488lb of bombs could be carried.

The two-seat XA-8 was ordered in 1930 and first flew the following year. After comparative tests of the two contenders the Curtiss design was judged superior and a production contract for five YA-8 and eight Y1A-8 service-test aircraft was awarded on September 29. Service trials with the 3rd Attack Group began in June 1932 and a production order for 46 A-8Bs was placed in February 1933.

By this time, however, the Army had reviewed its policy on the choice between liquid-cooled in-lines and radial air-cooled powerplants and had decided that the cheaper and less vulnerable radial should be adopted for its attack aircraft, even though some performance was sacrificed. Thus the YA-10 of 1933 was a YA-8 with a 625 hp Pratt & Whitney R-1690-9. By the time that the 46 production aircraft began tests in March 1934 they too had undergone a change in designation and engine, becoming A-12s powered by the 670 hp Pratt & Whitney R-1820-21. Other changes affected the crew accommodation: the two cockpits were closer together, with the pilot's open and the gunner's semi-enclosed beneath a canopy.

47

Boeing B-9

Boeing YB-9

Boeing B-9

In the late 1920s and early 1930s Boeing began to benefit significantly from the stagnation in design and development being suffered by Keystone, hitherto one of the largest suppliers of bomber aircraft to the Air Corps.

As early as April 1931, when the private-venture Boeing XB-901 first flew, Boeing had incorporated into its design such advanced features as retractable landing gear and all-metal construction—and in a monoplane, too. Power was provided by two 575 hp Pratt & Whitney R-1860-13 engines, and the crew of four—pilot, navigator/bombardier and two gunners— were accommodated in separate open cockpits along the fuselage.

After the first flight the XB-901 was delivered to Wright Field for evaluation by the Air Corps. The trials were extremely successful and in August the Army bought the prototype and six service-test aircraft for a total of more than $730,000. Re-engined with supercharged R-1860-11 engines, the prototype was re-designated YB-9, while the other five service-test aircraft, similarly powered, were designated Y1B-9A. The second prototype, designated Y1B-9, was originally powered by two Curtiss V-1570-29 in-line engines, but tests revealed inferior performance and R-1860s were later substituted.

The B-9 was essentially an interim design and did not enter quantity production, even though its performance was markedly superior to that of the contemporary Keystones. Top speed was 188 mph and bomb load some 2,260lb, but even these impressive figures were to be eclipsed within a few months by the new monoplane bombers taking shape at the Glenn Martin works at Cleveland, Ohio.

Douglas Y1C-21, December 1931

Douglas C-21 series

The Douglas Dolphin was a good-looking twin-engined commercial amphibian that first appeared in 1931. The new eight-seat aircraft attracted immediate interest from the armed forces in the United States, which needed a larger-capacity amphibian to supplement the two-seat Loenings that had been in service since 1924.

The Army ordered ten of the metal-hulled aircraft in 1932: eight as seven-seat Y1C-21s powered by two 350 hp Wright R-975-3 Whirlwind engines, and two eight-seat Y1C-26s with 300 hp Pratt & Whitney Wasp Juniors. Additional orders were later placed for eight C-26As and six C-26Bs. Two of the C-26Bs were subsequently re-engined and re-designated C-29.

A further change in designation took place in 1933 and 1934 when the C-21s and C-26s were converted to OA-3 and OA-4 observation types. Similarly, the C-26A and C-26B became the OA-4A and -4B respectively. In 1936 a number of the amphibians had their wood-skinned wings replaced by new units built of stainless steel, and all were redesignated OA-4C.

Boeing P-26A, 1939

Boeing P-26

Boeing's compact P-26 (Model 248) was both the Army's first monoplane fighter and its first fighter to feature all-metal construction.

The design of the Private-Venture Model 248 was evolved during 1931, and a contract was signed for construction of three Boeing-financed prototypes in December that year. First flight of the prototype was made on March 20, 1932, and from the start both handling and performance were well up to expectations, with a top speed of more than 230 mph at 6,000ft. During early tests the two flight prototypes were designated XP-936 (the third airframe was retained for static tests). The results were so good that the Army bought all three aircraft, designating them XP-26 (later progressing through YP-26 to P-26, although none was ever issued to an operational unit).

A production contract for 111 (later increased to 136) slightly revised P-26As was signed in January 1933 and deliveries began in January 1934, continuing until late June. The P-26—often called the "Peashooter" by its pilots—remained front-line equipment from 1934 until replaced by the Seversky P-35 and Curtiss P-36A between 1938 and 1940. The type operated with Air Corps pursuit squadrons in the US, Hawaii and the Panama Canal Zone, equipping the 1st, 16th, 17th, 18th, 20th, 32nd and 37th Pursuit Groups. Although the P-26 was considered a "hot ship" because of its high landing speed, the more experienced pilots appreciated its manoeuvrability and speed.

During 1934 Boeing received an order for an additional 25 aircraft, two of which were delivered as P-26Bs with SR-1340-33 fuel-injection engines while the other 23, with the standard engine, were designated P-26C.

Formation of Boeing P-26Es

Martin B-10 series

The deep-bellied Martin monoplane bombers of the 1930s were developed from the private-venture Model 123 (XB-907), which first appeared at Wright Field in July 1932. Powered by a pair of 600 hp Wright SR-1829-E Cyclones, it had a top speed of 197 mph. After tests it was substantially rebuilt and emerged that October as the XB-10, complete with larger wings and the first rotating transparent nose gun turret to be fitted to an American bomber. The 675 hp R-1829-19 had replaced the original powerplant and top speed had increased to 207 mph.

On January 17, 1933, the Army ordered 48 B-10s at a unit cost of $50,840. At that time the B-10 was faster than any fighter in Army service and Glenn Martin was awarded the 1932

Collier Trophy for the machine. The first 14 aircraft were delivered as YB-10s with 675 hp R-1820-25s, seven YB-12s had 775 hp Pratt & Whitney R-1690-11 Hornets, and 25 were delivered as B-12As. Two experimental aircraft were included in the original order: a YB-10A with turbo-supercharged R-1820-31s and the XB-14 with 950 hp YR-1830-9 Twin Wasps.

Tests of the first aircraft began in June 1934, and main production deliveries took place in 1935-36, when the Army received 103 B-10s. The type remained in service with Air Corps bomber squadrons until it was progressively replaced by the B-17 and B-18 in the late 1930s. The Martin's creditable performance also led to a total of 189 being sold abroad.

Martin B-10B of the 28th Bombardment Squadron

Martin B-10B used for target towing, 1941

Martin YB-12A on floats

Northrop A-17 Nomad

Northrop's big radial-engined A-17 attack aircraft originated in the military versions of the Gamma and Delta commercial monoplanes. Completed as a private venture in August 1933, the prototype Model 2-C was bought by the Army the following June and designated XA-13. Successful trials resulted in a $2 million order for 110 production aircraft. The powerplant selected for the production aircraft was the 950 hp Pratt & Whitney R-1830-9, an example of which was installed in the prototype in March 1935, leading to a change in designation to XA-16.

Results with the XA-16 were disappointing, however, and Northrop informed the Army that the aircraft was overpowered and that either a larger vertical tail or a smaller engine would be needed. Since the type was already in production the Army opted for a smaller engine, the 750 hp R-1535-11. The Army received its first A-17 in August 1935 and the type equipped attack units such as the 3rd and 17th Attack Groups during 1936.

In December 1935 the Army ordered the retractable-undercarriage A-17A, powered by a 825 hp Pratt & Whitney R-1535-13. Total orders for the A-17A reached 129 and all were completed between August 1936 and September 1938. In June 1940 93 were returned to Douglas to be resold to Britain and France for training and emergency use. Of these, 32 were detained at the French colony of Martinique, while the remainder were reassigned to South Africa after a brief stay in Britain.

Northrop A-17

Formation of A-17s

Consolidated A-11

Consolidated P-30/PB-2

The all-metal, low-wing Consolidated P-30 was the only two-seat monoplane fighter to become operational with the Air Corps between the two world wars.

This aircraft was derived from the wood-skinned XP-900 designed by Lockheed, at that time a subsidiary of the ill-fated Detroit Aircraft combine. Powered by a 600 hp Curtiss V-1570-23 Conqueror, the prototype and four further examples were bought by the Air Corps in September 1931 and designated YP-24 and

Y1P-24 respectively. Four Y1A-9 attack versions were later added to the contract.

The YP-24 crashed at Wright Field in October 1931 and shortly afterwards Detroit Aircraft was forced to retire from aviation. The P-24's designer, Robert Wood, joined Consolidated in Buffalo and was able to resurrect the design, this time with all-metal construction. Two prototypes of the new aircraft were ordered, one as the turbocharged Y1P-25 and the second as an attack version, the XA-11, without turbocharger.

Tests of the Y1P-25 began towards the end of 1932 but the machine crashed in the following January. The Army Board had however been so impressed by the results obtained that it ordered a further four aircraft powered by the supercharged 675 hp Curtiss V-1710-57 engine. Designated P-30, they were delivered to Wright Field for trials in mid-1934. During these tests Army pilots complained that the rear gunner became virtually useless during all but the gentlest manoeuvres.

Nevertheless, 50 production P-30As were ordered in December 1934 at a total cost of $1,996,700.

The P-30A was the first Consolidated aircraft to be built at San Diego. Powered by the 700 hp V-1710-61, the type was redesignated PB-2A shortly after delivery; the P-30 became the PB-2.

The A-11 attack aircraft development was not followed up, although four YA-11 service-test aircraft were bought by the Army.

North American BT-9A

North American BT-9 and AT-6

The private-venture North American NA-16 first appeared in 1935. After evaluation by the Army at Wright Field it was adopted late that year as a basic trainer with the designation BT-9. Awarded a contract for 42 aircraft, the company took new production facilities at Inglewood, California, where the first BT-9 flew in April 1936, powered by a 400 hp Wright R-975-7 Whirlwind radial.

The 40 BT-9As built were fitted with a fixed forward-firing machine gun and recording camera and a flexible gun in the rear cockpit. In 1937 North American announced the substantially similar BT-9B. A total of 117 of this version were built, followed by 67 BT-9Cs for the Organised Reserve.

In 1938 North American began a redesign of the BT-9, changing the tail assembly and producing a new metal-covered fuselage. This new aircraft became the BT-14, powered by a 450 hp Pratt & Whitney R-985-25. Some 251 were built from 1940, and 27 of these were later converted to BT-14A standard with the 400 hp R-985-11 engine.

The AT-6 Texan was a descendant of the original NA-16, by way of the BC-1A and the retractable-undercarriage NA-26. Powered by a 600 hp Pratt & Whitney R-1340, the BC-1 won a 1937 Air Corps design competition for a new "Basic Combat" trainer, resulting in a contract for 41 aircraft. Further contracts increased the total of BC-1s ordered to 180. The 92 BC-1As featured only slight aerodynamic changes.

In 1940 the BC-1 underwent a change in designation to AT-6, indicating a change to the advanced trainer role. Production of this aircraft was prodigious, with more than 15,000 being built by North American alone between 1938 and 1945. Licence production accounted for as many as a further 5,000 during this aircraft's long life.

During the Second World War the Texan became the standard advanced trainer for all Air Force pilots. After the war more than 2,000 remained in service with the USAAF, being redesignated T-6A, T-6C, T-6D and T-6F, according to configuration, when the designation system was once again changed in June 1948.

During the Korean War a number of T-6Fs were used by the 6147th Tactical Air Control Squadron on "Mosquito" missions, carrying UN army observers low over the enemy's lines. These aircraft were later replaced by specially equipped LT-6Gs.

North American AT-6G

59

Douglas C-39, May 1939

Republic (Seversky) P-35

The Republic P-35 single-seat fighter was derived from a private-venture experimental fighter, the two-seat SEV-2XP, which was later rebuilt as a single-seater after an accident and redesignated SEV-1XP. Designed by Alexander Kartveli, it was built by the Seversky Aircraft Corporation for the US Army's 1935 pursuit fighter competition. Powered by an 850 hp Wright R-1820-G5 engine, the SEV-1XP managed to produce a top speed of only 289 mph against the manufacturer's guarantee of 300 mph.

Nevertheless, a limited production contract for 77 aircraft, described by Seversky as the AP-1 (Army Pursuit), was placed in May 1937, with deliveries beginning in July that year. Designated P-35 by the Army, production aircraft were powered by the 1,050 hp Pratt & Whitney R-1830-45.

In October 1940 the US Government requisitioned 60 aircraft under construction for export to Sweden and designated EP-106. Powered by the 1,050 hp Pratt & Whitney R-1830-45, they were designated P-35A by the Air Corps. By the end of 1941 some 48 had been shipped to the Philippines, where they were serving with Air Corps fighter units at the time of the Japanese attack. Most were destroyed on the ground and only eight remained airworthy after two days' fighting. The balance of the P-35As were eventually delivered to Ecuador.

Douglas C-32 series

The C-32 transport was a military variant of the commercial Douglas DC-2, which first flew in April 1934. The XC-32, ordered in 1936, differed from the commercial aircraft in minor equipment details and was powered by two 750 hp Wright R-1820-25s.

The C-32 was followed into service by 18 C-33s, military cargo versions of the DC-2 with enlarged vertical tail surfaces, reinforced cabin floor and a large cargo-loading door on the port side. Normal load was either 2,400lb of cargo or 12 passengers. In service with Army transport squadrons from 1936, they were joined in 1939 by the first of 35 C-39s. This hybrid aircraft combined the C-33's fuselage and wings with the DC-3's centre section, tail assembly and undercarriage. Power was provided by a pair of 975 hp Wright R-1820-55s.

The last of the series to be delivered to the Army were 24 commercial DC-2s impressed for military service during 1942. Designated C-32A, they were generally similar to the sole C-32.

Other minor variants were the YC-34, two of which were bought with Fiscal Year 1936 funds; the C-38, which served as aerodynamic prototype for the C-39; and the C-41 and C-42, single examples of which were built as staff transports.

Seversky P-35

Stearman PT-13A

Stearman PT-13 and PT-17

In 1934 the Stearman Division of United Aircraft became a wholly owned subsidiary of the Boeing Aircraft Company at Wichita, Kansas, and in the same year the company produced the private-venture X75 training biplane, which entered production for the Air Corps as the PT-13 in 1936. Some 26, powered by the 215 hp

Lycoming R-680-5, were ordered, followed in 1937 by 92 PT-13As with 220 hp R-680-7s.

The PT-13 was a perfect primary trainer for service pilots, with its big, slow-revving radial engine, robust structure and sturdy undercarriage. Further production contracts quickly followed, and between

1939 and 1941 the Army ordered 225 PT-13Bs fitted with the 280 hp R-680-11. In 1942 the type was adopted as a primary trainer by both the Army and Navy, and a further 318 PT-13Ds were bought by the Army.

More numerous than even the PT-13 was the Continental-engined PT-17

Kaydet, the name adopted for the Canadian PT-27 but used indiscriminately for all aircraft in the series. In all, nearly 3,000 were acquired by the Army during the war. So tough was the type that about 2,000 survived to be converted post-war as cropspraying aircraft, and many are still airworthy today.

Stearman PT-17

North American O-47A

North American O-47

The solid North American O-47 was a two-seat observation monoplane powered by a single 975 hp Wright R-1820-49 engine. The design originated in 1934 with General Aviation, a successor to the American Fokker Aircraft Corporation (also known as Atlantic Aircraft), and was the standard Army observation aircraft from 1937 until the American entry into the Second World War.

The prototype XO-47 was built at the General Aviation plant at Dundalk, Maryland, while the 164 production O-47As were built during 1937 at the new North American facility at Inglewood, California. A further 74 O-74Bs powered by the 1,060 hp Wright R-1820-57 were delivered during 1939.

Although the O-47 was not used operationally during the war, the examples that survived the Japanese attacks in the Pacific in December 1941 and early 1942 were used as trainers and for such utility tasks as target towing.

Douglas B-18 and B-23

During the early 1930s the Army began to cast around for a new bomber to replace the Martin B-10, and in 1934 issued a specification for a multi-engined type with double the range and payload. Three companies submitted proposals: Boeing put forward the four-engined Type 299 (later designated XB-17), Martin an enlarged B-10, the twin-engined Type 146, and Douglas the snub-nosed DB-1 (Douglas Bomber).

The DB-1 bore a definite family resemblance to the contemporary DC-2 transport, having similar wings, tail and powerplant. Preliminary flight trials were held at Wright Field in August 1935, followed in January 1936 by production contracts for 13 Boeing YB-17s and 123 B-18s, as the Douglas aircraft was by then designated. Production B-18s were similar to the prototype DB-1, though equipment changes raised the gross weight by some 1,000lb. The last production B-18, with a power-operated nose turret and designated DB-2, was delivered in October 1937.

In June 1937 the Army ordered 177 B-18As from Douglas at a cost of more than $65,800 each. The first was delivered in April 1938 and was equipped with a modified bomb-aimer's nose position. By June of that year orders for a further 40 B-18As had been received, bringing the total to 217.

By 1940 the B-18 and B-18A equipped most Air Corps bomber squadrons and were still in front-line service when the US entered the Second World War in December 1941. In 1942, when the B-17 had superseded the B-18 in front-line bomber squadrons, 122 were fitted with radar noses and Magnetic Airborne Detector (MAD) gear and used for anti-submarine patrols in the Caribbean as B-18Bs.

The Douglas B-23 was a development of the B-18A with a slimmer fuselage and more powerful engines. The first B-23 flew for the first time on July 27, 1939, and a single production order for 38 was placed, with deliveries taking place between February and September 1940. The type was used briefly for patrols of the US Pacific coast before being relegated to training duties.

Douglas B-18A, August 1940

Douglas B-23, September 1940

Boeing XB-15

Boeing XB-15

As early as 1933 the Army Air Corps at Wright Field had been studying the problem of producing a bomber capable of reinforcing Hawaii, Panama or Alaska without refuelling. This called for a 5,000-mile range and a payload of at least 2,000lb. In May 1934 the Air Corps opened negotiations with Boeing and Martin, both of which tendered for the Army's "Project A".

On June 28, 1934, Boeing was awarded a contract for design data, wind-tunnel tests and a mock-up of its proposed XBLR-1 (Model 294). A contract for a prototype was awarded a year later, in July 1935, and first flight of the huge aircraft, now designated XB-15, was carried out on October 15, 1937, by Eddie Allen.

In its time the largest aircraft ever built in the US, the XB-15 had a wing span of 149ft and had a gross weight of 70,700lb, but its four 1,000 hp Pratt & Whitney R-1830-11s left it greatly underpowered.

Only the prototype was built and in 1943 this was converted to the XC-105 transport, with gross weight increased to 92,000lb.

Boeing B-17 Flying Fortress

The B-17 Flying Fortresses of the US Army Air Force's British-based 8th Air Force formed the main strategic daylight bombing force used against occupied Europe during the Second World War. Tough and heavily armed, the Fortress enjoyed a measure of affection from its crews out of all proportion to its performance and effectiveness as a fighting aircraft.

Work on a four-engined bomber to meet Army requirements was initiated by Boeing in August 1934. The resulting Model 299 was entirely separate from the much larger Model 294 project, which reached a dead-end with the XB-15. Named Flying Fortress, the prototype Model 299 was flown for the first time at Seattle on July 28, 1935, by Boeing test pilot Les Tower. Powered by four 750 hp Pratt & Whitney

R-1690-E Hornets, the aircraft could carry a bomb load of 4,800lb and had a crew of eight.

After preliminary trials the Army ordered 13 service-test aircraft, designated Y1B-17, plus a fourteenth for structural tests. The first of these flew for the first time on December 2, 1936, and differed from the Model 299 in having four 930 hp Wright GR-1820-39s together with minor changes to the undercarriage and systems.

The first Y1B-17s were delivered in March 1937 to the 2nd Bombardment Group at Langley Field, Virginia, where they were used to develop operational techniques for long-range bombing missions. The first production contract—placed in 1938 and covering 39 B-17Bs—was exceptionally modest on account of the protests of the US Navy, which claimed the

privilege of defending America's coastline from attack. A further 38 aircraft were ordered in 1939, however. These were B-17Cs, the first of which flew on July 21, 1940, powered by four 1,000 hp R-1820-65s. Range with 4,000lb of bombs was increased to 2,400 miles. Some 20 B-17Cs were diverted to Britain, where they were operated by the RAF as Fortress Is.

Also ordered in 1940 were 42 B-17Ds, differing only slightly from the B-17C, some 17 of which were brought up to D standard in 1941. First flown in February 1941, the B-17D became the first USAAF Fortress to be deployed overseas when the 19th Bombardment Group flew 21 examples to Hawaii in May that year. Many of these aircraft were destroyed during the Japanese attack on Pearl Harbor on December 7, 1941.

The B-17E introduced the new enlarged vertical tail assembly which became standard for all subsequent Fortress variants. It also carried improved defensive armament, comprising 12 0.50in machine guns distributed amongst the tail, waist, radio compartment and belly, with a pair of 0.30in guns in the nose. First flown in September 1941, the B-17E was soon in quantity production by Boeing, Vega and Douglas, a total of 1,023 having been built by May 1942. First unit in Europe to be equipped was the 8th Air Force's 97th BG based at Polebrook, Northants, which began operations in August 1942.

First flown in May 1942, the B-17F featured a new one-piece Plexiglas nose, new propellers and numerous other detail changes. Gross weight ultimately rose to 72,000lb, compared with 32,500lb for the

Boeing B-17E Fortress
Boeing B-17F-70

original Model 299. When production ended in September 1943 a total of 3,405 B-17Fs had been built.

Last and most numerous production variant was the B-17G, which introduced the new "chin" turret. Production totalled more than 8,600 aircraft, built by Boeing, Vega and Douglas.

Although a total of 12,677 "Forts" were delivered to the USAAF during the war, the maximum number in service at any one time was 4,574 in August 1944. The type dropped more than 640,000 tons of bombs on Europe, compared with 452,508 for the more numerous B-24 Liberator.

Some B-17s—such as the B-17H search and rescue aircraft, which remained in service until 1956—continued to serve with the Air Force after the war.

Boeing B-17G-15

Bell XFM-1

Bell YFM-1 Airacuda

The five-seat Bell XFM-1, designed by Robert J. Woods, was the first and only twin-engined pusher fighter to be built in the US. It first flew on September 1, 1937, powered by two 1,150 hp Allison V-1710-13 engines.

The characteristic feature of the aircraft was the positioning of gunners in nacelles ahead of the turbocharged engines. The nacelle guns were to have been 37mm cannon, but these weapons were not available in time and dummies were installed in their place. Other armament included two 0.50in machine guns in blisters on either side of the fuselage and a pair of 0.30in machine guns mounted above the nacelle cannon.

The first of nine service-test YFM-1s (ordered in May 1938 at a cost of more than $3 million) flew for the first time on September 28, 1939. Powered by two V-1710-23 engines, the YFM-1 had underwing racks for up to 340lb of bombs; defensive armament was also increased by a further two 0.50in and two 0.30in machine guns.

Three YFM-1As, introduced in 1940, incorporated a tricycle undercarriage. Two of the YFM-1s fitted with V-1710-41 engines were redesignated YFM-1B. The type did not enter operational service.

Curtiss P-36C

Curtiss P-36 series

The Army's requirement for a P-26A replacement led to a series of design competitions in the mid-1930s. For the first, in May 1935, only the Curtiss Design 75 was ready. A second, held in August 1935, yielded the Seversky SEV-1XP (later P-35), while a third, held in April 1936, attracted prototypes from Consolidated (P-30A) and Vought (V-141). Only the Curtiss and Seversky designs were to enter service with the Air Corps, however, and then only in limited quantities.

For the first two competitions the Curtiss Design 75 was powered by the generally unsatisfactory 900 hp Wright R-1670-5 two-row radial. For the final competition this was changed to the 950 hp Wright R-1820-39 single-row engine, and the aircraft's designation became Model 75B.

Although the competition was nominally won by the Seversky design, Curtiss received a contract for three service-test Y1P-36s in July 1936. Powered by the 1,050 hp Pratt & Whitney R-1830-13 Twin Wasp, the first was delivered in March 1937. Following flight tests at Wright Field in July 1937 Curtiss

received a production contract for 210 P-36As, valued at more than $4 million. This was the largest single order for fighters to be placed by the Army since 1918. Deliveries to Air Corps pursuit squadrons began in April 1938, initially to the 20th Pursuit Group at Selfridge Field, Michigan. While production was under way, however, a great deal of necessary development was being carried out and the last 30 aircraft were delivered as P-36Cs, powered by the 1,200 hp Pratt & Whitney R-1830-17 and armed with two wing-mounted 0.30in machine guns in addition

to the standard armament of two cowl-mounted machine guns.

The P-36 was plagued by a multitude of problems from the start of its Air Corps service, and by the time that the US entered the Second World War the type was obsolescent and had been largely supplanted by its successor, the Allison-engined P-40. Nevertheless, a number were still operational at that time and, although they were severely mauled, P-36s in the Pacific theatre scored the first Air Corps kills against Japanese aircraft.

Ryan PT-20

Ryan PT-16 series

The smart tandem two-seat Ryan Army trainers of the war years were derived from Claude Ryan's S-T (Sport Trainer), which first flew in June 1934. This exceptionally clean low-wing aircraft was powered by a 95 hp Menasco Pirate in-line engine, later changed to the more powerful 125 hp Menasco L-365-1 on the S-T-A.

In June 1939 the US Army awarded Ryan a contract for 16 Y1PT-16 primary trainers, based on the S-T-A. These aircraft were successfully operated by the Ryan School of Aeronautics at Lindbergh Field, San Diego, which became the first of many Civilian Pilot Training (CPT) schools operated by the US armed forces during the Second World War.

In 1940 the PT-16 was supplemented by 40 basically similar PT-20s. During the following year the Menasco engine was replaced by the 132 hp Kinner R-440-3 radial, and 100 of the re-engined aircraft were ordered under the designation PT-21.

Most numerous of the variants was the PT-22. Production of the Recruit, as this version was popularly known, exceeded 1,000 aircraft, all of the orders having been placed during 1941. Powerplant was the 160 hp Kinner R-540-1. Production ended in 1942 and Ryan was then contracted to investigate production of a variant constructed entirely from non-strategic materials. This turned out to be the YPT-25, five of which were delivered during 1942-43. No production order was forthcoming, however, and the PT-22 was thus the last of the wartime Ryan primary trainers.

Ryan YPT-16s at San Diego, 1939

Vultee BT-13 and BT-15 Valiant

Flight training in the US during the Second World War was divided into three stages: primary, basic and advanced. The first and last categories were carried out mainly on the PT-13/17 Stearman biplanes and AT-6 Texan respectively, while basic training was almost exclusively the preserve of the low-wing fixed-undercarriage Vultee BT-13.

Developed originally as the private-venture Vultee Model 54, the BT-13 had a 450 hp Pratt & Whitney R-985-25 engine and was selected by the Army in 1939. An initial order for 300 was followed by contracts totalling 6,407 production BT-13As. The BT-13B incorporated minor changes, and production of this variant ran to 1,125 aircraft.

The BT-15 was a version powered by a 450 hp Wright R-975-11 in place of the Pratt & Whitney, which was in short supply because of the extremely rapid build-up in BT-13 production.

By the end of the war the basic trainer had largely been supplanted by the advanced, and when the BT category was dropped the Army soon retired its remaining Valiants.

Vultee BT-13

Bell P-39 Airacobra

The Bell P-39 was unusual among single-seat fighters of the period in having its Allison V-1710 engine buried in the fuselage behind the pilot's cockpit, the propeller being driven by a long shaft passing beneath the pilot's seat. Behind this unorthodox arrangement lay a desire for increased manoeuvrability (the engine being more or less on the aircraft's centre of gravity), heavy nose armament, improved pilot visibility, and room for a nosewheel undercarriage. As it turned out, the Airacobra was disappointing as an interceptor, being practically useless above 17,000ft, but excellent as a ground-attack aircraft.

The XP-39 was first flown by James Taylor at Dayton on April 6, 1939, and a batch of 13 service-test aircraft—12 YP-39s and one YP-39A without turbosupercharger—were then ordered. A number of changes to the prototype following flight tests resulted in its redesignation as the XP-39B, in which guise it first flew on November 25, 1939. The type was ordered into quantity production in August 1939, the first contract being for 80 P-39Cs with non-turbocharged V-1710-37 engines. Deliveries began in January 1941.

After the first 20 aircraft had been built the designation was changed to P-39D, reflecting a number of equipment changes, including an increase in armament to four wing-mounted 0.30in machine guns in addition to the two nose-mounted 0.50in guns and the 37mm cannon firing through the centre of the propeller spinner. Additional orders brought the total of P-39Ds built to 923.

The Airacobra was also produced in quantity for export to Britain and the Soviet Union, and a number of these aircraft were repossessed by the US in December 1941, following the Japanese attack on Pearl Harbor, and redesignated P-400. US Army Air Force P-39s initially saw service in the Pacific theatre, operating out of Port Moresby, and in July 1942 the 31st Fighter Group began operations from Tangmere in the South of England. Airacobras were later deployed in most theatres, including North Africa, where the type won a reputation as a formidable ground-attack aircraft, achieving a lower loss rate per sortie than any other USAAF fighter employed in the area.

The majority of the later variants were destined for service in Russia—which absorbed nearly 5,000 of the 9,558 Airacobras built—and by late 1944 the type was being replaced in AAF service by the P-47 Thunderbolt, P-51 Mustang and P-38 Lightning.

Fairchild PT-19 series

Although featuring the same basic configuration as the Ryan PT-16 and PT-21 series of primary training aircraft, the Ranger-engined Fairchild PT-19 was both larger and heavier.

Developed as the private-venture M-62, the design was first bought by the US Army and designated PT-19. Production totalled 270. By far the most numerous variant was the PT-19A, powered by the 200 hp Ranger L-440-3. Production of this version totalled more than 3,100 by Fairchild alone, with a further 500 or so being built by other contractors.

The PT-19B was an improved version fitted out for blind-flying instruction. Production totalled 917. The first major change came in 1942 with the substitution of the 220 hp Continental R-670 radial for the Ranger in-line, then in short supply. Production of this variant, designated PT-23, totalled 869 by five manufacturers. Production of the PT-23A with blind-flying equipment totalled 256 aircraft.

Bell P-39 Airacobra

Fairchild PT-23

Consolidated B-24 Liberator

Second only to the B-17 among USAAF aircraft in terms of bomb tonnage dropped on Europe during the war, the B-24 Liberator was actually produced in greater quantities than the Fort.

The Liberator was developed in answer to a demand for a strategic bomber with greater range than the B-17. Preliminary design studies began in January 1939, a prototype contract was placed in March that year and the XB-24, with its new high-lift Davis wing, flew for the First time from Lindbergh Field, San Diego, on December 29, 1939.

In April 1939 the Air Force ordered seven pre-production YB-24s, followed in 1940 by 36 B-24As. The first production Liberators to be delivered were however destined for the RAF.

The first USAAF delivery was made in May 1941, when the only YB-24 completed was handed over. Only nine of the 36 B-24As were actually completed to that standard; a further nine aircraft were completed as B-24Cs and delivered by February 1942.

The first version to be produced in quantity was the B-24D, powered by four 1,200 hp R-1830-43s. Total production reached 2,738, most of which were built by Consolidated Vultee at San Diego. Armament ultimately consisted of ten 0.50in machine guns and a bomb load of some 12,800lb. First operational use of the type came during the attack against the Romanian oilfields at Ploesti on June 11-12, 1942. Liberators of the 8th Air Force began operations from Britain in October that year.

The B-24E introduced a number of minor changes, as did the B-24G, and a total of 1,232 of these variants were built by Ford and North American. The majority of the North American-built B-24Gs were fitted with an Emerson or Consolidated upper nose turret with twin 0.50in machine guns.

The first Consolidated-built Liberator with upper nose turret was the B-24H, total production of which reached 3,100. More numerous still was the B-24J, no fewer than 6,678 of which were built. A number of Gs and Hs were later brought up to J standard. Production continued with 417 Consolidated-built and 1,250 Ford-built B-24Ls and 2,593 B-24Ms.

Although large numbers of Liberators were used in Europe alongside the B-17, these long-range aircraft were particularly valuable in the Pacific theatre. Towards the end of 1944 the total USAAF B-24 inventory was more than 6,000 aircraft, equipping some 45 bomber groups.

Its particularly capacious fuselage made the Liberator an ideal candidate for conversion to the transport role. Designated C-87, this version could accommodate 25 passengers and five crew. A total of 276 C-87s and six C-87As were built.

Consolidated B-24E

Consolidated B-24J

79

SPECIAL TRANSPORT

SPECIAL TRANSPORT
B-87 B-24
NO.72
W.O. NO. 213
72

SPECIAL TRANSPORT
B-24
NO. 71
W.O. NO. 213
71

Consolidated C-87 on the production line

Curtiss P-40 Warhawk

The Curtiss P-40 was essentially a development of the radial-engined P-36/Hawk 75. In fact the prototype XP-40, ordered in July 1937, was a conversion of the tenth production P-36A, on which the R-1830-13 engine was replaced by a 1,160 hp supercharged Allison V-1710-19 liquid-cooled in-line. First flown in October 1938, it originally had a radiator mounted under the rear fuselage; this was later moved to a location under the nose. Armament was one 0.30in and one 0.50in machine gun mounted on the upper nose.

Having an airframe and engine that were both proven, Curtiss was able to put the P-40 into production with relatively little trouble. Following an evaluation at Wright Field in May 1939, the Air Corps placed an order for 524 P-40s, worth about $13 million, and the first of these appeared the following spring. After the first 200 had been built production was switched to the similar H-81A Tomahawk for France and Britain. Army production was

resumed in September 1940 with the P-40B, which had two additional wing guns; some 131 were built, the first of which entered service in February 1941. The P-40C, some 193 of which were built for the Air Corps, incorporated a number of minor improvements.

The Japanese attack on Pearl Harbor resulted in the destruction of more than 70 P-40Bs and Cs, and by December 10 only 22 P-40s remained airworthy in the Philippines. The type was also in use early in the war with General Clair Chennault's American Volunteer Group—the Flying Tigers—which helped to defend China against the Japanese. About 90 P-40Bs were flown by the volunteers, the aircraft having been diverted from British contracts.

The P-40D, which entered production in 1941, was powered by the 1,150 hp Allison V-1710-39. The nose-mounted guns were removed and the calibre of the four wing guns was increased to 0.50in. Of the 582 built, only 22 were acquired

by the USAAF, the remainder going to the RAF as Kittyhawk 1s. Similar to the P-40D was the P-40E with six 0.50in guns, some 2,230 of which were built. Of this total, about 1,500 were allocated to Britain under Lend-Lease contracts.

A change to the Packard-built Merlin V-1650-1 produced the P-40F, built in parallel with the Allison-engined P-40K. A total of 2,611 of these two versions were built. The partially stripped P-40L, commonly called the "Gipsy Rose Lee," was designated P-40M. Like previous USAAF Warhawks, this version saw service in the Middle and Far East.

Most numerous of the P-40 variants was the P-40N, which entered production in the latter part of 1943. Powered by the 1,200 hp Allison V-1710-81, early P-40Ns had a top speed of 378 mph.

By the time Warhawk production ended in December 1944 more than 13,700 of all versions had been built, with Air Force strength peaking at 2,500 of the type in April of that year.

Curtiss P-40

Curtiss P-40B

Curtiss P-40E

Lockheed C-56 Lodestar

Lockheed C-56 Lodestar series

The C-56 series of twin-engined personnel, troop and freight transports were military derivatives of the Lockheed Model 18 17-passenger commercial transport, which first flew in early 1940 and was itself developed from the Models 10, 12 and 14.

In May 1941 the US Army ordered a single C-56, powered by a pair of Wright R-1820-89 radials, and three C-57s, powered by two Pratt & Whitney R-1830-53s. A further 10 C-57s were ordered later. After America's entry into the Second World War a large number of commercial Lodestars were impressed into military service, receiving a variety of designations depending on engine type and interior fittings.

The series as a whole embraced a single C-57A, small numbers of C-57Bs and Cs and a single C-57D. Largest production run was the total of 325 C-60As with R-1820-87s. The C-66 was a commercial Model 18-10 with 11-passenger interior and a pair of R-1830-53s.

Douglas DB-7

Douglas A-20 Havoc

The twin-engined Havoc, originally put into production for foreign air forces as the DB-7, was later to become the most numerous AAF attack aircraft.

Designed by Jack Northrop and Ed Heinemann at the Douglas company's El Segundo division, the aircraft flew for the first time as the Douglas Model 7B from Mines Field, Los Angeles, on October 26, 1938. A number of modifications and design changes led to the DB-7, which was ordered in quantity by France in February 1939. After the fall of France in 1940 surviving aircraft passed to the RAF, which operated the type as the Boston and Havoc.

The Air Corps remained interested throughout the development phase, and on June 30, 1939, a total of 186

DB-7s were ordered: 63 as A-20s powered by the turbo-supercharged 1,700 hp Wright R-2600-7, and 123 as A-20As with a pair of 1,600 hp R-2600-3s. Most of the A-20s were later converted to P-70 night fighters, and the initial batch of A-20As were soon joined by a further 20; this version was first operated by the 3rd Bombardment Group, based at Savannah, Georgia.

The A-20B was powered by R-2600-11 engines and featured a modified glazed nose and bomb bay. Ordered in October 1940, a total of 999 were built at Long Beach.

In 1941 production was moved to Santa Monica, where it resumed with the A-20C. Most of the 808 A-20Cs ordered were

intended for Lend-Lease delivery to the RAF and Soviet Air Force, but after Pearl Harbor a substantial number were taken over by the AAF. This model was the first to see operational service with the Air Force, equipping the 15th BS in Britain from July 1942.

The next major production variant was the A-20G, with a solid nose typically containing four 20mm cannon and two 0.50in machine guns in early production models and six 0.50in machine guns in later aircraft. A total of 2,850 were built at Santa Monica, followed by 412 A-20Hs with 1,700 hp R-2600-29s in place of the -23s of the A-20G.

Later versions, the A-20J and

K, were again fitted with the glazed nose to accommodate a bombardier. A total of 863 were built, almost 260 of which were destined for service with the RAF as Boston IVs and Vs.

F-3A was the designation allocated to 46 A-20Js and Ks modified at the Daggett Modification Center from February 1944 for use as night photographic-reconnaissance aircraft.

The AAF's radar-equipped night-fighter version was the P-70. A total of 269 were acquired by modifying a variety of A-20 models. Most were used in the Pacific, where they were eventually replaced by the Northrop P-61 Black Widow in late 1944.

Douglas A-20C, April 1942

North American B-25 Mitchell

This twin-engined light bomber, which carried the name of the Army's renegade but far-sighted prophet of air power, was one of the outstanding aircraft of the Second World War. Production approached 11,000 of all versions and the type served on every major front.

The B-25 originated in the three-seat private-venture North American NA-40, designed in response to a 1938 Air Corps request. First flown in January 1939, the NA-40 was powered by a pair of 1,100 hp Pratt & Whitney R-1830-56C3-Gs, later changed for Wright GR-2600-A71s. Following the loss of this aircraft during its Wright Field trials, development continued with the NA-62, which featured a number of design changes, including a wider fuselage, lowered wing position and more crew stations. In this

form it was ordered by the Air Corps, a contract for 184 production aircraft designated B-25 being placed in September 1939. The first of these flew for the first time on August 19, 1940, powered by two 1,700 hp R-2600-9s.

The first operational variant was the B-25A, which entered service during 1941 with the 17th Bombardment Group (Medium) at McChord Field, Washington, flying anti-shipping patrols from the US West Coast. A total of 40 B-25As were followed by 120 B-25Bs, which completed the original 1939 contract. The B-25B earned almost instantaneous fame as the aircraft which attacked Tokyo in April 1942 under the command of Lt Col James Doolittle.

First major production variant

was the B-25C, the first of which entered service towards the end of 1941. A total of 1,619 were built at Inglewood, California, while 2,290 essentially similar B-25Ds were built at Kansas City. Bomb load for short-range missions was increased to 5,200lb. The C and D models were the first Mitchells to see widespread operational service, equipping the 12th BG in Egypt in August 1942.

A requirement for increased firepower for Pacific-based Mitchells led to the field modification of 175 aircraft to carry ten 0.50in machine guns, four of them in a "solid" nose, four in blisters on either side of the front fuselage and two in the top turret. Another heavily armed version was the B-25G, which mounted a 75mm cannon in the nose. A total of 405 were

built at Inglewood, followed by 1,000 B-25Hs, in which the 75mm gun was supplemented by no fewer than 14 0.50in machine guns.

In December 1943 the B-25J replaced the B-25D on the Kansas City line; this version reintroduced the glazed nose. A total of 4,318 were built between 1943 and 1945 and most served on low-level missions in the Pacific theatre. Many were later fitted with the solid nose, since a bombardier was superfluous on this type of mission.

Maximum AAF inventory was more than 2,600 B-25s in July 1944. After the war the Mitchell served with both SAC and TAC for a number of years before being relegated to the training and staff transport roles. The last was retired from USAF service in January 1959.

North American B-25C

North American B-25H

Martin B-26 Marauder

The twin-engined B-26 Marauder was burdened with a reputation as something of a "hot ship" when it first appeared in 1941, and a succession of fatal accidents during conversion training led Army Air Force pilots to call it the "Widow-maker". Yet by 1944 Marauders of the 9th Air Force were returning the lowest loss rate on operational missions of any US aircraft in the European theatre.

The aircraft was designed by the Glenn Martin Co in 1939 in response to an AAF requirement for a high-speed medium bomber with a bomb load of 2,000lb and a crew of five. No prototype was ordered, a

contract for 1,100 production B-26s being signed in September 1939. Powered by a pair of 1,850 hp R-2800-5s, the first B-26 was flown for the first time by Martin's chief engineer, William K. Ebel, on November 25, 1940.

The first 201 aircraft were completed as B-26s, followed by 139 B-26As with higher gross weight. First operational unit to be equipped was the 22nd Bombardment Group, which left Langley, Virginia, for the Pacific on December 8, 1941.

Production of the B-26B began in May 1942 after a break of some weeks while an Air Force board investigated the B-26's

worsening record of training accidents. A total of 1,883 B-26Bs were built by Martin. These aircraft differed markedly from one production block to another, the most significant of the changes affecting the B-26B-10-MA, which had its span increased by some six feet in an effort to reduce wing loading. Many changes were made to the Marauder's armament, and B-10 models carried some 12 0.5in Colt-Browning machine guns. The identical B-26C was produced at Omaha, where 1,235 were built.

By the end of 1942 Marauders were appearing in North Africa

with the 17th, 319th and 320th BG of the 12th Air Force. The type first appeared in Britain in February 1943, when the 8th AF took delivery of its first B-26s. All 8th AF Marauders were transferred to the 9th AF in November 1943.

Production during 1943 included some 300 B-26Fs, with increased wing incidence, and the first of 893 B-26Gs. Final production variant was the TB-26G unarmed trainer, only 57 of which were built before production of all Marauders was suspended on March 30, 1945. The type did not serve with the independent Air Force, set up in 1947.

Martin B-26B-10, Tunisia, July 1943

Martin B-26B

Lockheed P-38M

Lockheed P-38 Lighting

The unusually configured Lighting was built in smaller numbers than any of the other major US Air Force fighters of the Second World War—a total of 9,923 were produced between 1939 and 1945—but it had the distinction of serving on most battlefronts and in most roles.

Design work began in 1935 and the original configuration was much changed by the time that the prototype XP-38 was ordered in June 1937. First flight was on January 27, 1939, and two weeks later, on February 11, the aircraft set a coast-to-coast record, flying from March Field, California, to Mitchell Field, New York, in 7hr 2min with two refuelling stops.

Contracts for 13 service-test YP-38s had been placed before the prototype's first flight, and these were followed by an initial production batch of 66 P-38s, ordered in August 1939. Early development was relatively slow, however, and the Army did not receive its first production aircraft until June 1941. These early aircraft were powered by two opposite-rotating 1,150 hp Allison V-1710-27/29s and were armed with four 0.50in machine guns and a 37mm Oldsmobile cannon. The first 30 production Lightnings were completed as P-38s while the remaining 36 of the first contract became P-38Ds; the latter aircraft were delivered in August 1941.

Production continued with 210 P-38Es, which had a 20mm Hispano cannon in place of the Oldsmobile weapon. Some 99 were later converted to F-4 photo-reconnaissance variants with K-17 cameras in place of the nose armament.

First truly combat-ready version was the P-38F, some 527 of which were built from early 1942. The P-38G was similar to the F but was powered by 1,325 hp V-1710-51/55 engines in place of the 49/52s. A total of 1,082 were built during 1942, including 181 modified as F-5A photo-reconnaissance aircraft. The P-38H, which entered service in May 1943, had the more powerful F15 engines and

could carry a heavier bomb load. Lockheed built 600 of this version, followed by 2,970 P-38Js with the characteristic chin radiator beneath the propeller spinners. Numerically the most important version was the P-38L, some 3,923 of which were built. Final version was the black-painted P-38M night fighter, 75 of which were converted from P-38Ls.

The Lightning was particularly successful in the Pacific, where it is claimed to have destroyed more Japanese aircraft than any other Allied type. In Europe P-38s were used extensively on long-range escort and ground-attack missions with the 9th Air Force.

Lockheed P-38J

Douglas A-24B, April 1943

Douglas A-24 Dauntless

The A-24 two-seat dive bomber first flew as the XBT-1 in July 1935. This singular aircraft is probably better known by its Navy designations of SBD-1 to SBD-5, in which guise it sank more Japanese shipping than any other Allied weapon.

Prompted by the devastation wrought in France by German Ju87 Stuka dive bombers, the US Army ordered 78 A-24s in July 1940. Similar to the Navy aircraft apart from the deletion of deck operating equipment, they were delivered from the Navy production line at El Segundo, California, between June and October 1941. Powered by a 1,000 hp Wright R-1820-52 radial engine, they could carry up to 1,200lb of bombs; armament was two 0.50in Browning machine guns in the upper nose cowling and two 0.30in Brownings in the rear cockpit.

In November 1941 52 A-24s were sent by sea to the Philippines for use by the 27th Bombardment Group (L). After the outbreak of war in the Pacific Army A-24s were never as successful as the Navy's carrier-borne aircraft, and A-24s were frequently sent out on operations without adequate fighter cover and with insufficiently trained crews.

Despite its operational shortcomings the A-24 continued to be ordered. In 1942 170 A-24As were built at El Segundo, and the following year a further 615 A-24Bs, with 1,200 hp Wright R-1820-60 engines, were acquired from the Tulsa production line.

A handful of A-24s, redesignated F-24A and F-24B, remained in the inventory for a short while after the formation of the US Air Force as an independent service in 1947.

Douglas XB-19

Douglas XB-19, January 1942

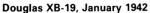

Douglas XB-19

Work on the vast Douglas XB-19 project, conceived essentially as a technology proving exercise, began in 1935. The Army Air Corps ordered engineering data from Douglas in October 1935, and after inspection of a mock-up the following March a prototype, at that time designated XBLR-2, was ordered on September 29, 1936.

Redesignated XB-19 in March 1938, the machine was not completed until 1941. Although obsolete by then, it was flown for the first time by Maj Stanley M. Ulmstead on June 27, the Army Materiel Division insisting that flight-test data would assist in future super-bomber projects.

Reported to have absorbed some $1.4 million of Air Corps funds and an estimated $4 million of Douglas's money, the XB-19 nevertheless furnished important information on structures and performance, much of which was used in the design of the giant six-engined Consolidated B-36 prototype. The XB-19 was used as a transport aircraft during the war before being scrapped in 1949.

Republic P-43 Lancer

During 1939 tests were held at Langley Field, Virginia, with the final production Seversky P-35 fitted with a turbosupercharged R-1830-19 engine. Designated XP-41, it had an inward-retracting undercarriage and slightly modified wing and was the work of a team led by Seversky designer Alexander Kartveli. A parallel line of development led to the AP-4 (Army Pursuit 4) proposal using the same semi-elliptical wing and a turbosupercharged

1,050 hp R-1830-SC2-G. Both the XP-41 and the AP-4 were evaluated at Wright Field, and the Air Corps was sufficiently impressed by the AP-4 to order 13 service-test aircraft under the designation YP-43 on May 12, 1939.

By this time Alexander Seversky had left the company he founded, which was reorganised and renamed Republic Aviation in October 1939. The new aircraft then

became the Republic YP-43 Lancer. Powered by the 1,200 hp Pratt & Whitney R-1830-35 Twin Wasp and armed with two 0.50in machine guns in the upper cowling and two wing-mounted 0.30in machine guns, the test aircraft were delivered between September 1940 and April of the following year.

A production contract for 54 P-43s and 80 P-43As was awarded in 1940, largely to keep the production line open during

development of Republic's follow-on fighter, the P-47 Thunderbolt. Deliveries of the P-43 began in May 1941, with P-43A deliveries starting in September of that year. Difficulties with the turbocharger limited the Lancer's operational usefulness, and in 1942 most production aircraft were converted for reconnaissance duties and redesignated P-43B (150 aircraft), P-43C (two aircraft) or P-43D.

Republic P-43 Lancer

Douglas C-47

Douglas C-47 Skytrain series

One of the most important aircraft in the history of aviation, the twin-engined Douglas DC-3 first flew as the DST (Douglas Sleeper Transport) on December 17, 1935, and had established itself as a commercial aircraft long before it put on uniform as the C-47 in 1940. (Pre-dating the C-47 in Air Force service, however, was the solitary Santa Monica-built C-41A, powered by two 1,200 hp Pratt & Whitney R-1830-21s,

which was delivered in September 1939 for use as a command transport.) The Air Force was later to become the main operator of the C-47, absorbing more than 10,500 of all versions, compared with the 448 civil versions built before the outbreak of the Second World War.

The first C-47 contract, for 147 Long Beach-built aircraft, was awarded in September 1940.

Powered by two R-1830-92s, they differed from commercial DC-3As principally in having large cargo doors on the port side. A total of 965 C-47s were eventually built at Long Beach, the first of which was delivered in late December 1941.

The C-47A was the most numerous of the family, a total of 5,235 being built at Long Beach and Oklahoma City. After the war a number were modified

as RC-47A reconnaissance aircraft, HC-47A search and rescue aircraft and VC-47A staff transports.

A prodigious number of C-47 Skytrain and C-53 Skytrooper variants—too many to catalogue here—were produced or modified. The aircraft has operated in all parts of the world under almost every flag and it has been used for almost every airborne role, including ground attack.

Douglas C-47As, April 1944

Beech AT-7

Beech C-45 and AT-11 series

The Beech C-45 was a military version of the twin-engined Model 18 light commercial transport, which first flew on January 15, 1937.

The first military purchase, in 1940, covered 11 C-45s for use as staff transports. Fitted out with six seats, they were joined in 1941 by 20 eight-seat aircraft designated C-45A. Subsequent orders called for 223 C-45Bs of increased gross weight, and 1,137 C-45Fs fitted with seven seats. In January 1943 the designation of all variants was changed to the UC category.

In 1941 the Army ordered a navigation trainer version designated AT-7. Some 1,141 of all AT-7 variants were eventually ordered, the final batch comprising 549 AT-7Cs powered by Pratt & Whitney R-985-AN-3s.

The AT-11 Kansan was a development of the AT-7; the majority of the 1,582 built were used for bombing and gunnery training.

Last of the significant wartime Model 18 variants was the photographic-reconnaissance F-2. Fourteen were produced in 1940 by modifying commercial B-18s, while the remaining 55 were modified UC-45As, Bs and Fs.

A number of military Model 18 variants survived the war and in 1951 no fewer than 900 C-45Fs, T-7s, T-11s and RC-45As (as the aircraft had been designated in June 1948) were re-manufactured as 468 C-45Gs and 432 C-45Hs. All were configured as six-seaters. Subsequently 96 C-45Gs became TC-45G navigation trainers. The last C-45s were retired by the Air Force in 1964.

Taylorcraft L-2 Grasshopper

In 1941 the Army obtained four Taylorcraft Model D tandem-seat high-wing light aircraft and used them, along with similar types from Aeronca and Piper, to evaluate the effectiveness of this type of machine for liaison and light observation duties.

Designated YO-57, the Continental YO-170-3-engined aircraft were joined by 70 production O-57s. The first fully militarised version was the O-57A, with modified cabin transparency and a cut-away wing-root trailing edge to improve crew vision.

In 1942 Army observation types were reclassified in the Liaison category; the O-57 became the L-2 and the O-57A the L-2A. A total of 336 O-57As were redesignated. These were followed by further production batches of 140 L-2As and 490 L-2Bs with special equipment for artillery spotting.

Final production model was the L-2M, of which 900 were built. This version had a fully cowled 65 hp Continental and wing spoilers for short-field operations.

Beech AT-11

Taylorcraft L-2A

Aeronca L-3 Grasshopper

Aeronca's entrant in the 1941 Army evaluation of light aircraft for observation and liaison duties was the Model 65TC Defender, a tandem two-seat training and sport aircraft powered by a 65 hp Continental. The four examples obtained initially were designated YO-58. They were joined later by 50 production O-58s and 20 O-58As with a four-inch-wider fuselage.

First full military-specification version was the O-58B. In common with other Army light observation types, the O-58 series was reclassified in 1942, the O-58 becoming the L-3, the 20 O-58As L-3As and the O-58Bs L-3Bs; a total of 875 were eventually built.

Last of the series-production Aeroncas was the L-3C, 490 of which were built. The L-3C had revised radio equipment and a gross weight of 1,800lb compared with the 1,850lb of the L-3B.

Aeronca L-3C

Piper L-4

Piper L-4 Grasshopper

Third of the contenders in the Army's 1941 light observation and liaison competition was the Piper Cub J3C-65, four of which were bought for preliminary investigation as the YO-59. Like the Taylorcraft and Aeronca submissions, the four Piper service-test aircraft were joined almost immediately by a number of basically identical production aircraft, in this case 20 O-59s. A contract for a further 120 O-59s followed soon after.

The O-59A was an improved version with modified cabin, and 649 out of a total order of 948 had been delivered when the type was re-classified in the liaison category as the L-4A. A contract for a further 980 L-4Bs, with different radio equipment, was placed in mid-1942.

The L-4 was by far the most numerous of the Grasshopper series, with the As and Bs being supplemented by a total of 1,801 L-4Hs towards the end of the war. Two contracts totalling 1,600 L-4Js (controllable-pitch propeller) had been completed and work on a further 350 was under way when the war ended; only 80 of the last batch were delivered before the contract was cancelled.

Beech AT-10

Beech AT-10

In 1940, at the request of the US Army Air Corps, T. A. Wells and other Beech Aircraft engineers began work on an advanced pilot trainer, the twin-engined Beechcraft Model 26.

Although it strongly resembled the standard Beechcraft twin-engined monoplanes, the AT-10 was an entirely new design. The first all-wood aircraft to be built by the company, it was also the first all-wood type to be accepted as an advanced trainer by the Army. Power was provided by a pair of 295 hp Lycoming R-680-9 radials.

Designed to demand the minimum of strategic materials, the AT-10 embodied metal only in the engine cowlings, pilot's cabin, undercarriage and engine bearers. Even the fuel tanks were made of wood lined with synthetic rubber.

Beech built 1,771 AT-10s at Wichita, and Globe (later Temco) built a further 600 at Dallas, Texas, between 1941 and 1943. For some reason details of this aircraft are relatively sparse, but it seems unlikely that many survived after the end of the war.

Lockheed A-29 and AT-18 series

The military A-28, A-29 and AT-18 series of twin-engined aircraft were derived from the successful commercial Model 14 of the late 1930s. The original military conversion was carried out to meet the British Purchasing Commission requirement for a coastal reconnaissance bomber. A contract for 250 aircraft, allocated the name Hudson, was placed in June 1938.

Although the majority of the Hudsons built went to the RAF and RAAF, a number of repossessed aircraft were used by the US Army Air Force as A-29s and A-29As. During 1942 some 24 repossessed aircraft were converted to A-29B photographic-reconnaissance configuration and were used by the 1st Photographic Group on survey and chartmaking flights.

Similar to the A-29A, the AT-18 was powered by a pair of 1,200 hp Wright R-1820-87s and fitted with a Martin dorsal turret. Lockheed built 217 of these air-gunner trainers and 83 similar AT-18A navigation trainers, which had the dorsal turret removed.

Lockheed AT-18

Lockheed A-28

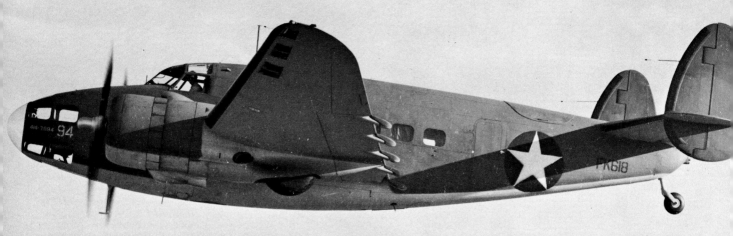

Lockheed B-34

Lockheed B-34 Lexington

Like the A-28 and A-29 series before it, the twin-engined B-34 Ventura was developed to meet a 1940 British requirement. Based on the larger commercial Model 18, the new bomber was built by Lockheed's Vega Aircraft subsidiary at Burbank, California.

The Ventura was larger and heavier than the Hudson and was powered by two 2,000 hp Pratt & Whitney R-2800-31s. The 675 ordered by the RAF in 1940 were designated B-34 by the US Army Air Force when Lend-Lease came into being in 1941.

The first Ventura was flown for the first time on July 31, 1941, and the first operational use of the type by the RAF came in November 1942.

The USAAF retained in the US about 200 aircraft (designated B-34 Lexington) for over-water patrols and navigation training. Biggest US operator of this type, however, was the US Navy, which designated its aircraft PV-1, PV-2 and PV-3.

Cessna AT-8, AT-17 and UC-78 Bobcat

The AT-8 was a military version of Cessna's first twin-engined aircraft, the T-50, which first flew in March 1939. Powered by a pair of 225 hp Jacobs radials, the five-seat civil T-50 was priced at less than $30,000 and was adopted in 1940 for use as a conversion trainer for the Commonwealth Joint Air Training Plan in Canada, where it was known as the Crane.

Late in 1940 the US Army ordered a small batch of T-50s for evaluation as advanced transition trainers for pilots destined to fly multi-engined operational aircraft. The 33 AT-8s ordered in 1940 were powered by two 295 hp Lycoming R-680-9 radials, while the 450 AT-17s built in 1941 were powered by 245 hp Jacobs R-775-9s. Minor equipment changes distinguished the AT-17A, B and C, of which a total of 749 were built.

In 1942 the type was adopted as a light personnel transport, designated C-78 (later UC-78) and named Bobcat. Cessna built 1,287 Bobcats, which were supplemented in Army service by 17 commandeered commercial T-50s designated UC-78A.

Final production variants were the UC-78B and C with two-blade fixed-pitch wooden propellers. Production totalled 1,806 UC-78Bs and 327 Cs. The last examples of this all-wood transport (popularly nicknamed the ''Bamboo Bomber'') had been declared surplus by 1949.

Cessna UC-78 Bobcat

Curtiss XP-55 Ascender

Douglas C-54A

Douglas C-54 Skymaster

Based on the pre-war commercial DC-4, the four-engined C-54 series was used in large numbers by the US Air Force from 1942, and a few were still in service as late as the 1970s.

The type had entered production for commercial customers when the Japanese attack on Pearl Harbor brought the US into the Second World War, and the civil aircraft were diverted to the USAAF as C-54s and C-54As. First flown at Santa Monica on February 14, 1942, the C-54 was powered by four 1,350 hp Pratt & Whitney R-2000-3s. The Air Force received 24 C-54s during 1942, all equipped with four long-range fuel tanks in the main cabin and fitted out for 26 passengers.

The C-54A, the first fully militarised version, could carry up to 50 troops or 32,500lb of cargo. A total of 97 were built at Santa Monica, with a further 155 being completed at Chicago. Of these 252 aircraft, some 56 were later transferred to the US Navy as R5D-1s. Powered by four 1,359 hp R-2000-7s, the first C-54A was delivered to the Air Force in October 1943.

The C-54B was similar to the A except for changes in fuel tankage. A total of 220 were built at Santa Monica and Chicago, and 30 were later transferred to the Navy as R5D-2s. The C-54Bs were followed by 380 Chicago-built C-54Ds, which differed from the B in being powered by the R-2000-11. The Santa Monica-built C-54E differed from the D only in the arrangement of its fuel tanks. Some 86 C-54Ds and 20 C-54Es were transferred to the Navy.

Final production variant was the C-54G troop carrier, 162 of which were built at Santa Monica; a number of these became Navy R5D-5s. The last production C-54 was delivered to the Air Force in January 1946. After the war some modified C-54s received new designations, including the 38 C-54M coal-carrying aircraft (originally C-54Es) used in the Berlin Airlift of 1948.

Curtiss XP-55 Ascender

In the years immediately before America's entry into the Second World War the Air Corps investigated a number of unusual fighter designs in its quest for increased performance. One of the more revolutionary proposals was the canard-wing Curtiss Model 24. As originally ordered in June 1940 the aircraft was to have been powered by a Continental XIV-1430-3 engine, but this was subsequently replaced by an Allison V-1710-95.

Lack of positive results from wind-tunnel tests led to a loss of official interest, and in order to keep the project alive Curtiss proposed the Model 24-B, a full-scale flying model powered by a 285 hp Menasco C-68-5 engine. Flight testing was carried out at Muroc Bombing Range between November 1941 and May 1942, and the results encouraged the Army to order three full-scale prototypes of the Allison-engined aircraft, designated XP-55 Ascender, in April 1942.

The first prototype began flight trials in July 1943 but was lost on November 15 during stalling tests; the pilot escaped by parachute. Testing of the second and third aircraft continued until the end of 1944, but official interest had again waned and no further development of this interesting design took place.

Vultee A-31 and A-35 Vengeance

The Vultee V-72 Vengeance was designed to meet a 1940 Royal Air Force requirement for a dive bomber for service in Europe. A total of 700 were ordered: 500 from Vultee and 200 to be built under licence by Northrop Corporation. In June 1941 further Lend-Lease contracts covered 100 Vultee-built A-31s and another 200 from Northrop. Deliveries had begun when the US entered the war in December 1941, and a number of aircraft were subsequently repossessed. These included 243 ordered under the original British cash contract, which retained their V-72 company designation.

Equipped to US Army standards, with four wing-mounted 0.50in machine guns and one 0.50in mounted in the rear cockpit, the aircraft was redesignated A-35A. The A-35B was fitted with the 1,700 hp Wright R-2600-13 engine and armed with six 0.50in wing-mounted machine guns; most examples of this version were supplied to Britain under Lend-Lease.

The Army made little operational use of the A-31 and A-35, and regarded the type as a waste of precious resources. Some were modified for use as target tugs.

Beech C-43 Traveler

The Beech C-43 Traveler, one of the most distinctive aircraft used by the Army during the Second World War, was essentially a civil Beech Model 17 in uniform.

The first product of the Wichita-based Beech Aircraft Corporation, this handsome aircraft flew for the first time on November 4, 1932. Known also as the Staggerwing because of the backwards stagger of its biplane wings, the four/five-seat Traveler was selected in 1939 for evaluation as a small communications aircraft, three examples being purchased and given the designation YC-43.

Production orders did not materialise until well into 1941, when an initial contract for 27 production UC-43s was placed. Further contracts brought the total to 207, most of which served in the US during the war.

102

Curtiss C-46 Commando

The C-46 Commando was the largest and heaviest twin-engined aircraft to see operational service with the USAAF during the Second World War. It originated in 1936 as a 36-passenger commercial transport known as the CW-20, the prototype of which flew for the first time on March 26, 1940.

Impressed by the capacity of the double-bulge fuselage, the Army ordered 25 militarised C-46s. Powered by two 2,000 hp Pratt & Whitney R-2800-43, the new transport could carry up to 40 passengers or about 12,000lb of freight.

Following the type's introduction into service with Air Transport Command and Troop Carrier Command in 1942, production orders quickly multiplied and a total of more than 3,300 of all versions were eventually built. The first variant, the C-46A, was powered by a pair of R-2800-51s. Because of its superior load-carrying capacity the Commando was used primarily in the Asian and Pacific theatres, flying the "Hump" supply route over the Himalayas between China and India.

Next major production variant was the C-46D, some 1,410 of which were built by Curtiss-Wright at Buffalo. These were followed by small numbers of C-46Es, Fs and Gs.

A number of C-46s continued to operate with Troop Carrier Command after the end of the war, and the last was retired from Air Force Reserve squadrons in 1960.

Republic P-47D-20

Republic P-47N-5 with zero-length rocket launchers

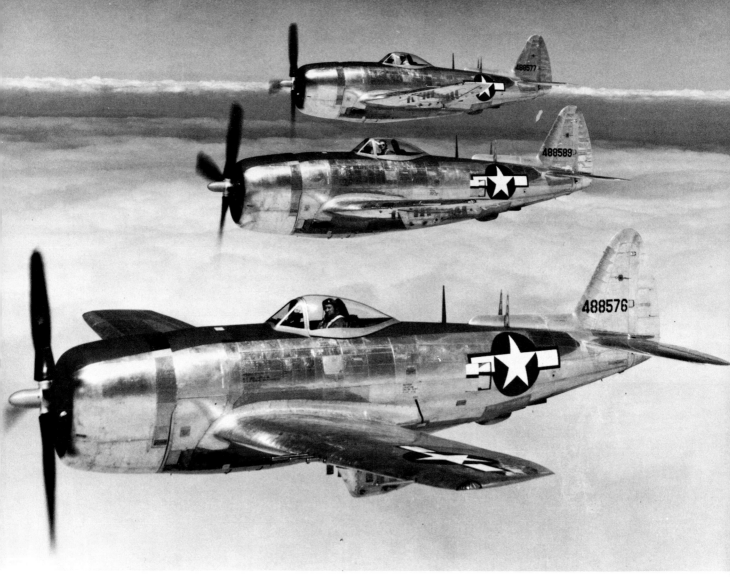

Republic P-47 Thunderbolt

An outstandingly successful heavy fighter, the Thunderbolt was built in larger quantities than any other fighter ever acquired by the Air Force. The P-47 was a development of the line started by the Seversky P-35 and which included the XP-41 and P-43 Lancer. The designations XP-47 and XP-47A were allocated to Allison-engined prototypes, and the first radial-engined prototype of the definitive fighter was the XP-47B, which was built around the 2,000 hp Pratt & Whitney R-2800 and was much larger and heavier. The prototype was flown for the first time in May 1941 but initial development was slowed by a number of problems and mass production did not begin until the spring of 1942, with the first P-47Bs reaching fighter

squadrons in June that year.

Production at Farmingdale switched to the P-47C after 171 P-47Bs had been completed. A total of 602 Cs were built; this version was distinguished by a slightly longer fuselage and an upright as opposed to forward-sloping radio antenna. The P-47C was the first Thunderbolt to see active service, equipping units of the 8th Air Force in Britain from January 1943.

In October 1941 the Air Force had ordered 850 improved P-47Ds from Republic, with a further 324 to be built by Curtiss at Buffalo (under the designation P-47G). Production of "razorback" P-47Ds eventually reached a total of 6,313, including 2,350 built at a new Republic facility at

Evansville, Indiana.

From production block 25 onwards all P-47Ds were fitted with the new "bubble" canopy giving good rearward visibility. A total of 6,289 late-model Ds were built at Farmingdale and Evansville, with a further 354 Curtiss-built P-47Gs.

In combat the Thunderbolt gradually built up a solid reputation for its ability to absorb battle damage and its stability as a gun platform, and the reputations of many pilots in the European and Pacific theatres were made on this hefty and demanding aircraft.

The P-47M, a high-speed version with a "sprint" engine, was capable of 470 mph at 30,000ft. Only 130 were built, however, and they equipped the 56th Fighter Group, based in Britain,

in the closing months of 1944.

Final production variant was the P-47N, intended specifically for service in the Pacific. These aircraft had a larger, strengthened wing able to carry 186 gallons of fuel and giving the aircraft a grand total of 1,266 gallons of internal fuel for a range of 2,350 miles. Republic built a total of 1,816.

Production of all versions of the "Jug" reached a staggering 15,579, some 5,222 of which were lost from all causes during the Second World War. Combat loss rate, however, was less than 0.7%. After the war Thunderbolts continued to serve for some years with SAC, TAC and ADC squadrons. The type then passed to ANG units and the last Thunderbolt was finally withdrawn from service in 1955.

North American P-51 Mustang

Justly one of the most famous aircraft ever built, the Mustang was also one of the most attractive of the Second World War fighters. Although designed and built in the US, it owed its existence to the British Air Purchasing Commission, which had gone shopping in America in 1940 for a P-40 substitute.

North American was selected to develop the aircraft and was given just 120 days to complete the prototype. Not only did the company meet the deadline but it also succeeded in producing a design of outstanding brilliance, featuring a laminar-flow wing and a radiator ingeniously positioned for minimum drag. Powered by a 1,100 hp Allison V-1710-F3R, the prototype NA-73 first flew in October 1940. First production aircraft were for the RAF, which designated them Mustang Is.

The Air Force received two examples of early production aircraft for evaluation at Wright Field under the designation XP-51. This resulted in an initial order for 150 P-51s armed with four wing-mounted 20mm cannon, followed by a further 310 P-51As with 0.50in machine guns and the more powerful Allison V-1710-81.

Performance at altitude with the Allison engine was not particularly good, and the Mustang was saved from mediocrity only by the substitution of the British Rolls-Royce Merlin for the American engine. First modifications were carried out in Britain in 1942 with Lend-Lease aircraft. US-built Mustangs later incorporated the 1,300 hp Packard-built V-1650-3, which conferred significant performance gains.

Subsequent versions were designated P-51B and P-51C, with the first P-51Bs being delivered to the 8th Air Force in Britain from December 1943. Deployment of these long-legged fighters to Europe was to prove extremely significant, giving the Air Force for the first time an aircraft capable of escorting the vulnerable B-17s and B-24s deep into enemy territory. By the end of the war Mustangs equipped all but one of the 8th Air Force's fighter escort groups.

Production of Merlin-engined P-51Bs and Cs totalled 3,738 from production lines at Inglewood and Dallas. Of this total, some 887 were supplied to the RAF as Mustang IIIs.

A further significant event was the 1944 introduction of the fully blown "bubble" canopy on the P-51D. With its cut-down rear fuselage top the P-51D provided the rearward view vital to survival in European operations. Production of the P-51D totalled 7,956 at Inglewood and Dallas.

The P-51D was numerically and operationally the most important of all the Mustangs. Armed with six wing-mounted 0.50in machine guns, it performed as a potent bomber escort in the dangerous skies over Northern Europe. The P-51K, 1,337 of which were built at Dallas, differed from the D only in the type of propeller fitted.

Last production version was the P-51H, some 555 of which were built at Inglewood out of a planned total of 1,445. This lightweight version was intended primarily for service in the Pacific and was powered by a 2,218 hp V-1650-9. Apart from the first 20 aircraft, all P-51Hs had a taller fin and rudder for improved directional stability. Production of 1,700 projected P-51Ls, with the more powerful V-1650-11, was cancelled.

At the war's end the Air Force had about 5,500 Mustangs in its inventory. Many of these continued to serve with the peacetime Air Force and, from 1946, with the newly created Air National Guard.

North American XP-51G

North American P-51B-10 Mustang

North American P-51D-5

Stinson L-5 Sentinel

Continuing its policy of adopting light aircraft for observation and liaison duties, the Army evaluated six three-seat Stinson 105 Voyager high-wing light aircraft in 1941 under the designation YO-54.

The O-62 production version had a larger fuselage and was somewhat heavier than the Voyager but incorporated the same 34ft-span wing. Powerplant was the 185 hp Lycoming O-435-1 flat-four engine.

With deliveries of the initial version totalling 1,731, and orders for later variants bringing the grand total to more than 3,000, the Sentinel was the second most numerous Army liaison aircraft after the Piper L-4. After 275 O-62s had been delivered the designation was changed to L-5; in 1943 some 688 L-5s were converted to L-5As with minor refinements to systems and mission equipment.

The ambulance version, with an upwards-hinged hatch aft of the cabin, was designated L-5B. A total of 679 were built, and this variant served in both the Pacific theatre during the Second World War and in the Korean War. The L-5C was a reconnaissance version with provision for a K-20 camera in the fuselage, while the L-5E was similar to the E but incorporated drooping ailerons coupled to flaps. A total of 758 of the two versions were built.

Stinson L-5 Sentinel
Boeing B-29A-30-BN Superfortress

Bell P-63 Kingcobra

Although it bore some external resemblance to the P-59 Airacobra, the P-63 Kingcobra was in fact an entirely new design. The first prototype XP-63 flew for the first time on December 2, 1942, powered by the 1,325 hp Allison V-1710-47.

Delivery of production P-63As began in October 1943. Bell built more than 3,300 of all variants, all but 882 of which went to the Soviet Union under Lend-Lease contracts. At least 300 of the remainder were supplied to the Free French Air Force.

The USAAF had no operational requirement for the aircraft, and of the 580 or so that remained in the US some 332 were used as RP-63 targets. The other 248 were used for a variety of experimental and non-operational purposes.

The RP-63 programme, begun during 1943, was directed at the production of a manned target aircraft which could be shot at with frangible bullets. Hits were registered by flashing lights on the wingtips and the type became known as the "Pinball Target". The RP-63A, C and G were later redesignated QF-63A, C and G respectively, although they were never flown as pilotless drones.

Bell P-63A Kingcobra

Boeing B-29 Superfortress

Best remembered as the aircraft which dropped the two atomic bombs on Japan in 1945, the B-29 Superfortress was not in fact a direct development of Boeing's B-17 Flying Fortress. Its origins lay in the huge XB-15 of 1937, from which it was evolved in a continuing series of design studies which culminated in the Model 347 "Hemisphere Defense Weapon".

Two XB-29 prototypes were approved in August 1940, and a third flying prototype was ordered the following December, together with a static-test airframe. The Air Force ordered 14 service-test YB-29s in 1941 and 500 production aircraft by January 1942. The first prototype flew for the first time at Seattle on September 21, 1942, by which time the Air Force had set up a production organisation involving not only Boeing but also Bell, North American and the Fisher Body Division of General Motors.

Powered by four 2,200 hp Wright R-3350-23 engines, production aircraft could carry up to 20,000lb of bombs internally and had a range of more than 3,000 miles with a useful load of 10,000lb. Like the B-17, the huge "Superfort" carried an awesome defensive armament consisting of four barbettes, each with twin 0.50in machine guns and sited above and below the fuselage, plus a tail station with twin 0.50s and a 20mm cannon. The General Electric fuselage barbettes were remotely controlled from sighting stations inside the pressurised fuselage, while the Bell tail turret was under the direct control of the gunner.

The first B-29 unit to be equipped was the 58th VHB (Very Heavy Bomber) Wing at Marietta, Georgia, in June 1943. This unit became active when the 40th, 444th, 462nd and 468th bombardment groups began operations against Japanese targets from bases in India in the spring of 1944.

As US forces began the reclamation of the Pacific islands from the Japanese during 1944 the Air Force was able to deploy increasing numbers of Superforts into the theatre, using a network of specially built airfields. Attacks on the Japanese homeland began in November 1944, and by the following January the aircraft had been switched from high-altitude daylight precision operations to low-level night raids with incendiary bombs, a move which contributed to the virtual elimination of a number of cities. The first atomic bomb was dropped on Hiroshima on August 6, 1945, and the second on Nagasaki three days later; Japan surrendered on August 14.

When the B-29 production line closed in May 1946 a total of 3,970 had been built. After the war the type continued to serve in a variety of roles, including reconnaissance and air rescue and as target drones and carriers for a number of research aircraft such as the Bell X-1, Douglas D-558-II and McDonnell XF-85 Goblin. The most significant modification of all turned a large number of B-29s into KB-29 tankers.

Boeing B-29A-5

Boeing B-29B-60-BA

Sikorsky R-4B Hoverfly
Sikorsky XR-6A

Sikorsky R-4, R-5 and R-6

The Sikorsky R-4 was the first US military helicopter to be supplied in production quantities. Flown for the first time as the XR-4 on January 13, 1942, it was powered by a 165 hp Warner R-500-3 and had accommodation for a crew of two.

The USAAF later ordered 30 evaluation machines, the first three of which were designated YR-4A and the remainder YR-4B. The YR-4B was powered by a 180 hp Warner R-550-1 and had gross weight increased from 2,450lb to 2,900lb. After extensive tests under a variety of environmental conditions the USAAF placed a production order for 100 R-4Bs.

The R-5 was based on the R-4 but was substantially larger and powered by a 450 hp Pratt & Whitney R-985-AN-5. First flown on August 18, 1943, the XR-5 was followed by 26 service-test YR-5As and 34 production R-5As. The latter were equipped with litter carriers on either side of the fuselage and were the Air Rescue Service's first helicopters. Some 21 R-5As were later modified to R-5D standard.

The commercial variant was the four-seat Sikorsky S-51, of which the USAAF bought 11 under the designation R-5F in 1947. During the following year Air Force aircraft designations were revised and the "R" was replaced by "H". Thus later purchases carried the designations H-5G and H-5H.

The Sikorsky R-6, developed in parallel with the R-5, was a refinement of the R-4, with the same rotor and transmission system in an improved fuselage. A total of 26 pre-production YR-6As and 193 R-6As were built under licence by the Nash Kelvinator Corporation.

Northrop P-61 Black Widow

US Army interest in night fighters was stimulated by the air war in Europe during 1940. To meet an Army Air Corps requirement for such a type Northrop offered a twin-engined, twin-boom design, the NS-8A, in November 1940. In January 1941 two prototypes were ordered on a fixed-price contract worth about $1.2 million. Designated XP-61, these aircraft were followed in March by an order for 13 service-test YP-61s. Airborne-intercept (AI) radar development was carried out at the Massachusetts Institute of Technology's Radiation Laboratory.

Production orders were placed before the prototype's May 26, 1942, first flight, some 150 having been ordered in September 1941 and a further

410 in the following February. The two-seat P-61 was the first US aircraft designed specifically for the night-fighter role and was as large as a medium bomber. Powerplant was two 2,000 hp Pratt & Whitney R-2800-10s and armament four 20mm cannon with 600 rounds in a bulge below the fuselage and four 0.50in machine guns with 1,600 rounds per gun in a remotely controlled barbette above the rear fuselage. The SCR-720 radar was mounted in the nose.

The first of 200 P-61As were delivered to the Air Force during October 1943; after the 37th had been delivered, however, the four-gun barbette was removed to lessen buffeting, and from the 46th aircraft the engines were changed to the -65 type, rated at 2,250 hp.

The first Air Force unit to be equipped with production Black Widows, in March 1944, was the 348th Night Fighter Squadron of the 481st Fighter Group, charged with training AAF night-fighter crews. In May the type was assigned to the European theatre, equipping the 422nd Night Fighter Squadron, based at Scorton. The 422nd was joined in June by the 425th NFS and aircraft from both units began operations from Hurn in early July.

Entering service in 1944 with the 18th Fighter Group in the South Pacific, where it replaced the P-70, the P-61 made its first kill in July and by the end of the year the Black Widow was standard equipment in all USAAF night-fighter squadrons. July 1944 also saw the first

deliveries of some 450 P-61Bs, which could carry four 1,600lb bombs or a 300-gallon drop-tank; the final 250 of this order had the top barbette re-installed, the buffeting problem having been solved in the meantime.

The P-61C, with turbo-supercharged 2,800 hp R-2800-73 engines, appeared in July 1945, but only 41 had been completed by VJ Day and a further 476 from this order were cancelled. A reconnaissance version, the F-15A Reporter, was also built, 36 being completed during 1946 after one XP-61E day fighter prototype and one P-61A had been converted as prototypes. Re-designated RF-61C in 1948, the Black Widow had been withdrawn from service by 1952.

Douglas XB-42A

Douglas XB-43

Douglas XB-42 and XB-43

The unorthodox three-seat Douglas XB-42 Mixmaster was one of the most advanced propeller-driven aircraft ever designed. With the striking range of the B-29 and combining the speed of the Mosquito B.XVI with twice its bomb load, the Mixmaster should have had a brilliant operational career. But, as with so many designs that appeared in the mid-1940s, it was rapidly overtaken in performance, reliability and economy of operation by jet-powered aircraft.

Originally a private venture, the design was submitted to the Bombardment Branch, Engineering Division, Air Technical Service Command, in May 1943 and a contract for two flying prototypes and one static airframe was awarded the following month.

The first prototype XB-42 was flown for the first time by Bob Brush on May 6, 1944, powered by two 1,800 hp Allison V-1710-125 engines. The second prototype, with an orthodox canopy replacing the individual blister canopies of the first aircraft, flew for the first time on August 1, 1944, but was destroyed on December 15, 1945.

The XB-43, the first US jet bomber, was first proposed in October 1943 as a straightforward development of the piston-engined XB-42.

Changes to the XB-42 design consisted of the installation of two General Electric TG-180 (later J35-GE-3) turbojets in the engine bays previously inhabited by the Allisons. Flush air intakes were located in the upper fuselage sides behind the two-seat cockpit and the lower fin was removed; an increase in the area of the upper fin restored the keel area thus lost.

So simple were the modifications to convert the XB-42 to jet power that the static-airframe XB-42 was selected to become the prototype XB-43. First flight—again with Bob Brush in charge—was made from Muroc on May 17, 1946. By this time plans to build a production batch of 50 aircraft had been shelved and the second aircraft, delivered to Muroc in May 1947, was used as an engine testbed.

Douglas XA-26, April 1943

Douglas A-26/B-26 Invader

The Douglas A-26 light bomber was designed to meet a 1940 USAAF requirement for a single successor to the Douglas A-20, Martin B-26 and North American B-25.

Two prototypes were ordered in June 1941. The first of these, the XA-26, was a three-seat attack bomber with a glazed nose, while the second, the XA-26A, was a two-seat night fighter with AI radar and fixed forward-firing armament. A third prototype, the XA-26B three-seat attack aircraft with a 75mm cannon in its solid nose, was added to the contract a few weeks later.

First flight was made by the XA-26 on July 10, 1942, from Mines Field. Following flight tests of all three prototypes the

A-26B was adopted as the initial production version. Armament was extensive, consisting typically of six nose-mounted 0.50in machine guns in place of the prototype's 75mm cannon, together with remotely controlled dorsal and ventral turrets. A total of 1,355 A-26Bs were built, with deliveries beginning in early 1944. The type made its operational debut in November 1944 with the 9th Air Force in Europe.

The A-29C differed from the A-26B in having a transparent nose but was also powered by two 2,000 hp Pratt & Whitney R-2800-27 or -79 engines. Delivery of 1,091 began in January 1945.

Large quantities of A-26Bs

and Cs remained in front-line service after the Second World War and the Invader was the primary attack aircraft with Tactical Air Command when this formation was created in 1946 from the old 9th and 12th Air Forces. In 1948 the attack category was discontinued and the aircraft were redesignated B-26B and B-26C.

In Korea the B-26 was widely used by the 3rd and later the 17th bombardment wings, flying tactical intruder missions from Iwakuni, Japan. Invaders were also used by the 12th Tactical Reconnaissance Squadron.

During the 1960s the Invader received a new lease of life when

it was used by the 1st Air Commando Group at Eglin AFB, Florida, to develop counter-insurgency tactics. For this purpose a remanufactured version, the YB-26K Counter Invader, was developed towards the end of 1962. Following extensive evaluation at Eglin the USAF ordered 40 B-26Ks powered by a pair of 2,500 hp R-2800-52Ws in October 1963. These aircraft were delivered between June 1964 and April 1965.

B-26Ks were used by the 606th Air Commando Squadron in the Vietnam War, operating out of Nakhon Phanom Air Base in Thailand on night intruder missions over the Ho Chi Minh Trail until phased out of service in November 1969.

Douglas B-26K

Bell XP-77

The diminutive Bell XP-77 appeared as a result of a shortage of strategic materials in the early war years, allied to a requirement for a lightweight single-seat fighter to combat the Japanese Zero, which was causing heavy losses in the Pacific.

Discussions between USAAF personnel and Bell designers and engineers began in October 1941 and led to an order for six prototypes and two static airframes in September 1942. Bell's heavy commitment to production and development of the P-39 and P-63 fighters slowed work on the little Ranger-engined all-wood fighter and official interest rapidly evaporated.

In August 1943 the contract was cut back to just two flying prototypes, the first of which was not ready to fly until April 1944. Following the loss on October 2 of the second aircraft after an unchecked inverted spin, the programme was terminated in December 1944 on the grounds that the aircraft showed no real advantage over more orthodox fighters.

Bell XP-77

Bell P-59 Airacomet

Bell P-59 Airacomet

The impetus behind America's first jet fighter programme, the Bell P-59 Airacomet, came from General Henry Arnold of the US Army Air Force, who had seen the Gloster E28/39 aircraft and its Whittle engine in Britain in April 1941, a few weeks before its first flight. On September 4 General Electric was invited to build 15 copies of the engine under licence and on the following day the Bell Aircraft Corporation, near neighbour of General Electric, was requested to design and develop a suitable airframe.

For security reasons the new aircraft was assigned the designation XP-59A in order to cause confusion with Bell's twin-boom pusher fighter project, the XP-59 (later quietly cancelled). Construction of the first prototype began in early 1942 and in September the completed airframe was crated up and moved by rail to Muroc

Bombing Range in California, later to become famous as Edwards Air Force Base. Powered by two General Electric Type I-A turbojets, the prototype made its first flight on October 1, piloted by Bell chief test pilot Robert M. Stanley. Three XP-59As and 13 YP-59A service-test aircraft were ordered, and the first two YP-59As arrived at Muroc in June 1943. The third service-test aircraft was shipped to Britain for comparative trials with the Gloster Meteor, an example of which was also shipped to the US. By then the engines had been substantially improved and, designated I-16 (later J31), they provided a nominal 1,600lb st each.

Production Airacomets were armed with one nose-mounted 37mm cannon and three 0.50in machine guns, with bomb racks under each wing. A production contract for 100 P-59As was

confirmed in March 1944 and deliveries began towards the end of the year. By that time, however, the Air Force had been able to evaluate the aircraft fully and it was decided to terminate the contract at 50 aircraft, a total composed of 20 P-59As and 30 P-59Bs.

The P-59A was used extensively on various research projects, operating with Air Force Proving Ground Command at Eglin Field, Florida, the Air Forces Board at Orlando, Florida, and with the Extreme Temperature Operations Unit of the Cold Weather Test Unit at Ladd Field, Alaska. Other P-59As were supplied to the 412th Fighter Group of the 4th Air Force for operational evaluation, the first unit working up at Muroc. Only 19 of the P-59Bs joined the 412th FG, which began re-equipping with the P-80 Shooting Star at the end of 1945.

General Motors (Fisher) P-75 Eagle

The P-75 Eagle was a curious hybrid built from the major components of several established types. In September 1942 the Fisher Body Division of General Motors submitted a proposal for a single-seat fighter using the untried Allison V-3420-19 liquid- cooled engine. A contract for two prototypes was awarded on October 10, resulting in a burst of feverish activity by Fisher. In order to assemble the prototypes as quickly as possible the company used Douglas A-24 Dauntless tail assemblies, F4U Corsair undercarriage and the outer wing panels of the Curtiss P-40. The big Allison engine was buried in the centre fuselage and drove contra-rotating propellers through twin shafts running under the cockpit.

By the middle of 1943 the USAAF was beginning to experience an urgent need for long-range escort fighters. Six XP-75s modified for long-range operation were accordingly ordered, with plans being made even at that stage for quantity production of 2,500 examples.

First flight of the prototype took place on November 17, 1943, and the first of the production P-75As, with modified canopy and tail, emerged in September 1944. Flight tests were not encouraging and the availability of the P-51 Mustang, P-47 Thunderbolt and P-38 Lightning rendered the Eagle superfluous. The production contract was terminated early in October 1944 after only six aircraft had been completed.

General Motors (Fisher) P-75A Eagle

Convair B-32 Dominator

Convair B-32 Dominator

The XB-32 Dominator was Convair's submission in response to the US Army Air Force's 1940 requirement for a "Hemisphere Defense Weapon". Although the requirement was later to be admirably met by the Boeing B-29 Superfortress, the Convair design was promising enough for three prototypes to be ordered in September 1940 as insurance against the possible failure of the B-29.

The first XB-32 flew on September 7, 1942, and had the same unbroken blunt nose profile as the B-29. Like the B-24 it had twin endplate fins mounted on a tailplane with marked dihedral. The second prototype embodied a stepped-down cockpit and flew for the first time in July 1943, while the third aircraft, which first flew on November 9, 1943, featured a tall single fin similar to that of the PB4Y-2 Privateer supplied to the US Navy by Convair.

Earmarked for low-altitude missions in the Pacific theatre, the production B-32 was completed without pressurisation or remotely controlled gun turrets in an effort to save weight. When deliveries began in November 1944, however, official opinion was that the aircraft was still overweight and that bombardier visibility was inadequate, and it was decided to cut back production and to equip only one combat group. At the end of the war only 115 out of a total order of 1,713 had been completed and the remainder were cancelled.

Lockheed C-69 and C-121 Constellation

The four-engined, triple-finned Lockheed Constellation was originally designed as an airliner for Howard Hughes' Trans World Airlines. Following the sudden entry of the US into the Second World War in December 1941, those aircraft already on the production line were requisitioned by the USAAF and designated C-69.

First flown from Burbank on January 9, 1943, the first C-69 was powered by four 2,200 hp Wright R-3350-35s. With a top speed of nearly 330 mph, it was the fastest transport to be acquired to date by the Air Force and could accommodate up to 64 passengers.

Only 22 out of a 1942 contract for 180 aircraft had been built by VJ Day, and these were operated by Air Transport Command until the end of the war, when they were declared surplus and re-sold to the airlines.

In 1948 the USAF ordered 10 C-121 Constellations for use by MATS on long-range VIP missions. These aircraft were designated C-121A, VC-121A or VC-121P, according to their seating arrangements; all were later redesignated PC-121A.

In 1951 the Air Force ordered 33 of a larger, improved model, the C-121C, powered by four 3,500 hp R-3350-34s. These were supplemented by 32 similar C-121Gs, which had originally been acquired by the US Navy and designated R7V-1.

Air Defense Command took delivery of its first RC-121C radar picket aircraft in October 1953, the aircraft going initially to the 552nd AEW & C Wing. The first 10 aircraft were converted C-121Cs and carried vast radomes above and below their centre fuselages. May 1954 saw the appearance of the first RC-121Ds, distinguished by their wing-tip fuel tanks.

Successive changes and improvements in equipment resulted in corresponding designation changes, with all variants later assuming the EC prefix. Several EC-121 Warning Stars continue to operate with Air Defense Command and Air Force Reserve units.

Lockheed C-69

Lockheed C-121C

UNITED STATES AIR FORCE

Lockheed RC-121

Lockheed F-80A

Lockheed T-33

Lockheed F-80

Lockheed P-80 and T-33 Shooting Star

The Lockheed P-80 was the first jet aircraft to be used operationally by the USAAF. Development began in June 1943 and the first contracts covered three XP-80 prototypes and 13 service-test YP-80As.

The first XP-80 prototype was built at Burbank and flew for the first time at Muroc on January 8, 1944, powered by a 3,000lb st de Havilland H-1 turbojet. The second two prototypes were powered by the Allison-developed General Electric J33 of about 4,000lb st and were designated XP-80A. The 13 service-test aircraft were fitted with production-standard J33-GE-9 or -11 engines and

armed with six nose-mounted 0.50in machine guns.

Planned production amounted to 5,000 P-80s by Lockheed and North American, but more than 3,000 were cancelled after VJ Day, and Lockheed's order was cut back to only 917 P-80As. The first of these were delivered during December 1945. Towards the end of the production run the J33-A-11 became the standard powerplant.

The P-80B, which first appeared in 1946, was powered by the 5,200lb st J33-A-21. A total of 240 late-production P-80As were either completed to this standard or were converted

later. Final production model was the P-80C, some 798 of which were built during 1948 and 1949. On June 11, 1948, "F" replaced "P" as the designation for US Air Force fighters and the Shooting Star was henceforth known as the F-80.

The type was used extensively in the Korean War, principally on ground-attack missions. After Korea the Shooting Star was rapidly downgraded as a result of the emergence of several more advanced aircraft, and most F-80s were redeployed as trainers or with Air National Guard units.

The RF-80A—originally

designated FP-80A—was an unarmed photographic-reconnaissance variant, some 53 of which were converted from F-80As. A number of F-80Cs were also converted to RF-80Cs.

Most enduring of all Shooting Star variants was the T-33 trainer conversion, produced by lengthening a standard F-80C airframe by more than 3ft to accommodate a second seat beneath a single canopy. Designated TF-80C, the first conversion flew on March 22, 1948. Production continued until August 1959, by which time Lockheed had built a total of 5,691.

Fairchild C-82A

Fairchild C-119F

Fairchild C-82 Packet and C-119 Flying Boxcar

The Fairchild C-82 was designed in 1941 to meet a USAAF requirement for a tactical freight and troop transport. Powered by two 2,100 hp Pratt & Whitney R-2800-85s, the prototype XC-82 flew for the first time on September 10, 1944, by which time the manufacturer had already received a production contract for 100 C-82A Packets. The type could carry 42 troops or 34 stretchers and was also suitable for glider towing and for air-dropping vehicles or freight. Deliveries ended in September 1948 after a total of 220 had been built.

In 1946 the C-82 was assigned to troop-carrier units of Tactical Air Command, although some examples were later allocated to MATS. All were declared surplus in 1954 and disposed of on the civil market.

An improved version of the Packet, under development since 1947, ultimately became the C-119A, which flew for the first time in November 1947 on the power of two 2,650 hp R-4360-4s. First production version was the C-119B with R-4360-20s, and delivery of 55 for the Air Force began in December 1949. These were followed by 347 C-119Cs with 3,500 hp R-4360-20WAs.

Most numerous of the Boxcar variants was the C-119G, some 480 of which were built to supplement 210 C-119Fs. Serving principally with Troop Carrier Command, the Flying Boxcar was used extensively during the Korean War and in Europe. Large numbers were also used by Air National Guard units.

In 1966 a batch of C-119Gs were brought up to C-119K standard by the installation of two 2,850lb st General Electric J85-GE-17 auxiliary turbojets and two 3,700 hp Wright R-3350-999s.

During the Vietnam War the USAF modified 52 C-119s as gunships. Designated AC-119G and AC-119K, they carried the names Shadow and Stinger respectively. Used for the suppression of enemy ground fire, they were normally armed with four side-firing 7.62mm General Electric Miniguns.

Northrop XB-35 and YB-49 Flying Wing

In 1941 Northrop began development of a series of long-range flying-wing bombers designed as a cheaper alternative to the massive strategic bombers from Boeing and Convair (the B-29 and B-36 respectively).

Northrop submitted its preliminary layout to the USAAF in September 1941 and detail design began in February 1942, with approval of the mock-up following in July that year. Design and construction of the XB-35 prototype proved to be a mammoth task and the aircraft was not completed until 1946. First flight, from Northrop's Hawthorne plant to Muroc (later Edwards AFB), was commanded by Max Stanley on June 25, 1946. The huge aircraft was powered by two 3,000 hp Pratt & Whitney R-4360-17s and two R-4360-21s, each driving pusher contra-rotating propellers. Full crew complement was 15, consisting of nine operational members and six reserves.

Aerodynamically sound, the XB-35 suffered from a succession of propulsion problems and the contra-props were eventually replaced by single-rotation units. But a production order for 200 B-35As was later cancelled and the aircraft never progressed beyond the prototype stage.

The YB-49 jet-powered version, with eight 4,000lb Allison J35-A-5 turbojets, first flew on October 21, 1947. The second YB-49 was destroyed in a fatal crash on June 5, 1948. The Air Force had earlier placed orders for 30 production aircraft, with more to follow, but the entire programme was terminated in late 1949 and all available funds were diverted to the B-36.

Northrop XB-35

North American P-82 Twin Mustang

North American F-82
Twin Mustang

The twin-engined, twin-boom North American F-82 was the last propeller-driven fighter to be acquired by the Air Force. Development began in January 1944, with the object of producing a long-range fighter with accommodation for two pilots, principally for operations in the Pacific theatre. Each consisting essentially of two P-51H fuselages joined together on a new centre wing and tailplane, the first two prototype XP-82 Twin Mustangs were powered by two Packard Merlins with opposite rotation. The third prototype, the XP-82A, had a pair of Allison V-1710-119s with common rotation. First flight of the new aircraft took place on April 15, 1945.

The initial order was for 500 P-82Bs, similar to the XP-82 prototype, but the order was cut back to only 20 after VJ Day. Two were equipped as night fighters and designated P-82C and P-82E. Finished in an all-black paint scheme, they carried an

SCR-720 and APS-4 radar respectively in a pod under the centre section; the co-pilot's cockpit on the starboard side was fitted out as a radar operator's position.

In March 1947 the Air Force ordered 250 Twin Mustangs, 100 of which were delivered as P-82E escort fighters, 91 as P-82F night fighters with APS-4 radar, and the final 59 as P-82Gs with SCR-720 radar. All 250 were powered by two 1,600 hp Allison V-1710-143/145 engines with opposite-rotating propellers. Designation of the B to G variants was changed to F-82 in June 1948.

When production ended in March 1949 the F-82 had replaced the P-61 Black Widow in Air Defense Command night-fighter squadrons. The type was used extensively by the 5th Air Force in the Korean War and on June 27, 1950, became the first US type to shoot down a North Korean aircraft.

Convair B-36

One of the largest aircraft ever built, the Convair B-36 generated a body of controversy almost equal to its size during its protracted development and service life. Its wing span was 230ft, or about the width of a full-size soccer pitch, and the later ten-engined versions had a gross weight of around 410,000lb—more than 180 tons.

Development of the Consolidated Model 37 began in response to a USAAF specification issued in April 1941 which called for a long-range strategic bomber capable of striking at European targets from bases in the US. It was to carry a 10,000lb load for 5,000 miles and be able to return without refuelling. Top speed was to be 240-300 mph and operating ceiling 35,000ft.

Two prototypes were ordered in 1941 but construction did not begin until the end of the following year. Designed initially with twin tail fins and rudders, the prototype XB-36 featured a single unit when it was rolled out in September 1945. First flight was made on August 8, 1946, under the power of six 3,000 hp Pratt & Whitney R-4360-25 engines buried in the huge wing and driving three-bladed pusher propellers no less than 19ft in diameter.

The second prototype, designated YB-36, introduced the domed cockpit roof which became standard on production aircraft. The initial production order for 100 aircraft was cut back in 1947 to 95, consisting of 22 unarmed B-36As, powered by R-4360-25s, and 73 B-36Bs powered by -41s.

The B-36As were delivered to the 7th Bombardment Wing of SAC at Carswell AFB from August 1947 and were used mainly for training and crew conversion, while the B-36Bs—the first of which flew for the first time on July 8, 1948—were fully operational, equipping SAC from November that year.

The B-36C, which was to have had six 5,500 hp Pratt & Whitney R-4360-VDT engines driving tractor propellers, was not built. The next production version was thus the B-36D, with four 5,200lb st General Electric J47-GE-19s paired in pods beneath the outer wing in addition to the six radial piston engines. Production ran to 86:

Prototype Convair XB-36 Peacemaker

Convair GRB-36F with GRF-84F Thunderstreak for FICON programme

64 converted from B-36Bs and 22 built from scratch. The first conversion was flown in July 1949 and deliveries to Eglin AFB, Florida, began in August 1950.

Another seven B-36Bs were converted to RB-36D strategic reconnaissance aircraft, followed by 17 built as new. During 1950 21 of the original B-36As, plus the YB-36, were converted to RB-36E standard. Production continued with 34 B-36Fs, powered by R-4360-53s, and 24 similar RB-36Fs.

The 83 B-36Hs, the first of which first flew in April 1952, featured an improved flight deck, while the B-36J, some 33 of which were built, had extra fuel tanks in the outer wings. Convair also built 73 RB-36Hs.

The B-36 was used for a variety of experimental programmes, including the FICON (Fighter Conveyor) parasite fighter programme using XF-85 Goblin and GRF-84F aircraft, and the NB-36H, which carried an airborne nuclear reactor.

SAC retired its last active B-36 in February 1959, when the B-52 began to enter service in

quantity.

In 1942 a parallel development of the B-36 for use as a long-range transport materialised as the XC-99. This outstandingly ugly aircraft combined the wings, tail assembly and powerplants of the bomber with a new double-deck fuselage capable of accommodating 400 fully equipped troops. First flown on November 23, 1947, it was delivered to the USAF in May 1949 and subsequently operated from Kelly AFB until retired in 1957.

Boeing B-50D

Boeing B-50 Superfortress

In 1944 Pratt & Whitney modified a B-29A Superfortress to take four 3,500 hp R-4360 engines, and this conversion was designated XB-44. Put into production by Boeing at Renton, Washington, in 1945 as the B-29D, the type was redesignated B-50 before deliveries began. In addition to uprated engines the new bomber featured a new, taller fin, revised undercarriage, a lighter wing structure and other detailed refinements.

The original order for 200 aircraft placed in July 1945 was later cut to 60 and production rate was sliced from 155 to only 20 a month. First flight took

place on June 25, 1947, and the B-50 became the first new bomber to be delivered to the recently formed Strategic Air Command (SAC).

A total of 79 B-50As were completed by January 1949 and were followed into production by 45 B-50Bs with strengthened wings and gross weight increased to 170,000lb. All but one of the B-50Bs were later converted to RB-50B standard for service with strategic reconnasissance squadrons. They were equipped with four camera stations with nine cameras, weather reconaissance equipment and provision for 700-gallon underwing fuel tanks.

In 1951 43 of the converted aircraft were again modified, 14 becoming RB-50Es, another 14 RB-50Fs with SHORAN, and 15 RB-50Gs with radar, electronics and armament changes.

A B-50C version with four Pratt & Whitney R-4360-51 engines was proposed, and the necessary airframe redesign was so extensive that the 43 aircraft ordered were given the designation B-54A. In April 1949, however, they were cancelled in favour of the giant Convair B-36. The production effort was then concentrated on the improved B-50D with R-3350-35 engines, 700-gallon underwing fuel tanks and one-piece Plexiglas nose

cone. Boeing built 222 B-50Ds and TB-50H trainers between May 1949 and February 1953.

As the B-50Ds reached the end of their operational lives many were converted for support duties, emerging as TB-50A and TB-50B trainers for B-36 crews, and KB-50 triple-hose refuelling tankers for Tactical Air Command (TAC). These tankers subsequently had J47 jet pods mounted under the wings in place of the wing fuel tanks. A total of 128 KB-50J and 50K jet-boosted tankers were converted by Hayes Aircraft Corporation, the first 50J making its maiden flight in December 1957.

Grumman SA-16 Albatross

The twin-engined G-64 Albatross was originally designed in 1946 to meet a US Navy requirement for a general-purpose type suitable for use as a transport, trainer or rescue aircraft. First flown as the XJR2F-1 on October 24, 1947, the type was adopted by the US Air Force almost immediately.

Earmarked for search and rescue missions, Air Force aircraft were designated SA-16A. Some 302 were delivered, each powered by a pair of 1,425 hp Wright R-1820-76s. Most of these were operated by the MATS Air Rescue Service from 1947 onwards.

The SA-16B was an improved version of the SA-16A with increased wing span, larger tail surfaces and more powerful de-icing boots. The first SA-16B flew for the first time on January 16, 1956. Beginning in January 1957, all SA-16As were brought up to SA-16B standard. In 1962 Air Force Albatrosses were redesignated in the Utility category as HU-16As or HU-16Bs.

The Republic F-84 Thunderjet, conceived in 1944 as a jet-powered successor to the P-47 Thunderbolt, was the first USAF single-seat fighter-bomber capable of delivering a tactical nuclear weapon.

The first of three prototype XP-84s was flown for the first time at Muroc on February 28, 1946, powered by a 3,750lb st General Electric J35-GE-7 turbojet. The first 15 production aircraft were designated YF-84As and were powered by the 4,000lb st Allison-built J35-A-15.

The first operational model was the P-84B, some 224 of which were built. Deliveries began in the summer of 1947 and the 14th Fighter Group at Dow Field was the first unit to receive the type. In June 1948 the designation was changed to F-84B.

A total of 345 F-84Cs and F-84Ds were built, the D models differing mainly in being fitted with the 5,000lb st J35-A-17D

Republic F-84B Thunderjet

Boeing C-97 Stratofreighter

The C-97 Stratofreighter was a transport variant of the B-29 long-range bomber, with which it had the wing, engines and tail assembly in common. Conceived in mid-1942 as the Boeing Model 367, the proposal was accepted by the USAAF and a contract for three prototype XC-97s was placed on January 23, 1943.

The first flight was made on November 15, 1944, and on January 9, 1945, the first prototype crossed the US with a 20,000lb payload at a speed of 383 mph. In July 1945 the Air Force ordered six YC-97, three YC-97A and one YC-97B service-test aircraft. Flying for the first time on March 11, 1947, the six YC-97s later went into service with Air Transport Command.

The three YC-97As incorporated features built into the B-50 bomber, including the taller fin and R-4360 engines, and first flew in January 1948. In December a production contract for 27 C-97As was increased to 50 aircraft, the first of which was delivered in October 1949. These aircraft were used by both MATS (Military Air Transport Services) and SAC (Strategic Air Command) crews and saw service during the Korean War.

Second production version was the C-97C, of which only 14 were built. Powered by R-4360-35A engines, the first was delivered in February 1951 and the type was mostly used for casualty evacuation.

The most important

development of the Stratofreighter was the KC-97 tanker. During 1948 and 1949 three C-97As were converted for flying-boom in-flight refuelling and redesignated KC-97A. First production version of the tanker was the KC-97E, 60 of which were built at Renton, Washington, in 1951 and 1952, with first deliveries in July 1951. The E could carry nearly 15,000 US gallons of fuel and could be converted for cargo carrying. The KC-97E was followed by 159 KC-97F tankers powered by four 3,800 hp Pratt & Whitney R-4360-59B engines, the first of which was delivered to SAC in April 1952. Deployment within SAC was usually 20 tankers to each wing of 45 Boeing B-47 bombers.

Last production variant was the KC-97G, first delivered in May 1953. Some 592 of this model were eventually built, the last one being rolled out at Renton on July 18, 1956.

All MATS Stratofreighters were progressively transferred to the Air National Guard from 1960, together with a number of Strategic Air Command tankers released by the introduction of the four-jet KC-135. In 1965 the Hayes International Corporation converted a number of ANG KC-97Gs to KC-97L configuration by fitting two General Electric J47-25 jets in pods under the outer wings to boost performance, especially at take-off.

Boeing C-97A

engine. The F-84D was the first of the Thunderjet series to serve in Korea, equipping the 27th Fighter Escort Wing by December 1950. Armament was four nose-mounted 0.50in machine guns, two wing-mounted guns and eight retractable rocket launchers beneath the wings.

The F-84E incorporated a number of improvements, including radar gunsight, improved wing-tip tanks and a longer fuselage. A total of 843 were built, with 100 allocated to Nato air forces in Europe.

Most numerous production version was the F-84G, deliveries of which began in 1951. This model was powered by the 5,600lb st J35-A-29 engine and was equipped with in-flight refuelling equipment. Republic built a total of 3,025 F-84Gs, of which nearly 2,000 were delivered straight to Nato air forces.

SAC had retired its F-84Gs by 1956, although Tactical Air Command retained its aircraft for some time afterwards.

Republic F-84E

McDonnell XF-85 Goblin

The XF-85 Goblin was a highly imaginative attempt to provide the Air Force with an inexpensive escort fighter for its long-range strategic bombers. Although the concept of parasite fighters had been briefly explored in the US during the early 1930s, it had been allowed to languish until revived in late 1942 as a way of stretching the range and endurance of early jet-powered aircraft.

The original McDonnell submission of 1944 called for a small but conventional fighter to be carried partially within a parent B-29, B-35 or B-36 bomber. In January 1945, however, the Air Force decided that the fighter should be carried entirely within the host bomber's fuselage. McDonnell's revised solution, the Model 27D, was a tiny egg-shaped fuselage with triple tail fins, stubby anhedral tailplane and foldable, sharply swept wings.

The Air Force issued a letter of intent for two prototype XF-85 Goblins in October 1945; this was confirmed in March 1947.

After making five captive flights attached to the trapeze of the EB-29B launch aircraft the Goblin made its first free flight on August 23, 1948, piloted by Edwin Schoch. The cockpit canopy was damaged during attempts to hook on to the trapeze, however, and Schoch made a successful emergency landing on a dry lakebed.

The original plan had been to order flight-test aircraft following prototype trials, but the XF-85 was so clearly a failure that the whole programme was cancelled after only 2hr 19min of test flying.

McDonnell XF-85 Goblin

North American B-45 Tornado

Early in the history of the jet-propelled bomber it became apparent that more than two engines would be needed if the performance required of the next generation of tactical aircraft was to be achieved. In April 1944 the Air Force invited proposals for a jet bomber with a speed of 500 mph, a tactical radius of 1,000 miles with a bomb load of 8,000lb, and a service ceiling of 40,000ft. Four designs were submitted: the North American XB-45, the Consolidated XB-46, Boeing's podded-jet XB-47 and the Martin XB-48.

Three prototypes of the XB-45 were ordered in December 1944, the first of which was flown for the first time at Muroc on March 17, 1947, by George Krebs. By this time a production contract for 96 B-45As had already been placed with North American. The XB-45 and first production B-45As were powered by four 4,000lb st Allison-built General Electric J35-A-11s paired in large nacelles under the wing, but later production aircraft had the 4,000lb st J47-GE-9.

The B-45A Tornado first entered service with the 47th Bombardment Group in November 1948 and the type also served in Europe with USAFE from 1952, remaining operational until mid-1958. Fourteen were later modified as TB-45A target tugs.

The B-45B, a projected version with updated radar and fire-control system, was not proceeded with. The first of ten B-45Cs, with a 1,200-gallon drop tank on each wing and powered by four 5,200lb st J47-GE-13/15s, was flown in May 1949. Production of a further 50 was cancelled to provide funds for B-36 procurement, but 33 RB-45C photo-reconnaissance aircraft were completed and delivered between June 1950 and October 1951. The type entered service with the 91st Strategic Reconnaissance Wing and later saw action during the Korean War.

North American F-86 Sabre

Design work on the USAF's first swept-wing fighter began in the closing stages of the Second World War. One static-test and two flying prototypes of a straight-winged aircraft designated XP-86 were ordered in May 1945, but evaluation of German research on swept wings led North American to adopt this radical feature and the XP-86 went back to the drawing board.

The first prototype was rolled out in August 1947 and, powered by a 4,000lb st Chevrolet-built Allison J35-C-3 turbojet, it was flown for the first time at Muroc on October 1 by George Welch.

By 1947 the Air Force had ordered 221 F-86As powered by the 4,850lb st General Electric J47-GE-1, and the first of these flew for the first time on May 18, 1948. On September 15 an F-86A flown by Maj Richard L. Johnson established a world air speed record of almost 671 mph.

Production of the F-86A totalled 554, comprising 33 F-86A-1s and 521 A-5s. First unit to be equipped was the 1st Fighter Group based at Marsh AFB, California, in early 1949, followed by the 4th and 81st FGs.

Neither the F-86B nor the F-86C progressed beyond the project stage, and the next production Sabre was the F-86E, fitted with an all-flying tailplane and powered by the J47-GE-13. A total of 336 were delivered between February 1951 and December 1952. The F-86F was basically similar to the E but was powered by the 5,970lb st

J47-GE-27.

The Sabre's baptism of fire occurred during the Korean War, the first F-86A unit to arrive being the 4th Fighter Interceptor Wing, which began its patrols in mid-December 1950. The F-86F arrived in Korea with the 8th and 18th Fighter Bomber Wings in early 1953. The F also introduced the ''6-3'' wing, which had increased chord and no slats. Production of the F totalled 1,079, mainly for USAF units. From 1954 large numbers were delivered to other nations under the auspices of MDAP, and further aircraft were built for export.

The F-86H was a full fighter variant and first flew in April 1953 powered by the 9,300lb st J73-GE-3. A total of 473 were built and all but the first 113

were armed with four nose-mounted 20mm cannon (early production aircraft carried six 0.50in machine guns).

All of the foregoing versions were essentially day fighters, and development of an all-weather interceptor Sabre did not begin until 1949. First flown at Muroc on December 22, 1949, the YF-86D was powered by the 7,650lb st J47-GE-17 and carried AN/APG-36 search radar above the nose intake. Armament consisted of 24 2.75in Mighty Mouse rockets in a retractable tray.

Production of the F-86D eventually totalled 2,504, and at the peak of its deployment in the 1950s some 20 Air Defense Command wings were equipped with the type in the US, Europe and Far East.

North American F-86F ▲

Douglas C-74 Globemaster

Douglas C-124 Globemaster II

The C-124 Globemaster II heavy cargo transport, conceived in 1947, was based on the earlier C-74 Globemaster I, which had been in production since 1945. Only 14 C-74s were built, and following retirement from the USAF a few surplus aircraft saw limited service with civilian cargo charter airlines.

The C-124 retained the wings, tail surfaces and four 3,500 hp Pratt & Whitney R-4360-49 engines of the C-74, mated to a new, substantially larger double-deck fuselage with double clamshell doors in the nose.

The prototype YC-124, which first flew on November 27, 1949, was actually the fifth C-74 and was followed by 204 production C-124As built at Douglas's Long Beach, California, facility. The Globemaster II could carry either 200 fully equipped troops or 123 stretchers, 45 walking patients and 15 medical attendants. Normal crew complement was five.

The first C-124As entered service with Military Air Transport Services (MATS) and Troop Carrier Command in May 1950 and were available at the start of the Korean War. The second production variant was the C-124C, some 243 of which were built. This version was distinguished by wing-tip combustion heaters and a thimble nose radome, features retrospectively fitted to most C-124As.

The Globemaster II gave valuable service for many years and the type was issued to troop-carrier squadrons of the Air Force Reserve and Air National Guard in 1961. They were eventually retired in the mid-1970s.

Douglas C-124 Globemaster II

Northrop F-89 Scorpion

The twin-jet two-seat F-89 Scorpion originated in a Northrop proposal of December 1945 for a jet-powered all-weather fighter to replace the P-61 Black Widow. The US Air Force accepted the proposal and ordered two prototypes in December 1946.

The first XF-89 was flown from Edwards AFB on August 16, 1948. Beginning in February 1949, trials were carried out with the new "decelerons,"

split-surface ailerons which could be deployed as airbrakes and which were adopted as standard on all production Scorpions.

First production orders were placed in July 1949 and the first of 18 F-89As was delivered in July 1951, followed by 30 F-89Bs. The F-89C incorporated numerous equipment changes as well as new elevators with internal mass balancing. Production of this variant

totalled some 164 aircraft, and all carried the same AN/APG-33 radar and armament as the A and B: six 20mm nose-mounted cannon and stores on underwing pylons.

The F-89C introduced wing-tip rocket pods containing 52 2.75in FFARs in addition to fuel. Some 682 were built. Neither the F-89E or F entered production, and the last production model of the Scorpion was the F-89H. Powered by two J35-A-35s, this

model had its wing-tip pods redesigned to carry three Hughes Falcon air-to-air missiles and 21 FFARs. Production totalled 156, and the F-89H began to equip Air Defense Command squadrons during 1956. In the same year 350 F-89Ds were modified to F-89J standard by the installation of a Douglas MB-1 Genie unguided nuclear-tipped rocket on each of two underwing pods.

Northrop F-89A Scorpion

Northrop F-89D Scorpion

137

Northrop F-89J Scorpion carrying two Genie missiles

Convair T-29C

Convair T-29 and C-131 Samaritan

The twin-engined Convair T-29 was a navigator/bombardier trainer version of the commercial Convair Model 240. First flight took place at Lindbergh Field, San Diego, on September 22, 1949. Production of 48 T-29As followed. Equipped to accommodate 14 student navigators, the first was delivered to the Air Force in February 1950. The T-29A was followed by 105 pressurised T-29Bs with provision for 10 student navigators and four student radar operators. Then came 119 T-29Cs with more powerful engines and 93 T-29Ds with "K" system bombsight and camera scoring equipment. The T-29E and YT-32 versions were both cancelled.

The USAF also operated a number of transport variants,

the first of which was the C-131A. A total of 26 were built, the first being delivered to MATS in April 1954. The C-131B was based on the commercial Convair 340 and a total of 36 were built; six were later equipped as JC-131Bs.

Staff transport variants for MATS were the 33 C-131Ds and VC-131Ds, of which 27 were fitted to Model 340 standard while the other six were to Model 440 standard. All could accommodate up to 44 passengers. In 1956 and 1957 Convair delivered 10 C-131Es to SAC as ECM trainers; six were later converted as RC-131Fs for photo-survey and mapping work with MATS, and one became an RC-131G for use by the Airways and Air Communications Service.

North American T-28 Trojan

The North American T-28 Trojan tandem two-seat trainer was designed in 1948 to meet a USAF requirement for a T-6 Texan replacement. Originally designated XBT-28 and later XT-28, the first prototype flew for the first time on September 26, 1949.

The Trojan was ordered in quantity during the following year, the initial contract covering 266 T-28As; subsequent orders brought the total up to 1,194 aircraft by 1953. Although powered by a 800 hp Wright R-1300-1A engine, making it one of the most powerful piston-engined aircraft to be used for ab initio training in the US Air Force, the T-28A was generally regarded as being underpowered.

The US Navy adopted the Trojan in 1952. The Navy's aircraft, designated T-28B, were much modified, with a new two-part cockpit canopy that was also applied to late-production Air Force T-28As, and powered by the 1,425 hp Wright R-1820-86.

In 1962 North American developed the T-28D for light counter-insurgency duties. More than 300 T-28As were converted to the new standard by the installation of the more powerful 1,300 hp Wright R-1820-56 and three stores points beneath each wing to carry up to 4,000lb of weapons. The type first served with the 1st Air Commando Group.

North American T-28As

Lockheed F-94C

Lockheed F-94 Starfire

Conceived in 1949, the two-seat radar-equipped night and all-weather F-94 Starfire was a development of the F-80 Shooting Star and T-33 trainer series. Two YF-94 prototypes were produced by converting existing T-33 airframes, the first of which had started out as an F-80 before being converted into the T-33 prototype. Changes included the installation of a 6,000lb st afterburning J33-A-33 engine, remodelled radar nose and revised accommodation for a pilot and radar operator. Armament comprised four 0.50in machine guns in the forward fuselage.

First flight by the YF-94 prototype was made on July 1, 1949. Production of 110 similar F-94As began during the same year and first deliveries, to the 319th All Weather Fighter Squadron, began in June 1950.

The F-94B incorporated several refinements, including tip tanks raised to the centreline of the wing and the installation of Sperry Zero Reader for blind landings. Production, which began in 1951, extended to 357 aircraft.

The F-94C was appreciably different from earlier variants, with a redesigned wing of lower thickness/chord ratio to raise the critical Mach number and a new nose containing 24 2.75in Mighty Mouse air-to-air rockets mounted in a ring round the centred radome. Changes were also made to the fin profile, and gross weight was raised to 20,000lb. Powerplant was the 8,500lb st afterburning Pratt & Whitney J48-P-5. A total of 387 F-94Cs had been delivered by February 1954.

The Starfire was used extensively by interceptor and all-weather fighter groups in the USA and abroad, principally in Japan. Some F-94s flew operationally in Korea.

Lockheed F-94B

Sikorsky H-19

The H-19 was a military version of the Sikorsky S-55 of 1948, itself a continuation of the line of Sikorsky helicopters which began with the R-4 in 1943. The US Air Force ordered five YH-19s for evaluation, and the first of these flew for the first time at Bridgeport on November 10, 1949. Capacity was ten troops or six stretchers in addition to the crew of two, a substantial increase over previous helicopters.

First production version was the H-19A, some 50 of which were ordered in 1951. These were followed by 250 H-19Bs with cranked tailbooms and more powerful 700 hp Wright R-1300-3 engines.

The H-19 initially followed the R-5 into MATS Air Reserve squadrons in Korea, where it was designated SH-19. For the rescue role it was equipped with a hoist on the starboard side of the fuselage, above the door.

The H-19 was also supplied to the Navy and Marine Corps as the HO4S and HRS respectively, and to the US Army as the H-19C and D Chickasaw.

In 1962 a change in the designation system resulted in the surviving H-19Bs becoming UH-19Bs and the MATS SH-19Bs becoming HH-19Bs.

Boeing B-47 Stratojet

At the peak of its career during the 1950s the six-jet B-47 was probably the most important military aircraft in the West. Preliminary design studies of this extremely handsome aircraft began as early as 1943, putting it well ahead of its time. The design passed through several stages, from the straight-winged Boeing Model 424 of March 1944 and Model 432 of December that year, through the swept-wing Model 448 with fuselage-mounted turbojets of the following September, to the Model 450 of October 1945, which incorporated podded twin engines under each wing and an additional nacelle close to each wing tip.

Two prototypes of the definitive design were ordered by the Air Force in May 1946 under the designation XB-47. The first flight, from Boeing Field at Seattle to Moses Lake AFB, was made on December 17, 1947, by Bob Robbins and Scott Osler. At that time power was provided by six 3,750lb st J35-2 turbojets, and to help the aircraft to take off at its gross weight of more than 125,000lb some 18 solid rockets were built into the rear fuselage.

The second XB-47 was first flown in July 1948 and a production contract for ten aircraft, valued at around $30 million, was placed that September. The B-47A was powered by the 5,200lb st J47-GE-11 and had a design gross weight of about 160,000lb.

First version of the Stratojet to be produced in quantity was the B-47B, some 380 of which were built (362 by Boeing at Wichita, ten by Douglas at Tulsa and eight by Lockheed at Marietta). Deliveries to SAC began in 1951, when the 306th Medium Bomb wing was equipped.

Main production version was the B-47E, which followed the B into production at Wichita, Tulsa and Seattle. This variant first flew in January 1953 and a total of 1,359 B-47Es and 255 RB-47Es were built, production ending in February 1957.

The B-47 was capable of carrying any airborne nuclear weapon of its day, and Stratojets were regularly deployed across the Atlantic and Pacific oceans when the Cold War was at its height. Peak strength in SAC was reached in 1957, when about 1,800 of all models were in service.

Many hundreds of B-47s were subsequently modified for a wide variety of specialist roles, resulting in a rash of new designations. These variants included the EB-47 electronic reconnaissance versions, RB-47H reconnaissance aircraft, TB-47 trainers and QB-47 drones. Although the last B-47E bomber wing was deactivated in 1966, a number of the specialist models lasted well into the 1970s.

Boeing B-47B

Boeing RB-47E with B-47E in background

Piasecki (Vertol) H-21 Workhorse

The Piasecki YH-21 was the first tandem-rotor helicopter to serve with the US Air Force, which ordered 18 in 1949. First flight was made on April 11, 1952, and successful trials resulted in an order for a further quantity of H-21As to operate with the Air Rescue Service, principally in the Arctic.

Powered by a derated 1,150 hp Wright R-1820-103 engine, the H-21A carried a crew of two (pilot and co-pilot or medical attendant) and could accommodate up to 12 stretchers or 14 troops. First flight of the production aircraft was in October 1953. That year also saw the first deliveries of the H-21B. This was an assault transport for service with Troop Carrier Command. Powered by a 1,425 hp Wright R-1820-103, it could accommodate 20 troops. Production for the US Air Force totalled 163.

In 1962 the designations were changed to CH-21A and CH-21B, while SH-21Bs became HH-21Bs.

Piasecki (Vertol) H-21D Workhorse in US Army markings

North American F-100C Super Sabre

North American F-100F

North American F-100
Super Sabre

The first of the US Air Force's Century-series fighters, the F-100 Super Sabre was also the first operational fighter in the world capable of maintaining supersonic speed in level flight.

Developed from the F-86 Sabre as a private venture between 1947 and 1949, the F-100 was originally known as the Sabre 45, a reference to the 45° sweep of the wing leading edge. Apart from being larger all round than the F-86, the new aircraft had a flattened oval intake for its twin-spool J57 turbojet and a slab tailplane mounted at the base of the rear fuselage.

Two YF-100A prototypes were approved in August 1952 and the first of these, powered by an XJ57-P-7 engine, was flown for the first time at Edwards AFB on May 25, 1953, followed by the second on October 14. The first of 203 production F-100As was flown on October 29, 1953. Powered by the 9,700lb st J57-P-7, they were armed with four M39E 20mm cannon.

The first production aircraft were delivered to the 479th Day Fighter Wing of Tactical Air Command at George AFB, California, in November 1953; this unit became operational the following September. F-100A production ended in March 1954; some aircraft were later modified as RF-100As, with cameras mounted in a slightly deeper front fuselage.

The F-100C which followed was a fighter-bomber with provision for 6,000lb of external stores. The first production aircraft flew in January 1955 and first equipped the 450th Day Fighter Wing at Foster AFB. A total of 476 were eventually built.

The improved F-100D featured an enlarged fin and rudder, external stores capacity increased to 7,500lb, and, for the first time on the type, landing flaps. Total production reached 1,274, with the first aircraft flying in January 1956.

The final production variant was the F-100F, a two-seat combat trainer which first flew in prototype form as the TF-100C in August 1956.

In late 1979 it was announced that the Air Force was planning to acquire 81 QF-100 target drones to succeed the Convair QF-102, supplies of which are likely to run out during the middle of 1983. A substantial number of F-100s are in store at Davis Monthan AFB, Arizona, and these aircraft will be converted by Sperry Flight Systems.

145

Republic F-84F Thunderstreak

Republic began development of a swept-wing fighter-bomber based on the F-84 Thunderjet at the end of 1949. Using some 60% of Thunderjet tooling, together with a standard F-84E fuselage, Republic was able to offer the aircraft to the US Air Force at a relatively low price. One prototype was ordered, initially under the designation YF-96A.

This aircraft first flew on June 3, 1950, on the power of a 5,200lb st Allison XJ35-A-25. The second prototype, powered by a Wright YJ65-W-1 and designated YF-84F, flew for the first time on February 14, 1951.

Production contracts had been placed by then and the first production F-84F flew in November 1952, with deliveries to Air Force units beginning in 1954.

Later production aircraft had an all-flying tailplane and were powered by the J65-W-3. Two experimental aircraft, designated YF-84J, were fitted with the 9,200lb st General Electric XJ73-GE-5, and two others, designated XF-84H, were powered by the Allison XT40-A-1 turboprop. A total of 2,711 F-84Fs were built, 1,301 of which were destined for Nato air forces in Europe.

Republic F-84F

Republic F-84F Thunderstreaks

Beech T-34A Mentor

Beech T-34 Mentor

The tandem two-seat Beech T-34 Mentor was derived from the four-seat Bonanza cabin monoplane and flew for the first time, as the Beech Model 45, on December 2, 1948. In early 1950, after several years of indecision over future pilot training policy, the type was evaluated by the US Air Force as the YT-34. After extensive trials it was ordered into production as the T-34A Mentor basic trainer in March 1953.

Deliveries to Air Training Command began in 1954, the type replacing elderly North American T-6s for primary training. Power was provided by a 225 hp Continental O-470-13 piston engine. A total of 450 were delivered to the Air Force, and more than 420 similar T-34Bs were also acquired by the US Navy from June 1954.

After the introduction of the more powerful North American T-28 Trojan the Mentor was used to provide student pilots with 30 hours of familiarisation flying before they progressed to the T-28 and jet-powered Cessna T-37. The T-34 was declared redundant following the introduction of all-through jet training in 1960.

Fairchild C-123K

Fairchild C-123 Provider

The Fairchild-built C-123B Provider tactical assault transport originated in the Chase Aircraft XCG-20 cargo glider of 1949, from which was derived the powered XC-123 Airtruc. The US Air Force ordered five pre-production C-123Bs from Chase in 1952, followed by 300 production aircraft from Kaiser-Frazer, after that company's acquisition of Chase in 1953.

Kaiser-Frazer failed to produce the aircraft and the contract was transferred to Fairchild, which flew the first refined C-123B on September 1, 1954.

In 1962 the single YC-123H was fitted with two auxiliary engines in underwing pods and flew for the first time on July 30 that year. In 1966 Fairchild Hiller was awarded a USAF contract to modify 183 C-123Bs to the auxiliary jet configuration, which involved fitting two pylon-mounted 2,850lb st General Electric J85-GE-17 turbojets outboard of the standard 2,300 hp Pratt & Whitney R-2800-99W radials. New Goodyear high-capacity wheels, brakes and anti-skid units and a new stall-warning system were installed at the same time. Designated C-123K, the first modified aircraft flew for the first time on May 27, 1966, and the last modified aircraft had been delivered by September 1969.

C-123s were used extensively in South-east Asia: several were armed as AC-123K gunships, while others were equipped as UC-123Bs for spraying defoliant.

Ten C-123Bs were converted to C-123J standard and were operated by the Alaska Air National Guard until 1976.

Fairchild C-123J Provider

Boeing B-52 Stratofortress

The B-52 strategic bomber has been in continuous service with SAC in one form or another since 1955, and versions will continue to operate until as late as the end of this century.

Development of this remarkable warhorse, which started life as a turboprop-powered project, began in 1945. A prototype contract for one XB-52 and one YB-52 was awarded to Boeing in July 1948, and by the end of that year the design had crystallised as an eight-turbojet aircraft with 35° wing sweep.

Both prototypes were built at Seattle and the XB-52 was flown for the first time on October 2, 1951, followed by the YB-52 on April 15, 1952. A production order for 13 B-52s had been

placed in February 1951, but large-scale production was not begun until completion of a comparative fly-off against the Convair XB-60. The initial aircraft were delivered to SAC as three B-52As and ten B-52Bs.

Production continued with 27 RB-52Bs and a further 23 B-52Bs, followed by 35 B-52Cs. The first unit to operate the type was the 93rd Heavy Bomb Wing at Castle AFB, California, which received its aircraft in June 1955. Boeing went on to build 101 B-52Ds at Seattle and a further 69 at Wichita. Deliveries of this version to SAC began in December 1956.

The B-52E introduced improvements to the avionics equipment and rearranged crew accommodation. Boeing built

100 B-52Es and 89 B-52Fs (which introduced the 13,750lb st J57-43W engine) at Wichita and Seattle. Deliveries of the F model to SAC began in June 1958, with production at Seattle ending in November of that year.

The B-52G, some 193 of which were built at Wichita, introduced a number of significant changes, including a wet wing, a shorter fin of increased chord and a remotely controlled tail turret. First flown in October 1958, this model was delivered to SAC from the following February. The B-52G could carry the North American AGM-28 Hound Dog air-to-surface missile.

Final production version was the B-52H, powered by the 17,000lb st TF33 turbofan, which

dramatically improved performance. The first of 102 examples of this model was flown for the first time on March 6, 1961, with deliveries to SAC beginning that May.

Three versions were still in front-line squadron service in 1980—the B-52D, G and H (in addition to the B-52F, used only for training)—and a total of around 350 remained operational at that time. Over the last few years the remaining aircraft have had their operational equipment progressively updated. The cancellation of the B-1 led to the improvement programme being accelerated, particularly as it affected the avionics and the type's ability to carry air-launched cruise missiles.

Boeing B-52E Stratofortress

Republic RF-84F Thunderflash

Republic RF-84 Thunderflash

Early in 1952 Republic Aircraft developed a single-seat reconnaissance version of the Thunderstreak with wing-root air intakes and cameras in the nose. This intake arrangement had first taken to the air on the second YF-84F and then on the YRF-84F prototype, which was flown for the first time in February 1952 by Carl Bellinger.

Deliveries to Strategic Air Command and Tactical Air Command reconnaissance units began in March 1954, and by the time that deliveries ended in 1958 production had reached 715, including 386 bought by the Air Force Mutual Defense programme and destined for users abroad.

In 1953 the type was fitted with a retractable hook in the nose for FICON (Fighter Conveyor) trials with the GRB-36 bomber. Acute dihedral was also added to the tailplane so that it would clear the B-36's bomb bay. Some 25 RF-84Fs

were subsequently modified, initially under the designation GRF-84F, and these aircraft equipped the 91st Strategic Reconnaissance Squadron in

1955. They were later restored for normal use, but their large number of non-standard features merited the new designation RF-84K.

A number of Thunderflashes were later transferred to Air National Guard squadrons, and a few still serve with Nato air forces.

Martin RB-57D in company with B-57B (background)

Martin B-57E

Martin B-57 Canberra

The Canberra is one of the very small number of European aircraft to have been adopted by the US Air Force in any significant quantity. The type was initially selected for use as a tactical bomber but was later developed into a high-altitude special reconnaissance aircraft.

The first Martin-built B-57A was modelled on the English Electric Canberra B.2, the first eight pre-production aircraft being powered by two 7,220lb st Wright J65-W-1 turbojets. First flown at Baltimore on July 20, 1953, the pre-production aircraft were followed by 67 RB-57As equipped with cameras in the rear of the bomb bay for dual-role missions. Delivered to Shaw AFB during 1954, they equipped the 363rd Tactical Reconnaissance Wing.

First true light bomber version was the B-57B with tandem two-seat cockpit and carrying a wing armament of either four 20mm cannon or eight 0.50in machine guns. Internal bomb load was a maximum of 6,000lb. First flown in June 1954, this model ran to 202 examples and

equipped TAC from January 1955. This variant was followed into production by 68 improved B-57Es.

The RB-57D was an extensively modified version with an extended-span wing and two Pratt & Whitney J57s. Martin built 20 of these reconnaissance bombers, which did much flying over Communist territory.

Following the grounding of the RB-57D in 1963 because of structural fatigue General Dynamics was contracted to build a new high-altitude version, the RB-57F. Powered by two 18,000lb Pratt & Whitney TF33 turbofans and two supplementary 3,300lb st J60-9 boost engines, the 21 RB-57Fs were extensively equipped with sensor equipment for a variety of reconnaissance and surveillance roles.

During the Vietnam War the US Air Force used its Canberras extensively on interdiction missions. The B-57G, a modification of early bomber variants, came too late to see service in that conflict.

Lockheed C-130 Hercules

The four-engined Lockheed Hercules is currently the most widely used and most numerous military transport aircraft in the world. Originally designed as a straight military cargo and personnel transport, since 1956 it has been modified for no fewer than 45 specialised applications and is in service with 46 nations.

Development began in 1951 following a general Air Force policy decision to re-equip with turboprop-powered transports. A contract for two prototype YC-130s was placed in September 1952, and the first made its maiden flight on August 23, 1954. Production contracts had already been placed and Lockheed laid down

a vast production line at Marietta, Georgia. The first C-130A built there flew for the first time in April 1955.

Deliveries of the first of 219 C-130As to Troop Carrier Command and TAC began in December 1956. Most of these aircraft later had the thimble radome which become standard on all subsequent Hercules variants. As production built up, a number of special variants were developed from the basic C-130A; they included the GC-130A drone launcher/director and the RC-130A for the Air Force's Air Photographic and Charting Service. A later and much more aggressive conversion was the AC-130A gunship, used with

devastating effect during the Vietnam War. These aircraft were usually armed with four 20mm Vulcan cannon and four 7.62mm Miniguns. Last of the major C-130A developments was the JC-130A, some 11 of which were converted for missile and spacecraft tracking.

The C-130B was a developed version with additional fuel tankage in the wings. Powerplant was four 4,050 shp Allison T56-A-7s. The first TAC aircraft flew in November 1958 and entered service in the following June.

The next major production variant for the Air Force was the C-130E, an extended-range version of the C-130B. A total of

389 were acquired by the Air Force, with deliveries beginning in April 1962. The USAF also took delivery of a number of rescue variants for the Aerospace Rescue and Recovery Service. Two initial contracts were awarded to Lockheed in 1963; a total of 66 HC-130Hs were eventually delivered.

Last production version for the USAF was the C-130H, deliveries of which began in 1975. Powered by four 4,910 shp T56-A-15s, it had a maximum payload of almost 44,000lb. Production of this variant was expected to run to about 36 aircraft per year through the early 1980s; most of these are for export.

Lockheed C-130E Hercules

Lockheed HC-130H Hercules

155

Convair F-102A Delta Dagger

Convair F-102 Delta Dagger

The sleek F-102 Delta Dagger had its origins in an ambitious USAF design exercise held in 1950 to define an advanced interceptor aircraft, fire-control and weapons system. Called MX1179 and led by Hughes Aircraft, this programme was intended to produce a working system by 1954.

The aircraft component of the system was to be the Convair F-102 (Model 8). This was a scaled-up version of Convair's experimental XF-92A, built in 1948 to produce data for a proposed Mach 1.5 fighter, the F-92 (Model 7).

The first YF-102 was flown for the first time at Edwards Air Force Base by Richard L. Johnson on October 24, 1953. Eight days later it was destroyed following an engine flame-out

on take-off. The following January flight tests with the second aircraft showed that the F-102 was incapable of reaching the speed of sound, transonic drag having exceeded the power available from the Pratt & Whitney J75-P-11 engine.

This would have been disastrous enough in any other programme, but matters were much more serious for Convair because the F-102 was being produced under the Cook-Craigie plan, which called for a slow initial rate of production paralleled by an intensive flight-testing programme. As a result, the San Diego production line had already been set up and was operating.

Fortunately, a solution was at hand in NACA engineer Richard Whitcomb's area-rule theory,

which called for a radical revision of the fuselage profile to the now familiar ''coke-bottle'' shape. This so reduced transonic drag that when Johnson made his first Mach run in the rebuilt YF-102A, on December 21, 1954, he achieved Mach 1.2 with no problems.

Thereafter the F-102 programme proceeded smoothly, and between 1953 and 1957 five production contracts called for a total of 873 F-102As, the last being delivered in April 1958. At the peak of its deployment in 1958 more than 25 Air Defense Command squadrons were equipped with the type, which was unique in being the first Air Force interceptor to rely entirely on missiles, in this case the Hughes

AIM-4A and AIM-4C Falcon and their MG-3 fire-control system.

In 1957 the armament was upgraded by General Dynamics Palmdale, which installed a full MG-10 fire-control system. The Air Force also operated 111 TF-102A combat trainers with a wider front fuselage seating two side-by-side. First flown in November 1955, the type retained the full operational equipment and armament of the F-102A.

The F-102 is no longer operational with Aerospace Defense Command squadrons, but several USAF aircraft have been rebuilt by Sperry as remotely piloted QF-102 and PQM-102 drones. The Dagger is however flown operationally in small numbers by Greece and Turkey.

156

North American F-107

The North American F-107 was to have been an advanced fighter-bomber development of the F-100 Super Sabre, designated F-100B. But so extensively redesigned was the aircraft that the designation was changed before the first YF-107A made its maiden flight.

Powerplant was a 24,500lb st afterburning Pratt & Whitney J75-P-9 turbojet with a bifurcated air intake on top of the fuselage behind the cockpit. Provision was made for four 20mm cannon and 10,000lb of bombs, tanks and other stores on underwing pylons.

The initial contract was for nine service-test aircraft, subsequently cut back to four. Of these, only three were completed, the first being flown for the first time on September 10, 1956, by North American test pilot Robert Baker. The second and third flew for the first time in November and December 1957 respectively. Performance was generally good and the aircraft exceeded Mach 2 on several flights, reaching a maximum of Mach 2.2. Nevertheless, in 1957 the programme was cancelled in favour of the Republic F-105 Thunderchief.

North American F-107A

Lockheed U-2R

Lockheed U-2 series

The Lockheed U-2 is one of the most controversial of all American post-war aircraft. Although designated a "utility" type, the U-2 originally had a far less innocuous role: strategic reconnaissance flights over communist-controlled territory.

Work on the U-2 began in 1954 at Lockheed designer D. L. "Kelly" Johnson's "Skunk Works" at Burbank, California. Designed from the outset as a high-altitude, very long-range espionage aircraft, it featured sailplane-like wings of high aspect ratio and a very light structure. The undercarriage was unorthodox, consisting of small centreline wheels and jettisonable outriggers. First flight was in 1955, under the power of a Pratt & Whitney J75-P-13 rated at 17,000lb st.

The U-2A initial production version was powered by the J75-P-37A engine. Entering service in 1956, it was supplemented by the more powerful U-2B, one of which was shot down over the Soviet Union on May 1, 1960, catapulting CIA pilot Francis Gary Powers into instant international notoriety and the USA into the centre of one of the hottest diplomatic rows for several years.

Current versions are the U-2C and two-seat U-2D, which make up most of the present fleet of about 40 aircraft (out of a total of 55 built), and the enlarged U-2R.

In 1978 it was announced that funding had been approved for a small number of high-altitude tactical surveillance and reconnaissance aircraft designated TR-1. This new aircraft is a single-engined, single-seat version of the U-2R and is apparently earmarked for what the Air Force calls "stand-off" battlefield surveillance, primarily in the European theatre. In late 1979 the Air Force announced that the first purchase would consist of two single-seat TR-1As and a single ER-2 Earth-resources observation aircraft to be used by NASA. The eventual USAF requirement is for 23 TR-1As and two TR-1B two-seat aircraft.

Configuration of the TR-1 does not differ greatly from that of the U-2 on which it is modelled. Wingspan is 103ft, ceiling in excess of 70,000ft and range more than 3,000 miles. Primary sensors will be the Advanced Synthetic Aperture Radar System (ASARS) being developed by Hughes.

Lockheed U-2A

Douglas B-66 Destroyer

The Douglas B-66 Destroyer, a development of the US Navy's A3D Skywarrior, was intended as a light tactical bomber and reconnaissance aircraft, although it ultimately served in a variety of roles, most notably electronic countermeasures (ECM).

The initial contract for five pre-production RB-66As was placed in February 1952, the first aircraft being flown from Long Beach to Edwards AFB by George R. Jansen on June 28, 1954. Superficially similar to the Skywarrior, the RB-66A was in fact substantially re-engineered, shedding such naval accoutrements as wing-folding

mechanisms, arrester hook and strengthened undercarriage. In all, some 400 alterations were made in the transition.

The three-seat RB-66A was powered by two 9,570lb st Allison YJ71-A-9 turbojets and was equipped as a reconnaissance aircraft with four cameras. It was not used operationally. The production version was the RB-66B, 145 of which were built at Long Beach. First flown in March 1955, it entered service with the 1st, 19th and 30th Tactical Reconnaissance Squadrons of the 10th Tactical Reconnaissance Wing in Europe in 1957. Also making its first

flight at around the same time was the B-66B, the only pure bomber version of the Destroyer, in which the camera bay was replaced with a weapons bay with a capacity of up to 5,000lb of bombs. A total of 72 were built at Long Beach, with deliveries commencing in March 1956.

The RB-66C was an all-weather electronic reconnaissance aircraft, designed to locate and identify enemy radar. A crew of seven were carried, five of them electronic warfare officers (EWOs). A total of 36 were built at the Tulsa plant, the first flying on October 29, 1955. These

aircraft were later redesignated EB-66C and fitted with upgraded ECM equipment.

The final production version was the Tulsa-built weather reconnaissance WB-66D. Thirty-six were completed, the first flying in June 1957.

During the 1960s the rapidly increasing need for ECM aircraft in South-east Asia resulted in the modification of B-66B and RB-66B types as EB-66Bs and EB-66Es. A total of 65 aircraft were modified, serving with distinction on numerous jamming missions during the Vietnam War. By 1974 the type had been withdrawn entirely from combat duty.

Douglas WB-66D

Douglas EB-66E

159

Boeing C-135 series

The Boeing C-135 series—which includes a variety of specialised aircraft, including tankers, electronic warfare types and transports—are all derived from the private-venture Boeing Type 367-80 jet transport prototype, which first flew in July 1954.

After evaluating the Dash 80 the US Air Force decided to buy 29 developed versions for service in the dual roles of tanker with SAC and transport with MATS.

The first of these aircraft, designated KC-135A, left the assembly line at Renton, Washington, in July 1956, flying for the first time on August 31. Initial deliveries to the 93rd Air Refuelling Squadron at Castle AFB, California, began the following June. By January 1965 a total of 732 had been supplied to SAC. A further 88 developed versions, including the C-135A Stratolifter, were also built during that time, most being powered by the 18,000lb st TF33 turbofan.

Boeing C-135

Boeing KC-135A

160

Cessna T-37

The twin-engined Cessna T-37 was the USAF's first jet-powered trainer to be designed as such from the start. The winner of a 1952 design competition, it was originally meant to be powered by a pair of Turboméca Marboré turbojets.

Two XT-37s were ordered by the Air Force, the first of which was flown by Bob Hogan at Wichita on October 12, 1954. An initial production batch of 11 T-37As, powered by two 920lb st Continental J69-T-9s, was ordered during 1954, the first of which flew in September the following year. Service use did not begin until 1957, however, after various modifications had been made. A total of 534 were built.

The T-37B first entered service with the Air Force in November 1959. Powered by two 1,025lb st

Continental J69-T-25s, the type featured a number of detailed equipment changes. T-37s will remain in the Air Force's

inventory until follow-on aircraft are introduced in the mid-1980s. Further modification is however ruled out by the type's age. The

Air Force is also critical of the T-37's limited all-weather capability, fuel consumption and noise level.

McDonnell Douglas C-133 Cargomaster

The vast C-133 Cargomaster was designed to meet a 1952 operational requirement for a heavy transport capable of carrying particularly bulky loads. There was no prototype, and 35 production C-133As were ordered in 1954.

Powered by four 7,000 ehp

Pratt & Whitney T34-7 turboprops, the first C-133A flew on April 23, 1956. All production aircraft were assigned to Military Air Transport Services (MATS)—later Military Airlift Command (MAC)—the first arriving at Dover AFB in August 1957. Later production aircraft were fitted with four 6,500 ehp

T34-P-7W or -7WA turboprops, and gross weight was raised by almost 30,000lb to 282,000lb.

The C-133B featured as standard the clamshell doors introduced on the last two C-133As. The first C-133B flew in October 1959 and the first of 15 production aircraft was

delivered to Travis AFB in March 1960. This model was powered by four 7,500 ehp Pratt & Whitney T34-9Ws and had a gross weight of 286,000lb.

Three MAC squadrons were equipped with the type. All Cargomasters had been withdrawn by early 1980.

McDonnell F-101 Voodoo

The McDonnell F-101 Voodoo penetration fighter was based on the company's earlier XF-88 prototype, flown for the first time on October 20, 1948, but cancelled in 1950 following a re-appraisal of the Air Force's tactical requirements.

In 1951 a USAF requirement for a long-range escort for Strategic Air Command resulted in a reworking of the XF-88 design, the new aircraft being substantially larger and heavier and powered by two Pratt & Whitney J57 turbojets in place of the original J34s. Designated F-101, it was at the time of its introduction the heaviest single-seat fighter ever accepted by the Air Force.

An initial order for 29 F-101As was placed in September 1952 and the first of these flew on September 29, 1954. Before that time, however, SAC had cancelled its requirement for the escort fighter and production was continued for Tactical Air Command, the quantity having been increased to 50 aircraft.

The F-101A, which first entered service with the 27th Tactical Fighter Wing at Bergstrom AFB, Texas, in May 1957, had a very long range and substantial armament: typically four 20mm M-39E cannon plus three Hughes Falcon air-to-air missiles and two FFAR rocket clusters.

The F-101A was followed into service by the F-101C, fitted with a strengthened wing capable of carrying a nuclear weapon in place of the Falcon missiles. A total of 47 were built, and the Voodoo eventually equipped nine squadrons in all. First unit to receive the F-101C, in 1955, was the 81st Tactical Fighter Wing at RAF Bentwaters, Suffolk, which also acquired a number of F-101As initially assigned to the 27th TFW.

Reconnaissance versions of both the F-101A and F-101C, designated RF-101A and RF-101B respectively, were also built. The first RF-101As were delivered in May 1957 to the 363rd Tactical Reconnaissance Wing at Shaw AFB, South Carolina. Both reconnaissance versions had a lengthened nose carrying either four KA-2 cameras, or one KA-2 and three KA-46 cameras for night

McDonnell RF-101Cs
McDonnell F-101B Voodoo of the 29th FIS

photography. Totals of 35 RF-101As and 166 RF-101Cs were built.

Although the tactical fighter variants were relatively short-lived, their RF counterparts were used in many major trouble spots from the late 1950s, their battle honours including the Cuban missile crisis of 1962 and extended service in South-east Asia. The F-101A and C took on a new lease of life when they were modified by Lockheed Aircraft Service Company to serve as the RF-101G and RF-101H with Air National Guard units through to the early 1970s.

The F-101B was a long-range all-weather interceptor in which a revised forward fuselage section was fitted with a tandem two-seat cockpit accommodating a pilot and radar operator. The aircraft was equipped with a new MG-13 fire-control system, flight-refuelling facilities and four GAR-1 or GAR-2 Falcon missiles plus two MB-1 Genie missiles with nuclear warheads. First flight was on March 27, 1957, and a total of 408 were built. In September 1962 McDonnell was awarded a contract to manufacture kits to bring 153 F-101Bs up to F-101F standard by updating the fire-control system and removing the in-flight refuelling probe, amongst other modifications.

Cessna U-3

The five-seat Cessna 310 (original military designation L-27A) was selected by the US Air Force in 1957 as a twin-engined light utility aircraft. Some 80 were initially bought by the Air Force in 1957.

This order was subsequently doubled, and in 1962 the designation was changed to U-3A.

First flown as a prototype in January 1953, the U-3A was powered by two 240 hp Continental O-470Ms. In 1960 Cessna introduced the Model 310D with swept vertical tail surfaces and increased cabin volume. The US Air Force ordered 35 of the improved aircraft, designated U-3B (Model 310E). Fitted with ''all-weather'' avionics and powered by two 285 hp Continental IO-520Ms, they were delivered between December 1960 and the end of June 1961.

Cessna U-3A

Lockheed F-104C Starfighters

Lockheed F-104 Starfighter

The single-seat, single-engined F-104 Starfighter was originally conceived as a day interceptor by Lockheed designer Kelly Johnson. As a result the design emphasised flight performance at the expense of both range and all-weather capability. These features, together with a rash of engine and other problems, made the Starfighter relatively unpopular with the US Air Force and it served as a front-line aircraft with Air Defense Command for just two years, from 1958 to 1960.

The US Air Force ordered two prototypes in March 1953 and the first XF-104, powered by the 10,000lb st afterburning Wright XJ65-W-6, was flown by Lockheed test pilot Tony Le Vier for the first time on February 7, 1954. Subsequent aircraft were powered by the 14,800lb st General Electric J79-GE-3.

A batch of 15 service-test YF-104As preceded 153 production F-104As, the first of which was delivered to the 83rd Fighter Interceptor Squadron at Hamilton AFB in January 1958. The F-104A was joined in Air Defense Command service by 26 tandem two-seat F-104B trainers, which had full operational capability. The first of these flew in February 1957, but by 1960 all As and Bs had been withdrawn from ADC squadrons and had been issued to the Air National Guard. They were subsequently recalled to ADC and 25 F-104As were re-engined with the 17,900lb J79-GE-19. Later still they were supplied to Taiwan, while 12 F-104As, with the J79-GE-11A engine, went to Pakistan and 18 similarly powered aircraft were supplied to Jordan. Some 24 examples were converted to QF-104 target drones in 1960-61.

Two versions were produced for service with Tactical Air Command: the single-seat F-104C and the two-seat F-104D. Powered by the 15,800lb J79-GE-7A, the first of 77 F-104Cs were delivered to the 831st Air Division of TAC at George AFB in October 1958. They were later transferred to the Air National Guard, as were the 22 F-104Ds.

Lockheed F-104C

Republic F-105 Thunderchief

The F-105 Thunderchief was the first supersonic tactical fighter-bomber to be developed from scratch for the US Air Force. Designed to succeed the Republic F-84F, the Thunderchief had as its primary mission in Tactical Air Command the delivery of nuclear and conventional weapons in all weathers at high speeds and over long ranges.

First contracts were placed in 1954 and the first of two YF-105As, powered by the stopgap J57-P-25 engine, was first flown on October 22, 1955.

The first developed version was the single-seat F-105B, powered by the 25,000lb st afterburning Pratt & Whitney J75-P-3. The first of these was flown for the first time on May 26, 1956, and the initial production aircraft was delivered to the 335th Tactical Fighter Squadron at Eglin AFB, Florida, in May of the following year. Production was completed in 1959 after 75 had been built.

Most numerous of the Thunderchief variants was the single-seat F-105D, some 600 of which were built. Equipped with NASARR monopulse radar and Doppler navigation, the first F-105D flew in June 1959, with deliveries to the 4th Tactical Fighter Wing beginning in the following May. About 350 were modified during the Vietnam War to carry the T-Stick bombing system, and about 30 of these aircraft were subsequently equipped with the later T-Stick II. Modified aircraft could be identified externally by the saddle-back, housing

avionic equipment, which ran from aft of the cockpit to the base of the fin.

In 1962 the USAF ordered 143 two-seat F-105F trainers. With dual controls and full operational equipment, the F was slightly longer than the F-105D and had a slightly taller fin. The first F-105F flew for the first time in June 1963. About 30 were later converted to Wild Weasel ECM aircraft and were redesignated F-105G. The large ECM pod was carried externally under the centre fuselage.

Republic F-105D

Republic F-105D Thunderchief

Kaman H-43 Huskie

Kaman H-43 Huskie

Kaman's unorthodox intermeshing twin-rotor system appeared on the company's first helicopter, the K-125 "synchropter," which first flew in January 1947. This was followed by the K-190 and K-225 twin-rotor helicopters, the latter entering service with the US Navy as the HTK-1 trainer and HOK-1 observation and utility type.

The first Kaman helicopter bought in quantity by the US Air Force was the H-43, developed from the Navy HOK-1 in response to an Air Force requirement for a firefighting and crash rescue aircraft. An initial production batch of 18 was ordered in 1957 and delivered as H-43As between November 1958 and mid-1959. Powered by the Pratt & Whitney R-1340-48, they were initially assigned to Tactical Air Command.

The H-43B was powered by a 860 ehp Lycoming T53-L-1A turboshaft to improve load-carrying ability; 116 were ordered (later increased to 193), with deliveries beginning in June 1959. The H-43B was deployed throughout all flying commands in the US for crash and fire-rescue missions, and was operated by detachments of MATS Air Rescue Service. During the Vietnam War the type was also used extensively for picking up downed airmen.

Convair F-106A Delta Dart

Convair F-106 Delta Dart

Though the F-106 was originally designated F-102B to indicate its family connection with the earlier Delta Dagger, it was to all intents a new design. Incorporating area rule from the start, a much more powerful Pratt & Whitney J75-17 engine and a new weapons system, the Dart was first flown on December 26, 1956, by Richard L. Johnson. Careful design work, benefiting from the lessons learned on the YF-102, paid off in the form of a maximum speed of more than Mach 2.3, roughly twice as fast as the Dagger.

The initial production contract, placed in April 1956, was for only 17 aircraft, increasing to 33 by the time of the first flight in December. Most of these aircraft were retained for development flying and the first operational unit was the 539th Fighter Interceptor Squadron, which received its aircraft in June 1959. By late 1960 deliveries totalled 277, together with 63 dual-control F-106Bs, which retained the full operational capability of the F-106A.

Unlike the Dagger, the F-106A Delta Dart is still in service in the USA, equipping selected squadrons within Aerospace Defense Command and the Air National Guard. The type's armament has been progressively updated and currently includes an internal 20mm M-61 multi-barrel cannon in a semi-retractable mount in the forward weapon bay, two Genie unguided rockets and four Falcon air-to-air missiles.

Convair F-106A

Convair B-58 Hustler

The first supersonic bomber to enter production for the US Air Force, the B-58 Hustler resulted from 1949 design studies of a B-36 successor by Consolidated Vultee at Fort Worth. A development contract was placed in August 1952 and the project was allocated a weapon system designation, WS-102A.

The Convair engineers' ingenious solution to the problem of carrying a large weapon load over a long distance at high speed in a relatively small airframe was to put all the weapons in a large external pod mounted beneath the centre fuselage. Power was provided by four podded General Electric J79-GE-1s, replaced from the 13th aircraft onwards by -5As.

The first contract called for 13 flight-test aircraft, the first of which was flown for the first time by B. A. Erickson on November 11, 1956. A further 17 pre-production aircraft were ordered in 1957, and all 30 aircraft were later passed to the Air Research and Development Command's 6952nd Test Squadron and the 3958th Operational Evaluation and Training Squadron at Carswell AFB.

Convair B-58A Hustler

Flight testing lasted for almost three years. A number of pre-production aircraft were subsequently brought up to operational standard to serve alongside the 86 production B-58As, the first of which were delivered during September 1959. Production ended in late 1962.

First operational unit to be equipped with the Hustler was the 43rd Bomber Wing of Strategic Air Command (SAC), which was activated at Carswell AFB in March 1960, later moving to Little Rock AFB. The only other wing to be equipped with the type was the 305th Bomber Wing at Bunker Hill AFB, near Penn, Indiana, which received the first of its Hustlers during 1961.

During its relatively short service life the Hustler established no fewer than 19 records, the last of which, set on October 16, 1963, was the longest supersonic flight: from Tokyo to London in slightly over 8½ hours.

The last B-58A was withdrawn from service in January 1970 following the introduction of the swing-wing General Dynamics F-111.

Convair B-58A Hustler

Rockwell International
T-39 Sabreliner

The T-39 originated in the private-venture North American NA-246, designed in response to the US Air Force's August 1956 UTX requirement for a combat-readiness trainer and utility aircraft. Design work continued throughout 1957 and the prototype was completed by the following May. Non-availability of a suitable engine delayed the first flight until September 16, 1958. Phase II evaluation was completed at

Edwards AFB in December, and in January 1959 an initial production order for seven flight-test aircraft was placed.

The first production T-39A flew for the first time on June 30, 1960. Flight testing was completed by the following March and full certification was awarded in March 1962. Deliveries of operational aircraft began in June 1961, and by the end of 1963 the Air Force had taken delivery of 143 T-39As.

Despite their Trainer designation, the majority of early T-39s were used as six-seat utility transports and were farmed out to almost all of the major Air Force commands. Sabreliners delivered to Air Training Command were assigned to the Instrument Pilot Trainer School at Randolph AFB.

In 1961 the Air Force ordered six T-39Bs as Doppler/NASARR trainers for F-105 Thunderchief pilots. All of these aircraft

entered service with the 4520th Combat Crew Training Squadron at Nellis AFB, the USAF's F-105 training base in Nevada.

Final Sabreliner variant was the T-39F, a designation assigned to three former T-39As modified in 1968 to carry the F-105G's Wild Weasel ECM fit. Known as ''Teeny Weeny Weasels,'' they were operated by the 66th Fighter Weapons Squadron at Nellis.

Rockwell T-39A

Northrop T-38 Talon

Northrop's 1954 study for a lightweight fighter—the N-156F, which eventually led to the F-5 Freedom Fighter—also generated a tandem two-seat trainer, the N-156T. After two years of private-venture development by Northrop the US Air Force authorised construction of three prototypes in December 1956. The contract was later amended in June 1958 to seven service-test YT-38s, including one static-test airframe.

The first prototype was flown for the first time at Edwards AFB on April 10, 1959, powered by two non-afterburning YJ85-GE-5 turbojets. Production aircraft were fitted with two 3,850lb st afterburning J85-GE-5s. When production ended in January 1972 a total of 1,187 Talons had been delivered. The first production aircraft was delivered to the 3510th Flying Training Wing at Randolph AFB in March 1961.

Although most were delivered to the US Air Force, 46 were acquired by the Luftwaffe but retained USAF markings, while the US Navy bought five and NASA had 24 on charge as astronaut proficiency trainers. The USAF's Thunderbirds aerobatic team switched to the T-38 from the F-4E in 1974.

The N-156F fighter prototype first flew on July 30, 1959, and, named Freedom Fighter, was selected for supply to foreign air forces under the Military Assistance Programme (MAP). Production orders for the single-seat F-5A and tandem two-seat F-5B were placed in October 1962. The US Air Force evaluated the F-5A in Vietnam but did not accept the type as front-line equipment.

Northrop T-38
Northrop YF-5As

Lockheed C-140 JetStar

The C-140 JetStar was designed initially to meet a US Air Force requirement for a multi-engined jet utility transport and training aircraft. The first prototype, built as the private-venture Model 1329, flew for the first time on September 4, 1957, only 241 days after the start of design. The two prototype aircraft were each powered by two Bristol Siddeley Orpheus torbojets, but in December 1959 one was re-engined with four Pratt & Whitney J60-P-5s. This powerplant was later chosen for the production version, the first of which flew for the first time in the summer of 1960.

In October 1959 the US Air Force announced that the Model 1329 JetStar had been adopted as the C-140, and in June 1960 five C-140s were ordered for MATS Airway and Air Communication Service, the organisation responsible for inspecting US military navigation aids worldwide. The aircraft were delivered during the summer of 1962.

The Air Force subsequently bought five C-140B mission-support aircraft and six VC-140B VIP transports with accommodation for three crew and eight passengers. First delivered in late 1961, the VC-140Bs were used by the 1254th Air Transport wing.

Lockheed VC-140B JetStar

McDonnell Douglas
F-4 Phantom II

One of the most successful Western combat aircraft ever built, the McDonnell Douglas F-4 was originally conceived as a shipborne fighter for the US Navy. First flown on May 27, 1958, at St Louis as the XF4H-1, it entered service with Navy squadrons during 1960.

Impressed by the Phantom's spectacular performance, the US Air Force evaluated the F4H-1 in 1961 as a potential successor to the F-106 Delta Darts of Air Defense Command. In March 1962 it was announced that the Phantom was to be the standard interceptor and reconnaissance aircraft in Tactical Air Command (TAC), USAF Europe (USAFE) and Pacific Air Force (PACAF). Initially designated F-110A and YRF-110A, the prototypes were later redesignated F-4C for the fighter variant and RF-4C for the reconnaissance model.

The F-4C retained the folding wing and arrester gear of the naval Phantoms but incorporated different internal equipment. Powered by two 17,000lb st afterburning General Electric J79-GE-15 engines, it was capable of a maximum level speed with external stores of more than Mach 2. Armament was four Sparrow IIIs in recesses under the fuselage and up to 16,000lb of external ordnance. A total of 583 F-4Cs were delivered to the Air Force between November 1963 and February 1967. Some 36 were later transferred to Spain, where they are locally designated C.12, and enough for two squadrons were modified as EF-4Cs for the Wild Weasel role, carrying ECM sensors, jamming pods, chaff dispensers and anti-radiation missiles. A number of F-4Cs were transferred to the Air National Guard in January 1972.

The Air Force received a total of 503 RF-4Cs, the first of which was delivered in April 1964. This unarmed version was equipped with cameras, sideways-looking radar and infra-red sensors.

The F-4D, first flown in December 1965, was a developed version of the F-4C with improved avionics. The Air Force received a total of 793, deliveries beginning in March 1966. The F-4D was succeeded by the improved F-4E, which incorporated leading-edge wing slats, internal M61A1 multi-barrel cannon and advanced avionics. The first production aircraft was supplied to the Air Force in October 1967 and a total of 949 were eventually delivered, including a number for MAP supply to other countries.

Ultimate Air Force version was the F-4G. This designation was first adopted for 12 F-4Bs modified for a specialised naval role, but in 1976 it was announced that 116 Air Force F-4Es would be modified as F-4Gs for the Advanced Wild Weasel programme. First deliveries, to the 35th Tactical Fighter Wing at George AFB, California, began in October 1978.

McDonnell Douglas RF-4C Phantom

McDonnell Douglas F-4D

McDonnell Douglas F-4Es

Sikorsky CH-3

The twin-engined CH-3 general-purpose transport helicopter is a military version of the commercial S-61R. Developed for the US Air Force from the S-61A, the CH-3 introduced many important design changes, including provision of a hydraulically operated rear ramp for straight-in loading of wheeled vehicles, a 20,000lb-capacity winch for internal cargo handling, retractable tricycle undercarriage and many other minor features.

The first S-61R flew on June 17, 1963, followed by the first CH-3C a few weeks later. First deliveries to the Air Force were made in December 1963, to Tyndall AFB, Florida, where the aircraft were used for drone recovery duties. A total of 41 CH-3Cs, powered by two 1,300 shp General Electric T58-GE-1 turboshafts, were built, and subsequent deliveries went to Aerospace Defense Command, Air Training Command, Tactical Air Command, Strategic Air Command and Aerospace Rescue and Recovery Service.

In February 1966 the CH-3C was followed into production by the CH-3E, which differed from the earlier aircraft mainly in having uprated 1,500 shp T58-GE-5 engines. A total of 42 were built from new, and all surviving CH-3Cs were later brought up to this standard.

Third of the Air Force's CH-3 variants was the HH-35, equipped for the Aerospace Rescue and Recovery Service with limited armour, self-sealing fuel tanks, retractable flight-refuelling probe, rescue hoist and defensive armament. A total of 50 Jolly Green Giants, as they were dubbed in Vietnam, were converted from CH-3Es.

Sikorsky HH-3C

Douglas A-1H Skyraider

Douglas A-1 Skyraider

Designed by Ed Heinemann, the Douglas Skyraider was intended primarily for the US Navy, for which it performed an extraordinary variety of roles, ranging from night attack to airborne early warning.

The Air Force first showed interest in the Skyraider in 1949, when the A-1 was evaluated as a possible ground-attack aircraft, but it was to be more than a decade before the Air Force had any of the type in its inventory. This followed the establishment in April 1962 of the Special Air Warfare Centre at Eglin AFB in Florida, when the 1st Combat Applications Group acquired two Navy aircraft.

These machines were supplemented by a further 150 Navy-surplus A-1Es, which were fitted with dual controls to suit the special needs of the Air Force. This feature was needed not only for training Vietnamese pilots and converting USAF jet pilots to tailwheel, piston-engined aircraft, but also because USAF pilots of the 603rd and 604th fighter squadrons, 1st Air Commando Wing, operating as "advisers" in Vietnam, were initially required to have Vietnamese "co-pilots" to select targets and take responsibility for attacks.

These A-1Es were supplemented by large numbers of A-1Hs. In the large-scale war during the mid to late 1960s Air Force Skyraiders were flown from bases in South Vietnam and Thailand to support ground forces in South Vietnam, Cambodia and Laos, and on escort and fire-suppression sorties for helicopter and flying-boat rescue operations in the north.

Powered by a 3,000 hp Wright R-3350-26W radial engine, attack versions of the Skyraider were usually armed with four wing-mounted 20mm cannon and could carry up to 8,000lb of external stores on up to 15 pylons.

Douglas A-1E

North American XB-70

North American XB-70 Valkyrie

The XB-70 Valkyrie was a large tail-first delta-wing Mach 3 strategic bomber designed to replace Strategic Air Command (SAC) B-52s in the mid-1960s.

The initial USAF requirement was issued in October 1954, and the programme was designated Weapon System 110A in 1955. Both Boeing and North American submitted design proposals and in December 1957 it was announced that the latter company had been selected as prime contractor for the system. Simultaneously, General Electric was awarded a contract to develop the chemical-fuel J93-GE-5 turbojet. In 1959, however, it was decided that the added complication of using chemical fuel was unnecessary and the aircraft—by then designated B-70—was adapted to take six J93-GE-3 afterburning turbojets.

In December 1959 the B-70 programme was cut back to a single prototype and further development of most of its operational subsystems was cancelled. In October 1960, however, the budget was partially restored and $265 million was made available for B-70 development.

A further *volte face* by President Kennedy in 1961 regraded the aircraft as an aerodynamic test vehicle to be used, in the President's words: "...to explore the problems of flying at three times the speed of sound with an airframe potentially useful as a bomber, through the development of a small number of prototype aircraft...."

This "small number" turned out in March 1963 to be two aircraft designated XB-70A. The first of these was shown publicly for the first time in May 1964, making its first flight, from Palmdale to Edwards AFB, on September 21. The design cruising speed of Mach 3 was achieved on the 17th flight, on October 14, 1965.

The second XB-70A, with slight aerodynamic and other changes, flew for the first time on July 17, 1965, and on May 19 the following year it sustained Mach 3 for 32 minutes. Tragically, it was lost on June 8 when an F-104 chase aircraft collided with it. Management of the surviving aircraft was taken over by NASA in March 1967 and the programme was terminated in 1969.

**North American XB-70 Valkyrie
with T-38 chase aircraft**

Cessna T-41 Mescalero

The Cessna T-41A is the military version of the Cessna Model 172 Skyhawk. In July 1964 the US Air Force ordered 170 Model 172s under the designation T-41A for delivery between September 1964 and July 1965. Air Force student pilots complete about 30 hours of basic training on the type before passing on to the T-37B jet primary trainer. A second buy was ordered in July 1967 and a total of 237 had been built by the end of 1973. Powerplant is the 160 hp Lycoming O-320-H2AD.

The T-41C is the US Air Force's version of the more powerful Cessna Model R172E with 210 hp Continental IO-360-D. The Air Force acquired 45 in October 1967 for the USAF Academy in Colorado, and 52 had been built by 1976.

C-141B and KC-135

Lockheed C-141 StarLifter

In May 1960 the US Air Force issued a requirement for a jet-powered freighter for the Military Air Transport Services (MATS) fleet. The design competition was hotly contested, with Lockheed, Boeing and Convair all submitting proposals, and on March 13, 1961, it was announced that Lockheed-Georgia had won with its C-141 proposal.

The original contract of August 1961 covered five development, test and evaluation aircraft, followed by a production contract for 284 C-141As, all of which had been delivered by 1968. The StarLifter was the flying element of Logistics Support System 476L, designed to give MATS (later Military Airlift Command, MAC) a worldwide airlift capability in support of US Strike Command, which included the Strategic Army Corps and the Composite Air Strike Forces of Tactical Air Command.

First flight was on December 17, 1963, and the type first entered squadron service with MAC in April 1965. From August of that year C-141s made almost daily flights across the Pacific to and from Vietnam, carrying troops, cargo and wounded. With a fuselage cross-section the same as that of the C-130 Hercules, the longer C-141A was able to carry a packaged Minuteman ICBM.

Operational experience revealed the need for flight-refuelling capability, however. It was also sometimes found that the StarLifter's hold was packed to capacity without the gross weight limitation having been reached. As a result the Air Force awarded Lockheed Georgia a contract in May 1976 to extend the fuselage of an existing C-141A and to provide the aircraft with in-flight refuelling requipment.

Designated YC-141B, the prototype conversion was rolled out in January 1977 and made its first flight on March 24, complete with a plug conferring 13ft 4in of extra fuselage.

In June 1978 Lockheed began work on converting all 271 remaining C-141As in the MAC inventory to C-141B standard. This work, carried out at Lockheed's Marietta, Georgia, factory, was scheduled to be completed by July 1982. The modifications will in effect provide the Air Force with another 90 C-141s, since three C-141Bs will do the work of four C-141As.

The first production aircraft was handed over to the USAF in December 1979 and was flown to Charleston AFB for testing before assignment to Altus AFB for crew training.

Stretched C-141B StarLifter (foreground) with C-141A

Sikorsky HH-53

The Sikorsky HH-53 is a heavy assault transport helicopter developed originally for the US Marine Corps as the CH-53A. Deliveries began in mid-1966 and the aircraft were powered by two 2,850 ehp General Electric T64-GE-6 turboshafts.

In September 1966 the US Air Force ordered eight for the Aerospace Rescue and Recovery service under the designation HH-53B. First flown on March 15, 1967, they were powered by two 3,080 shp T64-GE-3 turboshafts.

An improved version, the HH-53C, was delivered to the USAF from August 1968. Powered by a pair of -7 engines, the HH-53C could carry up to 20,000lb on its external hoist. When production ended a total of 72 HH-53Bs and Cs had been built.

Under the Air Force's Pave Low 3 programme eight HH-53s were modified for night search and recovery operations, following first flight of a prototype modified to this standard in June 1975.

Sikorsky HH-53C

Sikorsky HH-53C

Lockheed SR-71 Blackbird

The high-altitude Lockheed SR-71 was developed as a strategic reconnaissance aircraft to succeed the U-2. The existence of the SR-71 was first publicly acknowledged by the US Government in February 1964, although detailed design work had begun in 1959. Known at that time as the A-11, it was designed by a small team led by Kelly Johnson in the Burbank "Skunk Works".

Several versions of this remarkable aircraft have been built: the first three A-11s ordered on a US Air Force contract of 1960 were redesignated YF-12A in 1964, when they were evaluated as experimental all-weather interceptor fighters in the Improved Manned Interceptor (IMI) programme. First flight, at Watertown Strip, Nevada, took place on April 26, 1962. Following the decision not to proceed with the advanced bomber defence system, the second and third YF-12As were allocated in late 1969 to the joint NASA/USAF AST (Advanced Supersonic Technology) programme.

The single YF-12C was the fourth aircraft built and was completed as the prototype SR-71. It was subsequently allocated to the AST programme, joining the YF-12As.

Development of the SR-71 itself began in February 1963, and the first production example flew for the first time at Edwards AFB on December 22, 1964. Evaluation by SAC began in 1965 and first deliveries were made to the 9th Strategic Reconnaissance Wing at Beale AFB, California. Production is believed to have reached at least 30 aircraft, including the SR-71B.

The SR-71B is a tandem two-seat operational training version with a second cockpit placed above and behind the pilot's cockpit. Two examples are known to have been built, one of which was subsequently lost in a crash. The sole SR-71C is a revised training version modified from a production SR-71A.

Lockheed SR-17A Blackbird

Lockheed YF-12A

Lockheed SR-71A Blackbird

Cessna O-2

The four/six-seat Cessna Model 337 Skymaster resulted from manufacturer's studies aimed at producing a twin-engined aircraft that would be cheap, simple to fly, and offering all of the advantages of two engines. The prototype flew for the first time in February 1961.

In 1966 the Skymaster was selected by the US Air Force, which equipped it for forward air controller (FAC) missions, including visual reconnaissance, target identification and marking and damage assessment. Designated O-2A and fitted with dual controls as standard, it could carry a variety of stores on four underwing pylons, including rockets, flares or a 7.62mm Minigun pack.

The O-2B is generally similar to the commercial Skymaster but is equipped for psychological warfare missions with an advanced communications system and high-power air-to-ground broadcasting system. A combined total of 544 O-2As and O-2Bs had been delivered by December 1970; 31 of the Bs were converted from commercial aircraft.

Cessna O-2

Cessna A-37B

Cessna A-37 Dragonfly

The Cessna A-37 development of the T-37 twin-engined two-seat side-by-side trainer was designed for attack and counter-insurgency (COIN) missions from short, unimproved airstrips.

Development began after evaluation of two T-37Cs by the Special Air Warfare Centre at Eglin AFB, Florida, in 1962, and a contract for two prototype YAT-37Ds was awarded to Cessna the following year. The first of these flew for the first time on October 22, 1963, and preliminary testing was carried out at Edwards AFB and Eglin during 1963 and 1964.

Following a resurgence of interest in COIN operations as US involvement in the war in Vietnam increased, 39 production A-37As were ordered in August 1966 under the USAF's Combat Dragon programme. These aircraft were to be produced by modifying existing T-37B trainers. Deliveries began in May 1967 and a squadron of 25 aircraft was deployed to Vietnam in August for a four-month evaluation. At the end of the trial period they were retained by the 604th Air Commando Squadron at Bien Hoa Air Base. All had been withdrawn from service by 1974.

The standard production version was the A-37B, and the first of an initial batch of 127 flew for the first time in September 1967. Powered by two 2,850lb st General Electric J85-GE-17As, the type has twice the take-off power of the trainer. The A-37B is also significantly heavier and stronger than the A-37A and can carry up to 5,880lb of external stores.

A total of 577 had been built when production ended in 1977. A number went to the US Air Force and Air National Guard, while most were delivered to Security Assistance Programme customers in South-east Asia and South America.

Cessna A-37B Dragonfly

General Dynamics F-111
General Dynamics FB-111A

General Dynamics F-111A

General Dynamics F-111 and FB-111 series

The F-111 variable-geometry aircraft grew out of the US Defence Department's TFX (Tri-service Fighter, Experimental) programme, aimed at finding a common multi-role aircraft for all three services.

Following evaluation of design proposals by both Boeing and General Dynamics, the DoD awarded the TFX contract to the latter company in November 1962, with Grumman as associate. From the start the programme was bedevilled by acrimony and controversy, beginning with Boeing's claim that it should have received the contract on the grounds that its proposal was technically superior.

The initial contract was for 23 development aircraft, comprising 18 F-111As for the

USAF and five F-111Bs for the Navy; Grumman concentrated on the latter model. The project lurched from problem to problem, however, and by the time that the first F-111A made its maiden flight on December 21, 1964, morale within General Dynamics was at a low ebb.

By the end of 1968 the F-111 programme was firmly on the rocks, following cancellation of the Navy's F-111B (which had flown for the first time in May 1965) and the United Kingdom's F-111K because of performance shortfalls and spiralling costs. In an attempt to restore confidence in the aircraft, in March 1968 the Air Force deployed a combat squadron to South-east Asia, where it suffered the loss of a number of aircraft, resulting in a succession of groundings. Once scheduled for a total run of more

than 1,700 aircraft, production ended at 562 of all variants when the last F-111F was delivered in December 1976.

The 141 production F-111As for Tactical Air Command were followed by 94 F-111Es with modified air intakes. Most of the F-111Es currently serve with the 20th Tactical Fighter Wing at Upper Heyford, Oxfordshire. Next production version was the F-111D, some 96 of which were built. This is similar to the F-111A but has Mk 2 electronics for improved navigation and weapons delivery. Production ended in 1973 and the type currently equips the 27th TFW at Cannon AFB, New Mexico.

Production of the F-111F began in August 1971 and extended to 106 aircraft.

Generally similar to the F-111D, it is powered by two TF30-P-100 turbofans. During 1978 a development programme allowed for the addition of electro-optical sensors and guided-weapon capability.

The FB-111A two-seat strategic bomber version for SAC incorporates Mk 2 electronics and TF30-P-7 engines. A total requirement for 210 to replace the B-52 was announced in 1965, but production ultimately reached only 76 aircraft. The first production aircraft flew for the first time on July 13, 1968. Weapons load is a combination of nuclear bombs or SRAMs.

The first FB-111A was delivered to the 340th Bomb Group at Carswell AFB, Texas, in October 1969.

Rockwell OV-10A Bronco

The twin-boom Rockwell International OV-10A Bronco was originally designed by North American to meet the US Navy's 1963 requirement for a Light Armed Reconnaissance Aircraft (LARA) suitable for counter-insurgency (COIN) missions.

Eleven US airframe manufacturers entered the competition, and of the seven projects chosen for evaluation by the Department of Defence North American's NA-300 was declared the winner in August 1964. Seven prototypes were built at Columbus, Ohio, under the designation YOV-10A Bronco, and the first aircraft flew for the first time on July 16, 1965, powered by a pair of Garrett AiResearch T76 turboprops.

Several modifications were made following the initial manufacturer's flight trials, including a 10ft increase in wing span and the fitting of uprated engines. The initial production version for both the USAF and the Marine Corps was the OV-10A, the first of which was flown for the first time in August

1967.

The Air Force ultimately acquired some 157 Broncos for use in the forward air control role, as well as for limited quick-response ground support pending the arrival on the scene of tactical fighters. First deliveries were made in February 1968 to the 4410th Combat Crew Training Wing at

Eglin AFB, Florida. By August the Bronco was in Vietnam, initially with the Air Force's 19th Tactical Air Support Squadron for evaluation. Although the original plan called for the Air Force's FAC Broncos to be unarmed, it was later decided to provide them with a pair of 7.62mm Miniguns and provision for underwing rockets or

missiles, up to a maximum of 3,600lb.

Production ended in 1969, but in 1971 some 15 aircraft were modified by LTV Electrosystems under the USAF's Pave Nail programme for use as night forward air control and strike designation aircraft. All were restored to standard OV-10A configuration in 1974.

McDonnell Douglas C-9A Nightingale

The C-9A is an aeromedical airlift version of the commercial McDonnell Douglas DC-9-30 airliner. Design study data on the DC-9—originally known as the Douglas Model 2086—were released in 1962 and preliminary design work began that year. The prototype DC-9 flew for the first time in February 1965, and

the first Series 30 flew on August 1, 1966, powered by two 14,000lb st JT8-D-7 turbojets.

The C-9A Nightingale, eight of which were originally ordered in 1967 for operation by the 375th Aeromedical Wing of Military Airlift Command, is powered by two JT8-D-9s. It can carry

between 30 and 40 litter patients or more than 40 ambulatory patients (or a combination of the two), plus two nurses and three aeromedical technicians.

The first C-9A was rolled out in June 1968 and was delivered to the Air Force at Scott AFB on August 10. Total orders reached 21, the last of which was

delivered by February 1973.

In December 1973 the Air Force ordered a further variant of the commercial Series 30 under the designation VC-9C. Three of these VIP transports were delivered in 1975 for service with the Special Air Missions Wing at Andrews AFB, Maryland.

Vought A-7D Corsair II

The Vought A-7 was originally designed as a single-seat carrier-based light attack aircraft to replace the US Navy's McDonnell Douglas A-4 Skyhawks. Based on the F-8 Crusader, it was first flown on September 27, 1965, and the first Navy A-7As began to equip carrier squadrons from October 1966.

After evaluating the Corsair the US Air Force selected the aircraft in 1966 as the least expensive and best way to fill its requirement for a heavily armed long-range tactical fighter to replace the A-1E and F-100 Super Sabre in the close air support role, particularly in South-east Asia. The Air Force insisted on a larger engine, however, which led to replacement of the TF30 in Navy aircraft by the more powerful Allison-built TF41 (Spey) turbofan. In fact, commonality between Navy A-7As and the Air Force's A-7D was only about 25%.

First flown on April 5, 1968, the A-7D was accepted by the Air Force in late December that year and was the first subsonic jet-powered fighter to enter service with the USAF for almost 20 years. Equipment included the continuous-solution navigation and weapon delivery system, which permits all-weather radar bomb delivery. First unit to receive the type was the 54th Tactical Fighter Wing at Luke AFB, Arizona, and the A-7D first went into combat in South-east Asia in October 1972 with the 354th Tactical Fighter Wing.

Production ended in 1977 after 459 examples had been built. At the end of that year there were 209 on the strength of the active Air Force, with another 183 with the Air National Guard. From mid-1978 the surviving aircraft were being modified to carry the Pave Penny laser designator pod.

Vought A-7D Corsair IIs

Lockheed C-5A Galaxy

Design studies for a very large transport for Military Airlift Command (then MATS) began in 1963, when the requirement was for a 600,000lb aircraft known by the designation CX-4. This and later requirements later crystallised into a specification known as CX-HLS (Cargo, Experimental—Heavy Logistics System).

Following an initial design competition in May 1964, Boeing, Douglas and Lockheed were contracted to develop their designs further. At this time the requirement was for a 700,000lb aircraft designated C-5A.

In October 1965 Lockheed was nominated prime contractor for the airframe. Construction started in August 1966 and the prototype flew for the first time on June 30, 1968. The initial fixed-price contract called for five test aircraft and 53 production units. Options were included for production of up to 57 additional aircraft in "Run-B" and 85 more in "Run-C". Target total price of the 115 aircraft was more than $1.9 billion. Total programme cost was estimated at more than $3.4 billion.

Because of escalating costs the Air Force exercised its option on Run B in January 1969 but

Lockheed C-5A Galaxy

limited the number to 23, bringing the total buy to 81 aircraft; all had been delivered by May 1973. Of this total 77 remained by late 1979; three were lost in ground accidents and one crashed in Vietnam in April 1975.

The Galaxy has been subjected to three major

modification programmes: changes to the cargo ramp fastening system, the failure of which was blamed for the Vietnam crash; replacement of the upper and cargo deck floors, corroded and delaminated by spillage of liquids; and redesign of the wing to increase service life from 8,750 hours to 30,000 hours. In January 1978 the Air

Force awarded a $24 million contract to Lockheed for the manufacture of two new wing sets, one for ground testing and the second for flight trials scheduled to begin in August 1980. If tests are successful the new wings will be progressively fitted to all Galaxies in operational service, beginning in 1982.

Northrop F-5E Tiger II

The Northrop F-5E single-seat light tactical fighter was selected in November 1970 as the winner of the International Fighter Aircraft (IFA) competition to find a successor for the F-5A Freedom Fighter. Basis of the new design are the aids to manoeuvrability first applied to Netherlands Air Force NF-5As and Bs. The aircraft also incorporate other features developed for the Canadian, Dutch and Norwegian F-5s, including two-position nose undercarriage and arrester hook.

Powered by two 5,000lb st afterburning General Electric J85-GE-21As, the prototype flew for the first time on August 11, 1972. First deliveries of the F-5E to the USAF's 425th Tactical

Fighter Squadron were made in the spring of 1973. Twenty aircraft had been supplied for the Air Force training programme by the end of September that year and deliveries to foreign countries began in late 1973.

In USAF service the type is used in Aggressor squadrons, simulating enemy aircraft in the training of front-line air combat pilots.

Two versions are currently in production: the F-5E and the tandem two-seat F-5F. Development of the latter version was approved by the Air Force in early 1974 and first flight was made on September 25 of that year. Deliveries of production aircraft began in the summer of 1976.

Northrop F-5E Tiger II

Boeing T-43A

The Boeing T-43A military derivative of the commercial Boeing 737-200 is claimed by the US Air Force to be the world's most advanced navigational trainer; it is also probably the largest.

After evaluation of both the 737 and the McDonnell Douglas DC-9, the Boeing aircraft was selected in May 1971 to meet an urgent requirement for a navigation trainer to replace the Convair T-29 and to form the airborne section of the Undergraduate Navigator Training System. This was the first fixed-wing military aircraft production contract awarded to Boeing since 1955. First flight was at Renton, Washington, on April 10, 1973.

The T-43A carries 12 students, twice as many as the T-29, and has twice the utilisation rate. The initial order was for 19 aircraft to replace the 57 T-29s based at Mather AFB in California.

To improve the utilisation rate further the aircraft is used in conjunction with a computer-based mission simulator, the Honeywell T-45B, which can reproduce any kind of mission up to Mach 2 at 70,000ft.

Boeing T-43

McDonnell Douglas F-15 Eagle

The McDonnell Douglas F-15 Eagle single-seat air-superiority fighter emerged from the F-X programme, first proposed to the USAF in the 1960s as a follow-on to the North American F-100 Super Sabre. In the course of this programme design proposals were sought from three airframe manufacturers—McDonnell Douglas, North American Rockwell and Fairchild Hiller—and in December 1969 McDonnell Douglas was selected as prime airframe contractor.

The winning design was a single-seat fixed-wing aircraft with a thrust-to-weight ratio in excess of 1:1, containing extremely advanced avionics and armed with the 25mm Philco-Ford GAU-7A multi-barrel cannon (later abandoned in favour of the proven General Electric M61A1). The aircraft was to be powered by two Pratt & Whitney F100 afterburning turbofans of approximately 25,000lb st each.

The contract called for 20 development aircraft, comprising 18 single-seat F-15As and two TF-15A two-seat trainers. After completion at St

Louis the first F-15A was transported to Edwards AFB, where it was flown for the first time on July 27, 1972, by Irving Burrows. First flight of the TF-15A—later redesignated F-15B—was made almost exactly a year later, on July 7, 1973.

First deliveries were to the 555th Tactical Fighter Training Wing at Luke AFB, Arizona, in November 1974, followed by other squadrons of the 58th TFTW and, from January 1976, by the 1st Tactical Fighter Wing at Langley AFB, Virginia. Overseas, US Air Force F-15s first became operational with the 36th TFW at Bitburg AFB, West Germany, in late 1977. Total procurement for the Air Force is set at 729 aircraft, of which more than 450 had been delivered by the beginning of 1980. This total comprises 350 F-15As, 54 two-seat F-15Bs, and 325 F-15C/Ds.

Following delivery of the 404th Eagle in June 1979 the USAF began procurement of the C/D models, the first of which flew on February 26, 1979. The remaining aircraft of this type will incorporate increased fuel tankage; the earlier A/B models will not be retrofitted.

McDonnell Douglas F-15B

McDonnell Douglas F-15A Eagle

McDonnell Douglas F-15B

Boeing E-4A

Boeing E-4

The Boeing E-4A and E-4B are modified versions of the commercial Boeing 747-200 transport aircraft designed for use as Advanced Airborne Command Posts (AABNCP).

In February 1973 the US Air Force's Electronic Systems Division announced that it had awarded Boeing a $59 million contract for the supply of two E-4As; a contract worth more than $27 million was awarded in July 1973 for a third aircraft, and in December $39 million was awarded for a fourth aircraft.

The fourth (and subsequent) aircraft are fitted out with more advanced equipment and are designated E-4B. In January 1976 it was announced that the total planned force was six E-4Bs, with the programme scheduled for completion in 1983; this also allowed for the conversion of the original three E-3As to B standard.

The force is designed to replace EC-135 Airborne Command Posts of the National Military Command System and Strategic Air Command. Installation of interim

equipment in the first three aircraft was carried out by E-Systems. This involved the transfer and integration of equipment removed from EC-135. The first operational aircraft was delivered to Andrews AFB, Maryland, in December 1974.

The Air Force took delivery of its first E-4B testbed aircraft in August 1975. Equipped for flight refuelling, it was the first to be equipped with the advanced Command, Control and Communications equipment.

Rockwell International B-1

Though the Rockwell International B-1 variable-geometry bomber is one of the most technologically advanced aircraft in the world today, it is unlikely that it will ever go into production for use as a front-line type.

The B-1 was the outcome of a succession of studies begun in 1962 and culminating in the Advanced Manned Strategic Aircraft (AMSA) requirement of 1965 for a low-altitude penetration bomber to replace the ageing B-52s of Strategic Air Command by 1980.

Requests for proposals (RFPs) were issued in November 1969, with Rockwell being selected to carry out airframe development and evaluation, and General Electric to develop the F101 turbofan, in June 1970. The original contracts were for five flying prototypes, two structural test airframes and 40 engines. But in January 1971 the quantities were cut back to three flight-test aircraft, one ground-test airframe and only 27 engines. Procurement of a fourth flight-test aircraft was approved in 1975, and at that time a requirement for up to 244 production B-1s had been expressed by the Air Force.

Construction of the first aircraft began at Palmdale, California, in late 1972 and roll-out followed in October 1974. First flight was made from Palmdale on December 23; this was also the first flight of the YF101 engine. The third prototype, used as a testbed for the electronic systems, first flew on April 1, 1976, and was followed by the second prototype on June 14 that year.

On June 30, 1977, President Carter announced that production of the B-1 was to be cancelled, with priority being given instead to cruise missiles. Nevertheless, the test and development programme, including completion of the fourth prototype, was allowed to continue as insurance against the possible failure of the alternative system.

Third prototype YB-1A

Rockwell B-1

Beech C-12

The Beech C-12 is a military version of the attractive twin-engined Beech Super King Air 200. Design of this executive transport began in the autumn of 1970 and the prototype first flew on October 27, 1972. Compared with the earlier King Air 100, the Super King Air 200 has wings of increased span, a T-tail, more powerful engines and additional fuel capacity.

In August 1974 Beech was contracted to build 34 modified versions designated C-12A. The US Army was to receive 20, with the balance going to the Air Force. The following year the Army and the Air Force exercised options on additional aircraft, with the USAF ordering a further 16. A number of C-12s were also acquired by the US Navy during 1977.

The aircraft are described as standard off-the-shelf Super King Airs modified slightly to meet military requirements. Accommodation is provided for eight passengers and a crew of two.

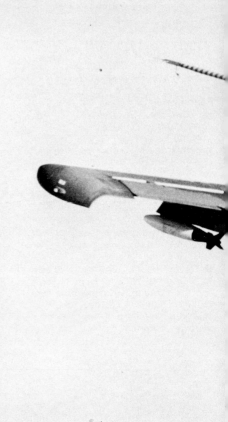

Fairchild Republic A-10A

Fairchild Republic A-10 Thunderbolt II

The Fairchild Republic A-10A grew out of the US Air Force's A-X programme, begun in 1967 to produce a highly battleproof, heavily armed close air support aircraft to replace the A-1 Skyraider.

In December 1970 Fairchild Republic and Northrop were selected from six competing companies to build two prototypes each for evaluation. Fairchild Republic's first YA-10A flew for the first time on May 10, 1972, and the competitive fly-off with Northrop's A-9 was completed in December that year. The A-10 was declared the winner in January 1973. The final development test and evaluation contract was for six aircraft, the first of which first flew in February 1975. This followed a second competitive fly-off with the Vought A-7D, which resulted in December

1974 in a production contract for 52 A-10As, later cut to 22 aircraft. Delivery of these aircraft to the 333rd Tactical Fighter Training Squadron at Davis-Monthan AFB, Arizona, began in the spring of 1976, and by the autumn of 1977 funds had been approved for the procurement of a total of 195 production A-10As. The 1978 and 1979 budgets allowed for a further 144 aircraft, with 144 more requested for 1980. Total requirement is put at 733 aircraft, the last of which should have been delivered by the end of 1983.

The first operational A-10A unit was the 354th Tactical Fighter Wing, based at Myrtle Beach, South Carolina, which received its first Thunderbolt II (soon dubbed "Warthog" because of its unlovely looks) in March 1977. This wing began

operating the aircraft with the Pave Penny laser designator in early 1978. This equipment complements the aircraft's formidable armament of a nose-mounted General Electric GAU-8/A Avenger 30mm seven-barrel cannon capable of a maximum rate of fire of 4,200 rounds/minute, and up to 16,000lb of external stores on eight wing and three fuselage stations. Powered by a pair of 9,065lb st General Electric TF34-GE-100 turbofans, the A-10A has a typical combat speed of 443 mph.

The type was first deployed overseas in January 1979, when 14 A-10As arrived at RAF Bentwaters and Woodbridge to equip the 81st Tactical Fighter Wing. Plans call for a total of six squadrons to be deployed in the United Kingdom. These aircraft will be rotated in small numbers

around the various forward bases in Nato's forward region, including the West German airfields at Sembach, Leipheim, Alhorn and Noervenich.

Following the expression of doubts about the suitability of the A-10A for all-weather operations, particularly in the European theatre, Fairchild Republic accelerated development of a company-funded two-seat version modified from one of the original evaluation aircraft. This flew for the first time at Edwards AFB on May 4, 1979. This version carries a back-seat weapons systems officer (WSO) who is responsible for navigation, ECM operation and target or threat acquisition and designation. Apart from the provision of the second seat, most of the changes concern improved mission avionics.

Fairchild Republic A-10A Thunderbolt II

Fairchild Republic A-10As

Two-seat night/adverse-weather A-10B

Boeing E-3A

Boeing E-3A Sentry

The Boeing E-3A Awacs (Airborne Warning And Control System), based on the Boeing 707-320 airframe, is currently in production for the US Air Force. Renamed Sentry in May 1978, the aircraft is equipped with extensive sensing, communications, display and navigational devices.

The Sentry is distinguished by a large mushroom radome mounted on the upper rear fuselage and housing a Westinghouse rotating radar system. The Sentry is capable of providing tactical air threat detection, surveillance and countermeasures direction. With its long-range, look-down AN/APY-1 radar and substantial jamming resistance the Sentry can operate as a self-contained force management centre or as a complement to an established ground control network.

Awacs grew out of the Air Force's over-land radar technology programme, begun in June 1963 to develop a large airborne radar with uncluttered look-down capability. Hughes and Westinghouse were chosen as radar competitors, with Westinghouse eventually being named winner in October 1972 after several months of airborne tests.

The number of aircraft to be bought has decreased several times during the programme, and the current Air Force requirement is for 34 aircraft, comprising 31 production models and three prototypes. By 1979 funding had been provided for the prototypes and 22 production aircraft.

The first production aircraft was delivered in March 1977 to the 552nd Airborne Warning and Control Wing, based at Tinker AFB, Oklahoma. A total of 19, including the three prototypes, had been delivered by the end of 1979.

General Dynamics F-16B

General Dynamics F-16A

General Dynamics F-16B

General Dynamics F-16

The single-seat General Dynamics F-16 air combat fighter was developed in response to a US Air Force request for proposals (RFP) of January 1972 for a lightweight fighter technology demonstrator. Nine companies originally received the RFP, of which five complied. In April 1972 the USAF selected the General Dynamics Model 401 and the Northrop P-600 for prototype construction, each company being awarded almost $40 million to build two demonstrators each.

The General Dynamics design—later redesignated YF-16—was powered by a single Pratt & Whitney F100 turbofan, and the use of many components common to other GD aircraft saved both time and money. The first of the prototypes was rolled out at Fort Worth, Texas, on December 13, 1973. It made an unscheduled first flight on January 20, 1974, during high-speed taxi tests, followed by an official first flight on February 2.

The General Dynamics and Northrop prototypes underwent a comparatively leisurely 300-hour USAF evaluation in the twelve months following the first flight. But the situation changed in 1974, when Defence Secretary Schlesinger announced the Air Combat Fighter programme, designed to produce a replacement for F-4 Phantom interceptors and to augment the F-15 inventory.

In January 1975, after a competitive fly-off between the YF-16 and Northrop's YF-17, the USAF chose the General Dynamics aircraft for development. The F-16 collected an additional boost in June 1975 when four Nato countries—Belgium, Denmark, the Netherlands and Norway—jointly announced their intention to buy the aircraft as an F-104 replacement, their combined order totalling some 348 aircraft.

The first development aircraft flew for the first time in December 1976 and the first two-seat F-16B on August 7, 1977. The USAF is to procure as many as 1,388 F-16s, and about 200, including prototypes and pre-production aircraft, had been delivered by the end of 1980. The first F-16 to enter operational service with the Air Force was delivered to the 388th Tactical Fighter Wing in January 1979.

Artist's impression of McDonnell Douglas KC-10

McDonnell Douglas KC-10A Extender

The KC-10A Extender, a military version of the trijet, wide-bodied DC-10 commercial aircraft, was the eventual winner of the US Air Force's Advanced Tanker Cargo Aircraft (ATCA) competition.

The history of ATCA is long and involved. The Air Force began studies of a follow-on to the Boeing KC-135 tanker in 1967 in anticipation of the proposed B-1 strategic bomber. As the studies proceeded the Air Force made known its preference for a completely new aircraft—at one time a stand-off missile-carrying capability was also required—even though it had invited both Boeing and

Lockheed to submit proposals based on the 747 and C-5A Galaxy respectively.

The whole programme slipped in concert with the eclipse of the B-1 and the consequent difficulty of justifying the added cost of developing and deploying a new companion tanker. At one time the bill was put at between $50 to $100 million in research and development plus another $2 million per copy over and above the commercial price.

By March 1973, however, the Air Force had affirmed its need for a new tanker to replace the ageing KC-135 fleet and to provide a wider range of

capabilities for both strategic and tactical forces. The number of possible contenders for the contract had increased to four with the appearance of the two tri-jet wide-bodied commercial aircraft from McDonnell Douglas (DC-10) and Lockheed (L-1011 TriStar).

Finally, on December 19, 1977, the Air Force announced that the McDonnell Douglas DC-10-30CF had been selected in preference to the Boeing 747; the C-5A Galaxy and L-1011 had already been eliminated on cost grounds.

The eventual requirement is for as many as 91 aircraft, with an initial production batch of 20

tanker/cargo aircraft at a unit cost of about $35.5 million; deliveries began early in 1980.

Powered by a military version of the General Electric CF6-50 turbofan, the KC-10 carries transfer fuel in standard DC-10 wing and centre-section fuel tanks and in special underfloor tanks, and is fitted with three underwing and tail refuelling booms controlled from an operator's station located beneath the aft fuselage. Typical tanker load will be 150,000lb of disposable fuel at a mission range of 2,500 nautical miles, while as a freighter the Extender will carry 148,000lb of cargo over 4,000 nautical miles.

Data

Type	Powerplant	Dimensions	Weights	Performance	Armament	Crew
Curtiss JN-4D	1×90 hp Curtiss OX-5 in-line	Span: 43ft 7in Length: 27ft 4in Height: 9ft 10½in Wing area: 352 sq ft	Empty: 1,580lb AUW: 2,130lb	Max speed: 75 mph at S/L Service ceiling: 11,000ft Range: 250 miles	None	2
Curtiss JN-6H	1×150 hp Wright-Hispano A in-line	Span: 43ft 7in Length: 26ft 11in Height: 9ft 10½in Wing area: 352 sq ft	Empty: 1,797lb AUW: 2,687lb	Max speed: 79 mph at S/L Service ceiling: 5,700ft Range: 250 miles	None	2
Nieuport 17	1×110 hp Le Rhône 9-J rotary	Span: 26ft 11½in Length: 18ft 10in Height: 7ft 7½in Wing area: 159 sq ft	Empty: 705lb AUW: 1,179lb	Max speed: 109 mph at S/L Service ceiling: 17,390ft Range: 186 miles	1×0.303in mg	1
Thomas-Morse S-4C	1×80 hp Le Rhône 9-C rotary	Span: 26ft 6in Length: 19ft 10in Height: 8ft 1in Wing area: 234 sq ft	AUW: 1,330lb	Max speed: 97 mph at S/L Service ceiling: 15,000ft Endurance: 2hr 30min	1×0.30in mg	1
SPAD VII	1×180 hp Hispano 8-Ab in-line	Span: 25ft 7in Length: 20ft 4in Height: 7ft 2½in Wing area: 194 sq ft	Empty: 1,102lb AUW: 1,553lb	Max speed: 127 mph at 10,000ft Service ceiling: 21,500ft Endurance: 1hr 30min	1×0.303in mg	1
SPAD XIII	1×235 hp Hispano 8-BEc in-line	Span: 26ft 6in Length: 20ft 6in Height: 8ft 6½in Wing area: 217 sq ft	Empty: 1,257lb AUW: 1,819lb	Max speed: 134 mph at 10,000ft Service ceiling: 22,500ft Endurance: 1hr 40min	2×0.303in mg	1
Standard E-1	1×100 hp Gnome 9-B rotary	Span: 24ft 0in Length: 18ft 11in Height: 7ft 10in Wing area: 153 sq ft	AUW: 1,144lb	Max speed: 102 mph at S/L Service ceiling: 14,800ft Endurance: 2hr 30min	None	1
Nieuport 28	1×170 hp Gnome 9-N rotary	Span: 26ft 8¾in Length: 21ft 0in Height: 8ft 2½in Wing area: 172 sq ft	Empty: 1,047lb AUW: 1,625lb	Max speed: 122 mph at S/L Service ceiling: 16,995ft Range: 155 miles	2×0.30in mg	1
de Havilland DH-4B	1×416 hp Liberty 12A in-line	Span: 42ft 5in Length: 29ft 11in Height: 9ft 8in Wing area: 439 sq ft	Empty: 2,939lb AUW: 4,595lb	Max speed: 118 mph at S/L Service ceiling: 12,800ft Endurance: 3hr 15min	4×0.30in mg; up to 450lb bombs	2
Breguet 14	1×310 hp Renault 12-Fcy in-line	Span: 47ft 3in Length: 29ft 2in Height: 10ft 9¾in Wing area: 527 sq ft	Empty: 2,392lb AUW: 3,771lb	Max speed: 110 mph at 6,560ft Service ceiling: 19,030ft Range: 435 miles	3×0.303 in mg; up to 660lb bombs	2
Packard-Le Pere LUSAC-11	1×400 hp Liberty 12A in-line	Span: 41ft 7in Length: 25ft 6in Height: 9ft 6in Wing area: 416 sq ft	AUW: 3,746lb	Max speed: 132 mph at 2,000ft Service ceiling: 20,200ft Range: 320 miles	4×0.30in mg	2
Sopwith 1A.2	1×135 hp Le Rhône 9-Jby rotary	Span: 33ft 6in Length: 25ft 3in Height: 10ft 3in Wing area: 346 sq ft	Empty: 1,159lb AUW: 2,041lb	Max speed: 99 mph at 6,500ft Endurance: 2hr 15min	2×0.303in mg; up to 100lb bombs	2
Sopwith 1B.1	1×135 hp Clerget 9-Ba rotary	Span: 33ft 6in Length: 25ft 3in Height: 10ft 3in Wing area: 346 sq ft	Empty: 1,305lb AUW: 2,150lb	Max speed: 100 mph at 6,500ft Endurance: 4hr 15min	2×0.303in mg	2
Martin MB-1 (GMB)	2×400 hp Liberty 12A in-line	Span: 71ft 5in Length: 44ft 10in Height: 14ft 7in Wing area: 1,070 sq ft	Empty: 6,702lb AUW: 10,225lb	Max speed: 105 mph at S/L Service ceiling: 10,300ft Range: 390 miles with 1,040lb bombs	5×0.30in mg; 1,040lb bombs	3

Type	Powerplant	Dimensions	Weights	Performance	Armament	Crew
Martin MB-2	2×420 hp Liberty 12A in-line	Span: 74ft 2in Length: 42ft 8in Height: 14ft 8in Wing area: 1,121 sq ft	Empty: 7,069lb AUW: 12,027lb	Max speed: 98 mph at S/L Service ceiling: 7,700ft Range: 400 miles with 2,000lb bombs	5×0.30in mg; 3,000lb bombs	4
Orenco/Curtiss D	1×300 hp Wright-Hispano H in-line	Span: 33ft 0in Length: 21ft 5½in Height: 8ft 4in Wing area: 273 sq ft	Empty: 1,908lb AUW: 2,820lb	Max speed: 140 mph at S/L Service ceiling: 18,450ft Endurance: 2hr 30min	1×0.50in mg; 1×0.30in mg	1
Thomas-Morse (Boeing) MB-3A	1×300 hp Wright H-3 in-line	Span: 26ft 0in Length: 20ft 0in Height: 8ft 7in Wing area: 229 sq ft	Empty: 1,716lb AUW: 2,539lb	Max speed: 141 mph at S/L Service ceiling: 19,500ft Endurance: 2hr 15min	2×0.30in mg	1
Consolidated TW-3	1×180 hp Wright E in-line	Span: 34ft 9in Length: 26ft 9in Height: 9ft 0in Wing area: 285 sq ft	Empty: 1,706lb AUW: 2,407lb	Max speed: 103 mph at S/L Service ceiling: 14,500ft Endurance: 3hr 45min	None	2
Consolidated PT-3A	1×220 hp Wright R-790-AB rotary	Span: 34ft 6in Length: 28ft 1in Height: 10ft 3in Wing area: 300 sq ft	Empty: 1,785lb AUW: 2,481lb	Max speed: 102 mph at S/L Service ceiling: 14,000ft Endurance: 3hr 45min	None	2
Barling NBL-1	6×420 hp Liberty 12A in-line	Span: 120ft 0in Length: 65ft 0in Height: 27ft 0in Wing area: 4,017 sq ft	Empty: 27,703lb AUW: 42,569lb	Max speed: 93 mph at 5,000ft Service ceiling: 7,275ft Range: 170 miles with 5,000lb bombs	7×0.30in mg; 5,000lb bombs	6
Curtiss PW-8	1×440 hp Curtiss D-12 in-line	Span: 32ft 0in Length: 22ft 6in Height: 8ft 10in Wing area: 287 sq ft	Empty: 2,191lb AUW: 3,151lb	Max speed: 162 mph at 6,500ft Service ceiling: 21,700ft Range: 440 miles	2×0.30in mg	1
Douglas DWC landplane	1×420 hp Liberty Vee	Span: 50ft 0in Length: 35ft 6in Height: 13ft 7in Wing area: 707 sq ft	Empty: 4,380lb AUW: 6,995lb	Max speed: 103 mph at S/L Service ceiling: 10,000ft Range: 2,200 miles max	None	2
Douglas DWC seaplane	1×420 hp Liberty Vee	Span: 50ft 0in Length: 39ft 0in Height: 15ft 1in Wing area: 707 sq ft	Empty: 5,180lb AUW: 7,795lb	Max speed: 100 mph at S/L Service ceiling: 7,000ft Range: 1,650 miles max	None	2
Loening OA-1	1×400 hp Liberty V-1650-1 Vee	Span: 45ft 0in Length: 34ft 7in Height: 12ft 1in Wing area: 495 sq ft	Empty: 3,440lb AUW: 5,010lb	Max speed: 119 mph at S/L Service ceiling: 11,825ft Endurance: 3hr 15min	2×0.30in mg	2
Douglas O-2H	1×450 hp Liberty V-1650-A Vee	Span: 40ft 10in Length: 30ft 0in Height: 10ft 8in Wing area: 362 sq ft	Empty: 2,857lb AUW: 4,550lb	Max speed: 135 mph at S/L Service ceiling: 16,900ft Range: 512 miles	3×0.30in mg	2
Douglas O-25A	1×600 hp Curtiss V-1570-7 Vee	Span: 40ft 0in Length: 30ft 8in Height: 10ft 10in Wing area: 364 sq ft	Empty: 3,400lb AUW: 4,805lb	Max speed: 157 mph at S/L Service ceiling: 22,180ft	3×0.30in mg	2
Douglas O-38B	1×525 hp Pratt & Whitney R-1690-5 radial	Span: 40ft 0in Length: 32ft 0in Height: 10ft 8in Wing area: 362 sq ft	Empty: 3,070lb AUW: 4,452lb	Max speed: 150 mph at S/L Service ceiling: 20,700ft Range: 275 miles	2×0.30in mg; 4×100lb bombs	2
Douglas BT-2B	1×450 hp Pratt & Whitney R-1340-11 radial	Span: 40ft 0in Length: 31ft 2in Height: 10ft 6in Wing area: 364 sq ft	Empty: 2,918lb AUW: 4,067lb	Max speed: 134 mph at S/L Service ceiling: 19,200ft Range: 320 miles	None	2
Boeing PW-9D	1×435 hp Curtiss D-12D Vee	Span: 32ft 0in Length: 24ft 0in Height: 8ft 8in Wing area: 241 sq ft	Empty: 2,328lb AUW: 3,234lb	Max speed: 155 mph at S/L Service ceiling: 18,230ft Endurance: 2hr 45min	2×0.30in mg	1

Type	Powerplant	Dimensions	Weights	Performance	Armament	Crew
Curtiss P-1C	1×435 hp Curtiss V-1150-5 Vee	Span: 31ft 6in Length: 23ft 3in Height: 8ft 6in Wing area: 252 sq ft	Empty: 2,136lb AUW: 2,973lb	Max speed: 154 mph at S/L Service ceiling: 20,800ft Range: 554-650 miles	2×0.30in mg	1
Curtiss P-3A	1×410 hp Pratt & Whitney R-1340-3 radial	Span: 31ft 7in Length: 22ft 5in Height: 8ft 9in Wing area: 252 sq ft	Empty: 1,956lb AUW: 2,788lb	Max speed: 153 mph at S/L Service ceiling: 23,000ft Range: approx 450 miles	2×0.30in mg	1
Curtiss P-6E	1×600 hp Curtiss V-1570-23 Vee	Span: 31ft 6in Length: 23ft 2in Height: 8ft 10in Wing area: 252 sq ft	Empty: 2,699lb AUW: 3,392lb	Max speed: 198 mph at S/L Service ceiling: 24,700ft Range: 570 miles max	2×0.30in mg	1
Curtiss O-1B	1×430 hp Curtiss D-12 Vee	Span: 38ft 0in Length: 28ft 4in Height: 10ft 1½in Wing area: 353 sq ft	Empty: 2,706lb AUW: 4,384lb	Max speed: 136 mph at S/L Service ceiling: 15,425ft	4×0.30in mg	2
Curtiss A-3B	1×435 hp Curtiss V-1150-5 Vee	Span: 38ft 0in Length: 27ft 2in Height: 10ft 6in Wing area: 353 sq ft	Empty: 2,875lb AUW: 4,476lb	Max speed: 139 mph at S/L Service ceiling: 14,100ft Range: 628 miles	6×0.30in mg; 200lb bombs	2
Huff-Daland LB-1	1×787 hp Packard 2A-2540 in-line	Span: 66ft 6in Length: 46ft 2in Height: 14ft 11in Wing area: 1,137 sq ft	Empty: 6,237lb AUW: 12,415lb	Max speed: 120 mph at S/L Service ceiling: 11,150ft Range: 430 miles with 2,750lb bombs	5×0.30in mg; 2,750lb bombs	4
Keystone LB-5A	2×420 hp Liberty V-1650-3 Vee	Span: 67ft 0in Length: 44ft 8in Height: 16ft 10in Wing area: 1,139 sq ft	Empty: 7,024lb AUW: 12,155lb	Max speed: 107 mph at S/L Service ceiling: 8,000ft Range: 435 miles with 2,052lb bombs	5×0.30in mg; 2,052lb bombs	5
Keystone LB-6	2×536 hp Wright R-1750-1 radial	Span: 75ft 0in Length: 43ft 5in Height: 18ft 1in Wing area: 1,148 sq ft	Empty: 6,863lb AUW: 13,440lb	Max speed: 114 mph at S/L Service ceiling: 11,650ft Range: 632 miles with 2,052lb bombs	5×0.30in mg; 2,052lb bombs	5
Keystone B-3A (LB-10A)	2×525 hp Pratt & Whitney R-1690-3 radial	Span: 74ft 8in Length: 48ft 10in Height: 15ft 8in Wing area: 1,145 sq ft	Empty: 7,705lb AUW: 12,952lb	Max speed: 114 mph at S/L Service ceiling: 12,700ft Range: 860 miles with 2,500lb bombs	3×0.30in mg; 2,500lb bombs	5
Keystone B-6A	2×575 hp Wright R-1820-1 radial	Span: 74ft 9in Length: 48ft 10in Height: 17ft 2in Wing area: 1,137 sq ft	Empty: 8,037lb AUW: 13,374lb	Max speed: 121 mph at S/L Service ceiling: 14,100ft Range: 363 miles with 2,500lb bombs	3×0.30in mg; 2,500lb bombs	5
Thomas-Morse O-19B	1×450 hp Pratt & Whitney R-1340-7 radial	Span: 39ft 9in Length: 28ft 4in Height: 10ft 6in Wing area: 348 sq ft	Empty: 2,722lb AUW: 3,800lb	Max speed: 137 mph at S/L Service ceiling: 20,500ft	2×0.30in mg	2
Boeing P-12B	1×450 hp Pratt & Whitney R-1340-7 radial	Span: 30ft 0in Length: 20ft 3in Height: 8ft 10in Wing area: 228 sq ft	Empty: 1,945lb AUW: 2,638lb	Max speed: 166 mph at 5,000ft Service ceiling: 27,450ft Range: 540 miles	2×0.30in mg	1
Boeing P-12F	1×600 hp Pratt & Whitney R-1340-19 radial	Span: 30ft 0in Length: 20ft 3in Height: 9ft 10in Wing area: 228 sq ft	Empty: 2,035lb AUW: 2,726lb	Max speed: 195 mph at 10,000ft Service ceiling: 31,400ft	2×0.30in mg	1
Curtiss B-2 Condor	2×633 hp Curtiss V-1570-7 Vee	Span: 90ft 0in Length: 47ft 6in Height: 16ft 3in Wing area: 1,499 sq ft	Empty: 9,039lb AUW: 16,516lb	Max speed: 132 mph at S/L Service ceiling: 17,100ft Range: 780 miles with 2,508lb bombs	6×0.30in mg; 2,508lb bombs	5

Type	Powerplant	Dimensions	Weights	Performance	Armament	Crew
Berliner-Joyce P-16/PB-1	1×600 hp Curtiss V-1570-25 Vee	Span: 34ft 0in Length: 28ft 2in Height: 9ft 0in Wing area: 279 sq ft	Empty: 2,803lb AUW: 3,996lb	Max speed: 175 mph at S/L Service ceiling: 21,600ft Range: 650 miles	3×0.30in mg	2
Douglas YO-31	1×675 hp Curtiss V-1570-53 Vee	Span: 46ft 4in Length: 33ft 5in Height: 10ft 7in Wing area: 308 sq ft	Empty: 3,496lb AUW: 4,654lb	Max speed: 186 mph at S/L Service ceiling: 24,300ft	2×0.30in mg	2
Douglas O-43A	1×675 hp Curtiss V-1570-59 Vee	Span: 45ft 11in Length: 33ft 11in Height: 12ft 3in Wing area: 335 sq ft	Empty: 4,135lb AUW: 5,300lb	Max speed: 190 mph at S/L Service ceiling: 22,400ft	2×0.30in mg	2
Douglas O-46A	1×725 hp Pratt & Whitney R-1535-7 radial	Span: 45ft 9in Length: 35ft 6¾in Height: 10ft 8in Wing area: 332 sq ft	Empty: 4,776lb AUW: 6,639lb	Max speed: 200 mph at 4,000ft Service ceiling: 24,150ft Range: 435 miles	2×0.30in mg	2
Curtiss A-8A Shrike	1×675 hp Curtiss V-1570-57 Vee	Span: 44ft 3in Length: 33ft 7in Height: 9ft 2in Wing area: 285 sq ft	Empty: 4,330lb AUW: 6,287lb	Max speed: 181 mph at S/L Service ceiling: 17,000ft Range: 624 miles	5×0.30in mg; 464lb bombs	2
Curtiss A-12	1×690 hp Wright R-1820-37 radial	Span: 44ft 0in Length: 32ft 3in Height: 9ft 4in Wing area: 285 sq ft	Empty: 3,898lb AUW: 5,900lb	Max speed: 174 mph at 5,000ft Service ceiling: 15,150ft Range: 510 miles with 400lb bombs	3×0.30 in mg; 4×100lb bombs	2
Boeing B-9A	2×600 hp Pratt & Whitney R-1860-11 radial	Span: 76ft 10in Length: 52ft 0in Height: 12ft 0in Wing area: 954 sq ft	Empty: 8,941lb AUW: 14,320lb	Max speed: 188 mph at 6,000ft Service ceiling: 20,750ft Range: 540 miles with 2,260lb bombs	2×0.30 in mg; 2,260lb bombs	4
Douglas C-21	2×300 hp Wright R-975-E radial	Span: 60ft 0in Length: 43ft 10in Height: 14ft 1in Wing area: 489 sq ft	Empty: 5,861lb AUW: 8,583lb	Max speed: 140 mph at S/L Service ceiling: 14,200ft Range: 550 miles	None	1-2 +5-6 passengers
Boeing P-26A	1×600 hp Pratt & Whitney R-1340-27 radial	Span: 27ft 11½in Length: 23ft 10in Height: 10ft 5in Wing area: 150 sq ft	Empty: 2,271lb AUW: 3,012lb	Max speed: 234 mph at 7,500ft Service ceiling: 27,400ft Range: 360 miles	2×0.30in mg; 112lb bombs	1
Martin B-10B	2×775 hp Wright R-1820-33 radial	Span: 70ft 6in Length: 44ft 9in Height: 15ft 5in Wing area: 678 sq ft	Empty: 9,681lb AUW: 16,400lb	Max speed: 213 mph at 10,000ft Service ceiling: 24,200ft Range: 1,240 miles max with 2,260lb bombs	3×0.30in mg; 2,260lb bombs	4
Northrop A-17A	1×825 hp Pratt & Whitney R-1535-13 radial	Span: 47ft 9in Length: 31ft 8in Height: 12ft 0in Wing area: 362 sq ft	Empty: 5,106lb AUW: 7,550lb	Max speed: 220 mph at 2,500ft Service ceiling: 19,400ft Range: 732 miles with 654lb bombs	5×0.30in mg; 654lb bombs	2
Consolidated P-30A	1×700 hp Curtiss V-1570-61 Vee	Span: 43ft 11in Length: 30ft 0in Height: 8ft 3in Wing area: 297 sq ft	Empty: 4,306lb AUW: 5,643lb	Max speed: 275 mph at 25,000ft Service ceiling: 28,000ft Range: 508 miles	3×0.30in mg	2
Consolidated A-11	1×675 hp Curtiss V-1570-59 Vee	Span: 43ft 11in Length: 29ft 3in Height: 9ft 10in Wing area: 297 sq ft	Empty: 3,805lb AUW: 5,490lb	Max speed: 228 mph at S/L Service ceiling: 23,300ft Range: 470 miles with 300lb bombs	5×0.30in mg; 300lb bombs	2
North American BT-9B	1×400 hp Wright R-975-7 radial	Span: 42ft 0in Length: 27ft 7in Height: 13ft 7in Wing area: 248 sq ft	Empty: 3,314lb AUW: 4,471lb	Max speed: 170 mph at S/L Service ceiling: 19,750ft Range: 630 miles	2×0.30in mg	2
North American BC-1	1×600 hp Pratt & Whitney R-1340-47 radial	Span: 43ft 0in Length: 27ft 9in Height: 14ft 0in Wing area: 225 sq ft	Empty: 4,050lb AUW: 5,200lb	Max speed: 207 mph at S/L Service ceiling: 24,100ft Range: 665 miles	2×0.30in mg	2

Type	Powerplant	Dimensions	Weights	Performance	Armament	Crew
North American AT-6A	1×600 hp Pratt & Whitney R-1340-49 radial	Span: 42ft 0in Length: 29ft 0in Height: 11ft 9in Wing area: 254 sq ft	Empty: 3,900lb AUW: 5,155lb	Max speed: 210 mph at S/L Service ceiling: 24,200ft Range: 629 miles	2×0.30in mg	2
Douglas C-33	2×750 hp Wright R-1820-25 radial	Span: 85ft 0in Length: 61ft 11¾in Height: 16ft 3¾in Wing area: 939 sq ft	Empty: 12,476lb Payload: 2,400lb AUW: 18,588lb	Max speed: 202 mph at 2,500ft Service ceiling: 20,000ft Range: 916 miles	None	2 +12 passengers
Douglas C-39	2×975 hp Wright R-1820-55 radial	Span: 85ft 0in Length: 61ft 6in Height: 18ft 8in Wing area: 939 sq ft	Empty: 14,287lb AUW: 21,000lb	Max speed: 210 mph at 5,000ft Service ceiling: 20,600ft Range: 1,600 miles max	None	2 +14 passengers
Republic (Seversky) P-35A	1×1,050 hp Pratt & Whitney R-1830-45 radial	Span: 36ft 0in Length: 26ft 10in Height: 9ft 9in Wing area: 220 sq ft	Empty: 4,575lb AUW: 6,723lb	Max speed: 290 mph at 12,000ft Service ceiling: 31,400ft Range: 600 miles at 260 mph	2×0.50in mg; 2×0.30in mg; 350lb bombs	1
Stearman PT-17	1×220 hp Continental R-670-5 radial	Span: 32ft 2in Length: 24ft 9in Height: 9ft 8in Wing area: 298 sq ft	Empty: 1,931lb AUW: 2,636lb	Max speed: 135 mph at S/L Endurance: 4hr	None	2
North American O-47A	1×975 hp Wright R-1820-49 radial	Span: 46ft 4in Length: 33ft 7in Height: 12ft 2in Wing area: 350 sq ft	Empty: 5,980lb AUW: 7,636lb	Max speed: 221 mph at 4,000ft Service ceiling: 23,200ft Endurance: 2hr	2×0.30in mg	2
Douglas B-18A Bolo	2×1,000 hp Wright R-1820-53 radial	Span: 89ft 6in Length: 57ft 10in Height: 15ft 2in Wing area: 959 sq ft	Empty: 16,321lb AUW: 27,673lb	Max speed: 216 mph at 10,000ft Service ceiling: 23,900ft Range: 900 miles	3×0.30in mg; 4,400lb bombs max	6
Douglas B-23 Dragon	2×1,600 hp Wright R-2600-3 radial	Span: 92ft 0in Length: 58ft 4¾in Height: 18ft 5½in Wing area: 993 sq ft	Empty: 19,089lb AUW: 32,400lb	Max speed: 282 mph at 12,000ft Service ceiling: 31,600ft Range: 1,455 miles with 4,000lb bombs	3×0.30in mg; 1×0.50in mg; 4,000lb bombs	6
Boeing XB-15	4×1,000 hp Pratt & Whitney R-1830-11 radial	Span: 149ft 0in Length: 87ft 7in Height: 19ft 5in Wing area: 2,780 sq ft	Empty: 37,709lb AUW: 70,700lb	Max speed: 197 mph at 6,000ft Service ceiling: 18,850ft Range: 3,400 miles with 2,511lb bombs	3×0.30in mg; 3×0.50in mg; 12,000lb bombs	10
Boeing B-17C Flying Fortress	4×1,200 hp Wright R-1820-65 radial	Span: 103ft 9in Length: 67ft 11in Height: 15ft 5in Wing area: 1,420 sq ft	Empty: 27,650lb AUW: 46,650lb	Max speed: 291 mph at 25,000ft Service ceiling: 36,000ft Range: 2,400 miles with 4,000lb bombs	6×0.50in mg; 1×0.30in mg; 10,500lb bombs	9
Boeing B-17E Flying Fortress	4×1,200 hp Wright R-1820-65 radial	Span: 103ft 9in Length: 73ft 10in Height: 19ft 2in Wing area: 1,420 sq ft	Empty: 32,250lb AUW: 53,000lb	Max speed: 317 mph at 25,000ft Service ceiling: 36,600ft Range: 2,000 miles with 4,000lb bombs	12×0.50in mg; 1×0.30in mg; 17,600lb bombs	10
Boeing B-17G Flying Fortress	4×1,200 hp Wright R-1820-97 radial	Span: 103ft 9in Length: 74ft 4in Height: 19ft 1in Wing area: 1,420 sq ft	Empty: 36,135lb AUW: 65,500lb	Max speed: 288 mph at 25,000ft Service ceiling: 35,600ft Range: 2,000 miles with 6,000lb bombs	13×0.50in mg; 17,600lb bombs	10
Bell XFM-1 Airacuda	2×1,150 hp Allison V-1710-13 Vee	Span: 69ft 10in Length: 44ft 10in Height: 13ft 7in Wing area: 684 sq ft	Empty: 13,376lb AUW: 17,333lb	Max speed: 271 mph at 20,000ft Service ceiling: 30,500ft Range: 800 miles	2×37mm cannon; 2×0.50in mg; 2×0.30in mg	5
Curtiss P-36A	1×1,050 hp Pratt & Whitney R-1830-13 radial	Span: 37ft 4in Length: 28ft 6in Height: 12ft 2in Wing area: 236 sq ft	Empty: 4,567lb AUW: 6,010lb	Max speed: 300 mph at 10,000ft Service ceiling: 33,000ft Range: 825 miles max	2×0.30in mg	1
Ryan PT-16	1×125 hp Menasco L-365-1 in-line	Span: 30ft 0in Length: 21ft 6in Height: 10ft 1in Wing area: 124 sq ft	Empty: 1,100lb AUW: 1,600lb	Max speed: 129 mph at S/L Service ceiling: 15,000ft Range: 350 miles	None	2

Type	Powerplant	Dimensions	Weights	Performance	Armament	Crew
Vultee BT-13A Valiant	1×450 hp Pratt & Whitney R-985-AN1 radial	Span: 42ft 0in Length: 28ft 10in Height: 11ft 6in Wing area: 239 sq ft	Empty: 3,375lb AUW: 4,496lb	Max speed: 180 mph at S/L Service ceiling: 21,650ft Range: 725 miles	None	2
Bell P-39N Airacobra	1×1,200 hp Allison V-1710-85 Vee	Span: 34ft 0in Length: 30ft 2in Height: 12ft 5in Wing area: 213 sq ft	Empty: 5,657lb AUW: 8,200lb	Max speed: 368 mph at 25,000ft Service ceiling: 38,500ft Range: 750 miles with 500lb bombs	1×37mm cannon; 2×0.50in mg; 2×0.30in mg; 500lb bombs	1
Fairchild PT-19A	1×175 hp Ranger L-440-1 in-line	Span: 36ft 0in Length: 28ft 0in Height: 10ft 6in Wing area: 200 sq ft	Empty: 1,845lb AUW: 2,545lb	Max speed: 132 mph at S/L Service ceiling: 15,300ft Range: 400 miles	None	2
Consolidated B-24D Liberator	4×1,200 hp Pratt & Whitney R-1830-43 radial	Span: 110ft 0in Length: 66ft 4in Height: 17ft 11in Wing area: 1,048 sq ft	Empty: 32,605lb AUW: 60,000lb	Max speed: 303 mph at 25,000ft Service ceiling: 32,000ft Range: 2,850 miles with 5,000lb bombs	10×0.50in mg; 8,800lb bombs	10
Consolidated C-87	4×1,200 hp Pratt & Whitney R-1830-65 radial	Span: 110ft 0in Length: 66ft 4in Height: 18ft 0in Wing area: 1,048 sq ft	Empty: 31,935lb AUW: 56,000lb	Max speed: 306 mph Service ceiling: 31,000ft Range: 2,900 miles	1×0.50in mg	5 +25 passengers
Curtiss P-40B Warhawk	1×1,040 hp Allison V-1710-33 Vee	Span: 37ft 4in Length: 31ft 9in Height: 12ft 4in Wing area: 236 sq ft	Empty: 5,590lb AUW: 7,600lb	Max speed: 352 mph at 15,000ft Service ceiling: 32,400ft Range: 730 miles	2×0.50in mg; 2×0.30in mg	1
Curtiss P-40K Warhawk	1×1,325 hp Allison V-1710-73 Vee	Span: 37ft 4in Length: 33ft 4in Height: 12ft 4in Wing area: 236 sq ft	Empty: 6,400lb AUW: 10,000lb	Max speed: 362 mph at 15,000ft Service ceiling: 28,000ft Range: 350 miles with 500lb bombs	6×0.50in mg; 500lb bombs	1
Lockheed C-56 Lodestar	2×1,200 hp Wright R-1820-71 radial	Span: 65ft 6in Length: 49ft 10in Height: 11ft 1in Wing area: 550 sq ft	Empty: 11,650lb AUW: 17,500lb	Max speed: 253 mph at S/L Service ceiling: 23,300ft Range: 1,600 miles	None	2 +16 passengers
Douglas A-20G Havoc	2×1,600 hp Wright R-2600-23 radial	Span: 61ft 4in Length: 48ft 0in Height: 17ft 7in Wing area: 464 sq ft	Empty: 16,993lb AUW: 27,500lb	Max speed: 317 mph at 12,400ft Service ceiling: 25,800ft Range: 1,025 miles with 2,000lb bombs	8×0.30in mg; 4,000lb bombs max	3
Douglas P-70	2×1,600 hp Wright R-2600-11 radial	Span: 61ft 4in Length: 47ft 7in Height: 17ft 7in Wing area: 464 sq ft	Empty: 16,031lb AUW: 21,265lb	Max speed: 329 mph at 14,000ft Service ceiling: 28,250ft Range: 1,060 miles at 270 mph	4×20mm cannon	4
North American B-25H Mitchell	2×1,700 hp Wright R-2600-13 radial	Span: 67ft 7in Length: 51ft 0in Height: 15ft 9in Wing area: 610 sq ft	Empty: 19,975lb AUW: 36,047lb	Max speed: 275 mph at 13,000ft Service ceiling: 23,800ft Range: 1,350 miles with 3,000lb bombs	14×0.50in mg; 1×75 mm cannon; 8×5in RP; 3,000lb bombs	5
Martin B-26G Marauder	2×2,000 hp Pratt & Whitney R-2800-43 radial	Span: 71ft 0in Length: 56ft 1in Height: 20ft 4in Wing area: 658 sq ft	Empty: 23,800lb AUW: 38,200lb	Max speed: 283 mph at 5,000ft Service ceiling: 19,800ft Range: 1,100 miles	11×0.50in mg; 4,000lb bombs	7
Lockheed P-38E Lightning	2×1,150 hp Allison V-1710-27/29 Vee	Span: 52ft 0in Length: 37ft 10in Height: 9ft 10in Wing area: 328 sq ft	Empty: 11,880lb AUW: 15,482lb	Max speed: 395 mph at S/L Service ceiling: 39,000ft Range: 500 miles	1×20mm cannon; 4×0.50in mg	1
Lockheed P-38L Lightning	2×1,475 hp Allison V-1710-111/113 Vee	Span: 52ft 0in Length: 37ft 10in Height: 9ft 10in Wing area: 328 sq ft	Empty: 12,800lb AUW: 21,600lb	Max speed: 414 mph at 25,000ft Service ceiling: 44,000ft Range: 450 miles	1×20mm cannon; 4×0.50in mg; 1,600lb bombs	1
Douglas A-24 Dauntless	1×1,000 hp Wright R-1820-52 radial	Span: 41ft 6in Length: 32ft 8in Height: 12ft 11in Wing area: 325 sq ft	Empty: 6,181lb AUW: 10,200lb	Max speed: 250 mph at 17,200ft Range: 950 miles	2×0.50in mg; 2×0.30in mg; 1,000lb bombs max	2

Type	Powerplant	Dimensions	Weights	Performance	Armament	Crew
Douglas XB-19A	4×2,600 hp Allison V-3420-11 Vee	Span: 212ft 0in Length: 132ft 4in Height: 42ft 0in Wing area: 4,285 sq ft	Empty: 92,400lb AUW: 140,230lb	Max speed: 265 mph at 20,000ft Service ceiling: 39,000ft Range: 4,200 miles with 2,500lb bombs	1×37mm cannon; 5×0.50in mg; 5×0.30in mg (not fitted); 37,100lb bombs max	16
Republic P-43 Lancer	1×1,200 hp Pratt & Whitney R-1830-47 radial	Span: 36ft 0in Length: 28ft 6in Height: 14ft 0in Wing area: 223 sq ft	Empty: 5,654lb AUW: 7,935lb	Max speed: 349 mph at 25,000ft Service ceiling: 38,000ft Range: 800 miles	2×0.50in mg; 2×0.30in mg	1
Douglas C-47A Skytrain	2×1,200 hp Pratt & Whitney R-1830-92 radial	Span: 95ft 6in Length: 63ft 9in Height: 17ft 0in Wing area: 987 sq ft	Empty: 17,865lb AUW: 26,000lb	Max speed: 230 mph at 8,800ft Service ceiling: 24,000ft Range: 1,600 miles	None	2 +27 troops
Beech C-45	2×450 hp Pratt & Whitney R-985-AN-1/3 radial	Span: 47ft 8in Length: 34ft 3in Height: 9ft 8in Wing area: 349 sq ft	Empty: 5,890lb AUW: 7,850lb	Max speed: 215 mph at S/L Service ceiling: 20,000ft Range: 700 miles	None	6
Taylorcraft L-2A Grasshopper	1×65 hp Continental O-170-3 flat-four	Span: 35ft 5in Length: 22ft 9in Height: 8ft 0in Wing area: 181 sq ft	Empty: 875lb AUW: 1,300lb	Max speed: 88 mph at S/L Service ceiling: 10,050ft Range: 230 miles	None	2
Piper L-4 Grasshopper	1×65 hp Continental O-170-3 flat-four	Span: 35ft 3in Length: 22ft 0in Height: 6ft 8in Wing area: 179 sq ft	Empty: 730lb AUW: 1,220lb	Max speed: 85 mph at S/L Service ceiling: 9,300ft Range: 190 miles	None	2
Aeronca L-3 Grasshopper	1×65 hp Continental O-170-3 flat-four	Span: 35ft 0in Length: 21ft 0in Height: 7ft 8in Wing area: 158 sq ft	Empty: 865lb AUW: 1,300lb	Max speed: 87 mph at S/L Service ceiling: 7,750ft Range: 190 miles	None	2
Beech AT-10	2×295 hp Lycoming R-680-9 radial	Span: — Length: — Height: — Wing area: —	Empty: — AUW: —	Max speed: 200 mph at 5,000ft Service ceiling: 19,800ft Range: 765 miles at 175 mph	None	2
Lockheed A-29 Hudson	2×1,200 hp Wright R-1820-87 radial	Span: 65ft 6in Length: 44ft 4in Height: 11ft 11in Wing area: 551 sq ft	Empty: 12,825lb AUW: 20,500lb	Max speed: 253 mph at 15,000ft Service ceiling: 26,500ft Range: 1,550 miles	5×0.30in mg; 1,600lb bombs	4
Lockheed B-34A Ventura	2×2,000 hp Pratt & Whitney R-2800-31 radial	Span: 65ft 6in Length: 51ft 5in Height: 11ft 11in Wing area: 551 sq ft	Empty: 17,275lb AUW: 27,250lb	Max speed: 315 mph at 15,500ft Service ceiling: 24,000ft Range: 950 miles	2×0.50in mg; 6×0.30in mg; 2,500lb bombs	5
Cessna UC-78 Bobcat	2×245 hp Jacobs R-755-9 radial	Span: 41ft 11in Length: 32ft 9in Height: 9ft 11in Wing area: 295 sq ft	Empty: 3,500lb AUW: 5,700lb	Max speed: 195 mph at S/L Service ceiling: 22,000ft Range: 750 miles	None	1 +4 passengers
Curtiss XP-55 Ascender	1×1,275 hp Allison V-1710-95 Vee	Span: 41ft 0in Length: 29ft 7in Height: 10ft 0¾in Wing area: 235 sq ft	Empty: 6,354lb AUW: 7,930lb	Max speed: 378 mph at 16,900ft Service ceiling: 35,800ft Range: 635 miles	4×0.50in mg	1
Douglas C-54A Skymaster	4×1,290 hp Pratt & Whitney R-2000-7 radial	Span: 117ft 6in Length: 93ft 10in Height: 27ft 6in Wing area: 1,460 sq ft	Empty: 37,000lb AUW: 73,000lb	Max speed: 265 mph at 10,000ft Service ceiling: 22,000ft Range: 2,000 miles with 22,000lb payload	None Cargo: 32,500lb	4 crew +50 troops
Vultee A-35B Vengeance	1×1,700 hp Wright R-2600-13 radial	Span: 48ft 0in Length: 39ft 9in Height: 15ft 4in Wing area: 332 sq ft	Empty: 10,300lb AUW: 16,400lb	Max speed: 279 mph at 13,500ft Service ceiling: 22,300ft Range: 2,300 miles	6×0.50in mg; 2,000lb bombs	2
Beech UC-43	1×450 hp Pratt & Whitney R-985-AN-1 radial	Span: 32ft 0in Length: 26ft 2in Height: 10ft 3in Wing area: 296 sq ft	Empty: 3,085lb AUW: 4,700lb	Max speed: 198 mph at S/L Service ceiling: 20,000ft Range: 500 miles	None	1 + 3 passengers

Type	Powerplant	Dimensions	Weights	Performance	Armament	Crew
Republic P-47B Thunderbolt	1×2,000 hp Pratt & Whitney R-2800-21 radial	Span: 40ft 9¼in Length: 35ft 4¼in Height: 14ft 2in Wing area: 300 sq ft	Empty: 9,346lb AUW: 13,360lb	Max speed: 429 mph at 27,800ft Service ceiling: 42,000ft Range: 550 miles	6 or 8×0.50in mg	1
Republic P-47D-25 Thunderbolt	1×2,300 hp Pratt & Whitney R-2800-59 radial	Span: 40ft 9¼in Length: 35ft 10in Height: 14ft 9in Wing area: 300 sq ft	Empty: 10,000lb AUW: 17,500lb	Max speed: 429 mph at 30,000ft Service ceiling: 42,000ft Range: 590 miles	6 or 8×0.50in mg; 2×1,000lb bombs	1
Republic P-47N-1 Thunderbolt	1×2,800 hp Pratt & Whitney R-2800-57 radial	Span: 42ft 6¼in Length: 36ft 1¾in Height: 14ft 6in Wing area: 322 sq ft	Empty: 10,988lb AUW: 13,823lb	Max speed: 467 mph at 32,000ft Service ceiling: 43,000ft Range: 800 miles	6 or 8×0.50in mg; 3×1,000lb bombs	1
North American P-51B Mustang	1×1,380 hp Packard V-1650-3 Vee	Span: 37ft 0½in Length: 32ft 2½in Height: 12ft 2in Wing area: 233 sq ft	Empty: 6,985lb AUW: 11,800lb	Max speed: 440 mph at 30,000ft Service ceiling: 41,800ft Range: 400 miles at 370 mph	4×0.50in mg; 2×1,000lb bombs	1
North American P-51D Mustang	1×1,490 hp Packard V-1650-7 Vee	Span: 37ft 0½in Length: 32ft 2½in Height: 12ft 2in Wing area: 233 sq ft	Empty: 7,125lb AUW: 11,600lb	Max speed: 437 mph at 25,000ft Service ceiling: 41,900ft Range: 950 miles at 362 mph	6×0.50in mg; 2×1,000lb bombs	1
North American P-51H Mustang	1×1,380 hp Packard V-1650-9 Vee	Span: 37ft 0½in Length: 32ft 2½in Height: 13ft 8in Wing area: 233 sq ft	Empty: 6,585lb AUW: 11,054lb	Max speed: 487 mph at 25,000ft Service ceiling: 41,600ft Range: 850 miles at 343 mph	6×0.50in mg; 2×1,000lb bombs or 10×5in RP	1
Stinson L-5 Sentinel	1×185 hp Lycoming O-435-1 flat-four	Span: 34ft 0in Length: 24ft 1in Height: 7ft 11in Wing area: 155 sq ft	Empty: 1,550lb AUW: 2,020lb	Max speed: 130 mph at S/L Service ceiling: 15,800ft Range: 420 miles	None	2
Bell P-63A Kingcobra	1×1,325 hp Allison V-1710-95 Vee	Span: 38ft 4in Length: 32ft 8in Height: 12ft 7in Wing area: 248 sq ft	Empty: 6,375lb AUW: 10,500lb	Max speed: 408 mph at 24,450ft Service ceiling: 43,000ft Range: 450 miles	1×37mm cannon; 4×0.50in mg; 3×500lb bombs	1
Boeing B-29A Superfortress	4×2,200 hp Wright R-3350-23, -41, or -57 radial	Span: 141ft 3in Length: 99ft 0in Height: 29ft 7in Wing area: 1,736 sq ft	Empty: 71,360lb AUW: 141,100lb	Max speed: 358 mph at 25,000ft Service ceiling: 31,850ft Range: 4,100 miles with 16,000lb bombs	10×0.50in mg; 1×20mm cannon; 20,000lb bombs	10
Sikorsky R-4	1×180 hp Warner R-550-1 or -3 radial	Rotor dia: 38ft 0in Length: 48ft 2in Height: 12ft 5in	Empty: 2,020lb AUW: 2,535lb	Max speed: 75 mph at S/L Service ceiling: 8,000ft Range: 130 miles	None	2
Sikorsky R-5B	1×450 hp Pratt & Whitney R-985-AN-5 radial	Rotor dia: 48ft 0in Length: 57ft 1in Height: 13ft 0in	Empty: 3,780lb AUW: 4,825lb	Max speed: 106 mph at S/L Service ceiling: 14,400ft Range: 360 miles	None	2
Sikorsky R-6A	1×240 hp Franklin O-405-9 flat-four	Rotor dia: 38ft 0in Length: 38ft 3in	AUW: 2,590lb	Max speed: 96 mph at S/L	None	2
Northrop P-61B Black Widow	2×2,000 hp Pratt & Whitney R-2800-65 radial	Span: 66ft 0in Length: 49ft 7in Height: 14ft 8in Wing area: 664 sq ft	Empty: 22,000lb AUW: 29,700lb	Max speed: 366 mph at 20,000ft Service ceiling: 33,100ft Range: 610 miles	4×20mm cannon; 4×0.50in mg; 4×1,600lb bombs	2
Douglas XB-42A Mixmaster	2×1,375 hp Allison V-1710-133 Vee	Span: 70ft 7in Length: 53ft 10in Height: 18ft 10in Wing area: 555 sq ft	Empty: 24,775lb AUW: 44,900lb	Max speed: 488 mph at 14,000ft Range: 2,100 miles	None	3
Douglas XB-43	2×3,750lb st General Electric J35-GE-3 turbojets	Span: 71ft 2in Length: 51ft 2in Height: 24ft 3in Wing area: 563 sq ft	Empty: 21,775lb AUW: 39,533lb	Max speed: 515 mph at S/L Service ceiling: 38,500ft Range: 1,100 miles	None	3

Type	Powerplant	Dimensions	Weights	Performance	Armament	Crew
Douglas A-26B-15	2×2,000 hp Pratt & Whitney R-2800-27 or -79 radial	Span: 70ft 0in Length: 50ft 0in Height: 18ft 6in Wing area: 540 sq ft	Empty: 22,370lb AUW: 35,000lb	Max speed: 355 mph at 15,000ft Service ceiling: 22,100ft Range: 1,400 miles with 4,000lb bombs	10×0.50in mg; 4,000lb bombs	3
Bell XP-77	1×520 hp Ranger XV-770-12 Vee	Span: 27ft 6in Length: 22ft 10½in Height: 8ft 2¼in Wing area: 100 sq ft	Empty: 2,855lb AUW: 4,028lb	Max speed: 330 mph at 4,000ft Service ceiling: 30,100ft Range: 550 miles at 274 mph	2×0.50in mg; 1×300lb bombs	1
Bell P-59A Airacomet	2×1,650lb st General Electric J31-GE-3 turbojet	Span: 45ft 6in Length: 38ft 1½in Height: 12ft 0in Wing area: 386 sq ft	Empty: 7,950lb AUW: 13,000lb	Max speed: 409 mph at 35,000ft Service ceiling: 46,200ft Range: 240 miles at 20,000ft	1×37mm cannon; 3×0.50in mg	1
General Motors (Fisher) P-75 Eagle	1×2,600 hp Allison V-3420-23 four-bank piston	Span: 49ft 4in Length: 40ft 5in Height: 15ft 6in Wing area: 347 sq ft	Empty: 11,495lb AUW: 18,210lb	Max speed: 433 mph at 20,000ft Service ceiling: 36,400ft Range: 2,050 miles max	10×0.50in mg; 2×500lb bombs	1
Convair B-32 Dominator	4×2,200 hp Wright R-3350-23 radial	Span: 135ft 0in Length: 83ft 1in Height: 32ft 9in Wing area: 347 sq ft	Empty: 60,278lb AUW: 120,000lb	Max speed: 357 mph at 30,000ft Service ceiling: 35,000ft Range: 2,500 miles with 8,000lb bombs	10×0.50in mg; 20,000lb bombs	8
Lockheed C-69 Constellation	4×2,200 hp Wright R-3350-35 radial	Span: 123ft 0in Length: 95ft 2in Height: 23ft 8in Wing area: 1,650 sq ft	Empty: 50,500lb AUW: 72,000lb	Max speed: 330 mph at S/L Service ceiling: 25,000ft Range: 2,400 miles	None	3 +60 troops
Lockheed EC-121 Warning Star	4×3,250 hp Wright R-3350-91 turbo-compound radial	Span: 126ft 2in Length: 116ft 2in Height: 27ft 0in Wing area: 1,654 sq ft	Empty: 80,611lb AUW: 143,600lb	Max speed: 321 mph at 20,000ft Service ceiling: 20,600ft Range: 4,600 miles Endurance: 20hr max	None	17—26
Lockheed F-80C	1×4,600lb st Allison J33-A-35 turbojet	Span: 39ft 11in Length: 34ft 6in Height: 11ft 4in Wing area: 238 sq ft	Empty: 8,240lb AUW: 16,856lb	Max speed: 594 mph at S/L (Mach 0.78) Service ceiling: 42,750ft Range: 1,380 miles	6×0.50in mg; 2×1,000lb bombs or 10×5in RP	1
Lockheed T-33A	1×4,600lb st Allison J33-A-35 turbojet	Span: 38ft 10½in Length: 37ft 9in Height: 11ft 8in Wing area: 238 sq ft	Empty: 8,048lb AUW: 11,965lb	Max speed: 600 mph at S/L (Mach 0.787) Service ceiling: 47,500ft Range: 1,345 miles	2×0.50in mg	2
Fairchild C-82A Packet	2×2,100 hp Pratt & Whitney R-2800-85 radial	Span: 106ft 5½in Length: 77ft 1in Height: 26ft 4in Wing area: 1,400 sq ft	Empty: 32,500lb AUW: 54,000lb	Max speed: 248 mph at 17,500ft Service ceiling: 21,200ft Range: 3,875 miles	None	4 +42 troops or 34 stretchers
Fairchild C-119G Flying Boxcar	2×3,400 hp Wright R-3350-89W radial	Span: 109ft 3in Length: 86ft 6in Height: 26ft 6in Wing area: 1,447 sq ft	Empty: 39,982lb AUW: 74,400lb	Max speed: 296 mph at 17,000ft Service ceiling: 23,400ft Range: 2,280 miles (max fuel)	None	4
Fairchild AC-119K Stinger	2×3,700 hp Wright R-3350-89B and 2×2,850lb st General Electric J85-17	Span: 109ft 3in Length: 86ft 6in Height: 26ft 6in Wing area: 1,447 sq ft	Empty: 58,282lb AUW: 80,400lb	Max speed: 250 mph at 10,000ft Service ceiling: 23,500ft Range: 1,980 miles	2×20mm cannon; 4×7.62mm multi-barrel Minigun	5
Northrop XB-35	4×3,000 hp Pratt & Whitney R-3350-17 and -21 radial	Span: 172ft 0in Length: 53ft 1in Height: 20ft 1in Wing area: 4,000 sq ft	Empty: 89,560lb AUW: 209,000lb	Max speed: 391 mph at 35,000ft Range: 720 miles with 51,000lb bombs	20×0.50in mg; 51,200lb bombs	7
Northrop YB-49	8×4,000lb st Allison J35-A-5 turbojet	Span: 172ft 0in Length: 53ft 1in Height: 20ft 1in Wing area: 4,000 sq ft	Empty: 86,000lb AUW: 168,000lb	Max speed: 495 mph at 20,000ft Range: 4,000 miles with 10,000lb bombs	10,000lb bombs	6

Type	Powerplant	Dimensions	Weights	Performance	Armament	Crew
Republic F-84G Thunderjet	1×5,600lb st Allison J35-A-29 turbojet	Span: 36ft 4in Length: 38ft 5in Height: 12ft 10in Wing area: 260 sq ft	Empty: 11,460lb AUW: 22,000lb	Max speed: 605 mph at 4,000ft Service ceiling: 40,500ft Combat radius: 1,000 miles (max)	6×0.50in mg; 32×5in RP; 2×1,000lb bombs	2
North American F-82G Twin Mustang	2×1,600 hp Allison V-1710-143/145 Vee	Span: 51ft 3in Length: 42ft 5in Height: 13ft 10in Wing area: 408 sq ft	Empty: 15,997lb AUW: 25,591lb	Max speed: 461 mph at 21,000ft Service ceiling: 38,900ft Range: 2,240 miles	6×0.50in mg; 4×1,000lb bombs	2
Convair B-36D	6×3,500 hp Pratt & Whitney R-4360-41 radial and 4×5,200lb st General Electric J47-GE-19 turbojet	Span: 230ft 0in Length: 162ft 1in Height: 46ft 8in Wing area: 4,772 sq ft	Empty: 158,843lb AUW: 357,500lb	Max speed: 439 mph at 32,120ft Service ceiling: 45,200ft Range: 7,500 miles	6×twin 20mm cannon; 86,000lb bombs	15
Boeing B-50A	4×3,500 hp Pratt & Whitney R-4360-35, -35A or -51 radial	Span: 141ft 3in Length: 99ft 0in Height: 32ft 8in Wing area: 1,720 sq ft	Empty: 81,050lb AUW: 168,408lb	Max speed: 385 mph at 25,000ft Service ceiling: 37,000ft Range: 4,650 miles	12×0.50in mg; 1×20mm cannon; 20,000lb bombs	6
Boeing KB-50J	4×3,500 hp Pratt & Whitney R-4360-35 radial and 2×6,620lb st General Electric J47-GE-23 turbojet	Span: 141ft 3in Length: 105ft 1in Height: 33ft 7in Wing area: 1,720 sq ft	Empty: 93,200lb AUW: 179,500lb	Max speed: 444 mph at 17,000ft Service ceiling: 39,700ft Range: 2,300 miles	None	6
Grumman SA-16A Albatross	2×1,275 hp Wright R-1820-76A radial	Span: 80ft 0in Length: 60ft 8in Height: 24ft 3in Wing area: 833 sq ft	Empty: 20,100lb AUW: 27,025lb	Max speed: 264 mph at 18,800ft Endurance: 23hr max with external tanks	None	4-6 +10 passengers or 12 stretchers
Boeing KC-97G Stratofreighter	4×3,500 hp Pratt & Whitney R-4360-59 radial	Span: 141ft 3in Length: 110ft 4in Height: 38ft 3in Wing area: 1,720 sq ft	Empty: 82,500lb AUW: 175,000lb	Max speed: 375 mph at 25,000ft Service ceiling: 35,000ft Range: 4,300 miles	None	5 +96 troops max
McDonnell XF-85 Goblin	1×3,000lb st Westinghouse J35-WE-22 turbojet	Span: 21ft 1½in Length: 14ft 10½in Height: 8ft 3¼in Wing area: 90 sq ft	Empty: 3,740lb AUW: 4,550lb	Max speed: 664 mph at S/L Endurance: 30min	4×0.50in mg	1
North American B-45C Tornado	4×5,200lb st General Electric J47-GE-13, -15 turbojet	Span: 89ft 0in Length: 75ft 4in Height: 25ft 2in Wing area: 1,175 sq ft	Empty: 48,903lb AUW: 112,952lb	Max speed: 579 mph at S/L Service ceiling: 43,200ft Range: 1,910 miles with 10,000lb bombs	2×0.50in mg; 22,000lb bombs	4
North American F-86D Sabre	1×5,700lb st General Electric J47-GE-17 turbojet	Span: 37ft 1½in Length: 40ft 3¼in Height: 15ft 0in Wing area: 288 sq ft	Empty: 13,518lb AUW: 19,975lb	Max speed: 693 mph at S/L (Mach 0.91) Service ceiling: 49,750ft Combat radius: 277 miles at 550 mph	24×2.75in FFAR rockets	1
North American F-86H Sabre	1×8,920lb st General Electric J73-GE-3E turbojet	Span: 39ft 1in Length: 38ft 8in Height: 15ft 0in Wing area: 313 sq ft	Empty: 13,836lb AUW: 24,296lb	Max speed: 692 mph at S/L (Mach 0.91) Service ceiling: 50,800ft Combat radius: 519 miles at 552 mph	4×20mm cannon; 2×1,000lb bombs or 16×5in RP	1
Douglas C-124C Globemaster II	4×3,800 hp Pratt & Whitney R-4360-63A radial	Span: 174ft 2in Length: 130ft 0in Height: 48ft 4in Wing area: 2,506 sq ft	Empty: 101,165lb AUW: 194,500lb	Max speed: 304 mph at 20,800ft Service ceiling: 21,800ft Range: 4,030 miles with 26,375lb payload	None	8
Northrop F-89D Scorpion	2×7,200lb st afterburning Allison J35-A-35, -33A, -41 or -47 turbojet	Span: 59ft 8in Length: 53ft 10in Height: 17ft 7in Wing area: 652 sq ft	Empty: 25,194lb AUW: 42,241lb	Max speed: 636 mph at 10,600ft Service ceiling: 40,000ft Ferry range: 1,370 miles	52×2.75in FFAR or 3×AIM-4 Falcon	2
Convair T-29B	2×2,400 hp Pratt & Whitney R-2800-97 radial	Span: 91ft 9in Length: 74ft 8in Height: 26ft 11in Wing area: 817 sq ft	Empty: 29,000lb AUW: 43,575lb	Max speed: 296 mph at 10,000ft Service ceiling: 23,500ft Range: 1,500 miles	None	4 +16 passengers

Type	Powerplant	Dimensions	Weights	Performance	Armament	Crew
Convair C-131B Samaritan	2×2,500 hp Pratt & Whitney R-2800-99W radial	Span: 105ft 4in Length: 79ft 2in Height: 28ft 2in Wing area: 920 sq ft	Empty: 29,248lb AUW: 47,000lb	Max speed: 305 mph at 16,000ft Service ceiling: 24,500ft Range: 1,900 miles	None	4 +48 passengers
North American T-28D Trojan	1×1,425 hp Wright R-1820-56S radial	Span: 40ft 7½in Length: 32ft 10in Height: 12ft 8½in Wing area: 271 sq ft	Empty: 6,521lb AUW: 8,495lb	Max speed: 352 mph at 18,000ft Range: 1,185 miles	2×0.50in mg	2
Lockheed F-94C Starfire	1×8,750lb st A/B Pratt & Whitney J48-P-5 or -5A turbojet	Span: 42ft 5in Length: 44ft 6in Height: 14ft 11in Wing area: 338 sq ft	Empty: 12,700lb AUW: 24,200lb	Max speed: 585 mph at 30,000ft Service ceiling: 51,400ft Ferry range: 1,200 miles	24×2.75in FFAR	2
Sikorsky UH-19B	1×800 hp Wright R-1300-3 radial	Rotor dia: 53ft 0in Length: 42ft 3in Height: 13ft 4in	Empty: 5,250lb AUW: 7,900lb	Max speed: 112 mph at S/L Range: 360 miles	None	2 +10 troops or 6 stretchers
Boeing B-47E-II Stratojet	6×7,200lb st A/B General Electric J47-GE-25 or -25A turbojet	Span: 116ft 0in Length: 109ft 10in Height: 27ft 11in Wing area: 1,400 sq ft	Empty: 80,756lb AUW: 206,700lb	Max speed 650 mph at 20,000ft (Mach 0.93) Service ceiling: 40,500ft Range: 3,200 miles	2×20 mm cannon; 20,000lb bombs	3
Piasecki (Vertol) H-21 Workhorse	1×1,425 hp Wright R-1820-103 radial	Rotor dia: 44ft 6in Length: 86ft 4in Height: 15ft 5in	Empty: 8,000lb AUW: 13,300lb	Max speed: 131 mph at S/L Service ceiling: 9,450ft	None	2 +14 troops or 12 stretchers
North American F-100D Super Sabre	1×17,000lb st A/B Pratt & Whitney J57-P-21A turbojet	Span: 38ft 9in Length: 54ft 3in Height: 16ft 2in Wing area: 385 sq ft	Empty: 21,000lb AUW: 34,832lb	Max speed: 864 mph at 36,000ft (Mach 1.3) Service ceiling: 44,900ft Tactical radius: 550 miles	4×20mm cannon; 7,500lb underwing stores	1
Republic F-84F Thunderstreak	1×7,220lb st Wright J65-W-3 turbojet	Span: 33ft 7¼in Length: 43ft 4¾in Height: 14ft 4¾in Wing area: 325 sq ft	AUW: 28,000lb	Max speed: 695 mph at S/L (Mach 0.91) Service ceiling: 46,000ft Combat radius: 450 miles	6×0.50in mg; 6,000lb external stores	1
Beech T-34A Mentor	1×225 hp Continental O-470-13 flat-six	Span: 32ft 10in Length: 25ft 10in Height: 9ft 7in Wing area: 178 sq ft	Empty: 2,055lb AUW: 2,900lb	Max speed: 189 mph at S/L Service ceiling: 20,000ft Range: 975 miles	None	2
Fairchild C-123B Provider	2×2,300 hp Pratt & Whitney R-2800-99W radial	Span: 110ft 0in Length: 75ft 9in Height: 34ft 1in Wing area: 1,223 sq ft	Empty: 29,900lb AUW: 71,000lb	Max speed: 253 mph at 6,000ft Service ceiling: 29,000ft Range: 1,340 miles with 19,000lb payload	None	2 +61 troops or 50 stretchers
Boeing B-52H Stratofortress	8×17,000lb st Pratt & Whitney TF33-P-3 turbofan	Span: 185ft 0in Length: 157ft 6¾in Height: 40ft 8in Wing area: 4,000 sq ft	Empty: 190,000lb AUW: 505,000lb	Max speed: 595 mph at 40,000ft (Mach 0.90) Service ceiling: 55,000ft Max range: 10,000 miles	1×20mm cannon; 60,000lb bombs max	6
Republic RF-84F Thunderflash	1×7,800lb st Wright J65-W-7 turbojet	Span: 33ft 7¼in Length: 47ft 7¾in Height: 15ft 0in	Empty: 26,800lb AUW: 28,000lb	Max speed: 679 mph at S/L (Mach 0.89) Service ceiling: 46,000ft Range: 2,200 miles with max external fuel	5×0.50in mg	1
Martin B-57B Canberra	2×7,220lb st Wright J65-W-5 turbojet	Span: 63ft 11½in Length: 65ft 6in Height: 15ft 7in Wing area: 960 sq ft	Empty: 26,800lb AUW: 55,000lb	Max speed: 582 mph at 40,000ft Service ceiling: 48,000ft Range: 2,300 miles	4×20 mm cannon; 8×0.50in mg; 5,000lb internal bombs+8×5in HVAR	2
General Dynamics/ Martin RB-57F Canberra	2×18,000lb st Pratt & Whitney TF33-11A turbofan and 2×3,300lb Pratt & Whitney J60-P-9 turbojet	Span: 122ft 5in Length: 69ft 0in Height: 19ft 0in Wing area: 2,000 sq ft	Empty: 36,000lb AUW: 63,000lb	Max speed: 500 mph Service ceiling: 75,000ft Range: 3,700 miles	None	2

Type	Powerplant	Dimensions	Weights	Performance	Armament	Crew
Lockheed C-130E Hercules	4×4,050 ehp Allison T56-A-7A turboprop	Span: 132ft 7in Length: 97ft 9in Height: 38ft 3in Wing area: 1,745 sq ft	Empty: 75,331lb AUW: 175,000lb Max payload: 45,000lb	Max speed: 386 mph at S/L Service ceiling: 23,000ft Range: 4,700 miles with 20,000lb payload	None	4 +92 troops max
Convair F-102A Delta Dagger	1×17,000lb st A/B Pratt & Whitney J57-P-23 or -25 turbojet	Span: 38ft 1½in Length: 68ft 4½in Height: 21ft 2½in Wing area: 662 sq ft	Empty: 27,700lb AUW: 31,500lb	Max speed: 825 mph at 36,000ft (Mach 1.25) Service ceiling: 54,000ft Combat radius: 550 miles	6×AIM-4A or AIM-4C Falcon; 24×2.75in FFAR	1
North American F-107A	1×24,500lb st A/B Pratt & Whitney J57-P-9 turbojet	Span: 36ft 7in Length: 60ft 10in Height: 19ft 8in	AUW: 42,000lb	Max speed: Mach 2.2 at 36,000ft	4×20mm cannon; 10,000lb under-wing stores	1
Lockheed U-2B	1×17,000lb st Pratt & Whitney J57-P-13 turbojet	Span: 80ft 0in Length: 49ft 7in Height: 13ft 0in Wing area: 565 sq ft	AUW: 19,750lb	Max speed: 528 mph at 60,000ft (Mach 0.8) Range: 4,000 miles Ceiling: 85,000ft	None	1
Lockheed U-2R	1×17,000lb st Pratt & Whitney J57-P-13 turbojet	Span: 103ft 0in Length: 63ft 0in Height: 16ft 0in	AUW: 29,000lb	Max speed: 430 mph at 60,000ft Range: 3,000 miles Ceiling: 90,000ft	None	1
Douglas B-66B Destroyer	2×10,200lb st Allison J71-A-13 turbojet	Span: 72ft 6in Length: 75ft 2in Height: 23ft 7in Wing area: 780 sq ft	Empty: 42,549lb AUW: 83,000lb	Max speed: 631 mph at 6,000ft Service ceiling: 39,400ft Combat radius: 900 miles	2×20mm cannon; 15,000lb internal bombs	3
Douglas RB-66C	2×10,200lb st Allison J71-A-13 turbojet	Span: 74ft 2in Length: 75ft 2in Height: 23ft 7in Wing area: 781 sq ft	Empty: 43,966lb AUW: 82,420lb	Max speed: 640 mph at S/L Service ceiling: 39,200ft Combat radius: 1,440 miles	None	7
Boeing KC-135A Stratotanker	4×13,750lb st Pratt & Whitney J57-P-59W turbojet	Span: 130ft 10in Length: 136ft 3in Height: 38ft 4in Wing area: 2,433 sq ft	Empty: 98,466lb AUW: 297,000lb	Max speed: 624 mph at 25,000ft Transfer radius: 1,150 miles	None	5
Boeing VC-137C	4×18,000lb st Pratt & Whitney JT3D-3 turbofan	Span: 145ft 9in Length: 152ft 11in Height: 42ft 5in Wing area: 3,010 sq ft	Empty: 137,500lb AUW: 328,000lb Max payload: 96,000lb	Max speed: 597 mph at 23,000ft Service ceiling: 38,500ft Range: 7,000 miles	None	7/8 +49 passengers
Cessna T-37B	2×1,025lb st Continental J69-T-25 turbojet	Span: 33ft 9¼in Length: 29ft 3in Height: 9ft 2in Wing area: 184 sq ft	Empty: 4,056lb AUW: 6,574lb	Max speed: 425 mph at 20,000ft Service ceiling: 39,200ft Range: 800 miles	Provision for 2 underwing armament pods	2
Douglas C-133B Cargomaster	4×7,500 ehp Pratt & Whitney T34-P-9W turboprop	Span: 179ft 7¾in Length: 157ft 6½in Height: 48ft 3in Wing area: 2,673 sq ft	Empty: 120,363lb AUW: 286,000lb Payload: 110,000lb	Max speed: 359 mph at 8,700ft Range: 4,000 miles with 52,000lb payload	None	5
McDonnell F-101A Voodoo	2×15,000lb st A/B Pratt & Whitney J57-P-13 turbojet	Span: 39ft 8in Length: 67ft 5in Height: 18ft 0in Wing area: 368 sq ft	Empty: 24,970lb AUW: 50,000lb	Max speed: 1,009 mph at 35,000ft Service ceiling: 55,800ft Range: 1,900 miles	4×20mm cannon; 1×3,721lb nuclear bomb	1
McDonnell F-101B Voodoo	2×16,900lb st A/B Pratt & Whitney J57-P-55	Span: 39ft 8in Length: 67ft 5in Height: 18ft 0in Wing area: 368 sq ft	Empty: 28,970lb AUW: 52,400lb	Max speed: 1,134 mph at 35,000ft Service ceiling: 54,800ft Range: 1,520 miles	2×MB-1 Genie; 4×GAR-1 or GAR-2 Falcon, or 6×Falcon	2
McDonnell RF-101A Voodoo	2×14,500lb st A/B Pratt & Whitney J57-P-13	Span: 39ft 8in Length: 69ft 4in Height: 18ft 0in Wing area: 368 sq ft	Empty: 25,335lb AUW: 51,000lb	Max speed: 1,012 mph at 35,000ft Service ceiling: 55,800ft Range: 1,100 miles	None	1
Cessna U-3A	2×240 hp Continental O-470-M	Span: 36ft 0in Length: 27ft 1in Height: 10ft 5in Wing area: 175 sq ft	Empty: 2,900lb AUW: 4,600lb	Max speed: 232 mph at S/L Range: 850 miles	None	4/5
Lockheed F-104A Starfighter	1×14,800lb st A/B General Electric J79-GE-3B turbojet	Span: 21ft 11in Length: 54ft 9in Height: 13ft 6in Wing area: 179 sq ft	AUW: 22,000lb	Max speed: 1,450 mph at 36,000ft (Mach 2.2)	1×20mm M-61 cannon; 2 or 4×Sidewinder AAM	1

Type	Powerplant	Dimensions	Weights	Performance	Armament	Crew
Fairchild Republic F-105D Thunderchief	1×26,500lb st A/B Pratt & Whitney J75-P-19W turbojet	Span: 34ft 11¼in Length: 64ft 3in Height: 19ft 8in Wing area: 385 sq ft	Empty: 27,500lb AUW: 52,546lb	Max speed: 1,480 mph at 38,000ft (Mach 2.25) Tactical radius: 230 miles with 12,000lb bombs	1×20mm M-61 cannon; 8,000lb internal ordnance; 6,000lb external stores	1
Fairchild Republic F-105F Thunderchief	1×26,500lb st A/B Pratt & Whitney J75-P-19W turbojet	Span: 34ft 11¼in Length: 69ft 1in Height: 20ft 2in Wing area: 385 sq ft	Empty: 28,393lb AUW: 54,000lb	Max speed: 1,480 mph at 38,000ft (Mach 2.25) Ferry range: 2,070 miles	1×20mm M61 cannon; 8,000lb internal ordnance; 6,000lb external stores	2
Kaman H-43B Huskie	1×860 ehp Lycoming T53-L-1A turboshaft	Rotor dia: 51ft 6in Length: 25ft 0in Height: 15ft 6½in	Empty: 4,469lb AUW: 8,800lb	Max speed: 120 mph at S/L Service ceiling: 25,700ft Range: 235 miles	None	3/4
Convair F-106A Delta Dart	1×24,500lb st A/B J75-P-17 turbojet	Span: 38ft 3½in Length: 70ft 8¾in Height: 20ft 3in Wing area: 662 sq ft	Empty: 24,083lb AUW: 34,510lb	Max speed: 1,525 mph at 36,000ft Service ceiling: 55,000ft Combat radius: 365 miles	1×20mm M61A1 cannon; 1×Genie; 4×Falcon AAM	1
Convair B-58A Hustler	4×15,600lb st A/B General Electric J79-GE-3B turbojet	Span: 56ft 10in Length: 96ft 9in Height: 31ft 5in Wing area: 1,542 sq ft	AUW: 163,000lb	Max speed: 1,385 mph at 40,000ft (Mach 2.1) Service ceiling: 60,000ft Tactical radius: 1,200 miles	1×20mm Vulcan cannon; mission pod of nuclear or conventional bombs	3
Rockwell T-39A	2×3,000lb st Pratt & Whitney J60-P-3 turbojet	Span: 44ft 5in Length: 43ft 9in Height: 16ft 0in Wing area: 342 sq ft	Empty: 9,300lb AUW: 17,760lb	Max speed: 595 mph at 36,000ft Service ceiling: 39,000ft Range: 1,725 miles	None	2+4—6 passengers
Northrop T-38A Talon	2×3,850lb st A/B General Electric J85-GE-5 turbojet	Span: 25ft 3in Length: 44ft 2in Height: 12ft 10in Wing area: 170 sq ft	Empty: 7,164lb AUW: 11,550lb	Max speed: 838 mph at 36,000ft (Mach 1.27) Service ceiling: 42,400ft Range: 1,267 miles	None	2
Lockheed C-140A JetStar	4×3,300lb Pratt & Whitney JT12A-8 turbojet	Span: 54ft 5in Length: 60ft 5in Height: 20ft 5in Wing area: 543 sq ft	Empty: 22,074lb AUW: 42,000lb	Max speed: 566 mph at 21,200ft Range: 2,235 miles	None	2+10 passengers
McDonnell Douglas F-4E Phantom II	2×17,900lb st A/B General Electric J79-GE-17A turbojet	Span: 38ft 7½in Length: 63ft 0in Height: 16ft 5½in Wing area: 530 sq ft	Empty: 30,328lb AUW: 61,795lb	Max speed: 1,485 mph at 40,000ft Service ceiling: 62,250ft Combat radius: 595 miles	1×20mm M61A1 cannon; Sparrow AAMs; air-to-ground ordnance	2
Sikorsky CH-3E	2×1,500 shp General Electric T58-GE-5 turboshaft	Rotor dia: 62ft 0in Length: 73ft 0in Height: 18ft 1in	Empty: 13,255lb AUW: 22,050lb	Max speed: 162 mph at S/L Service ceiling: 11,100ft Range: 465 miles	None	2+25 troops
Douglas A-1E Skyraider	1×3,020 hp Wright R-3350-26WA radial	Span: 50ft 0in Length: 38ft 2in Height: 15ft 5in Wing area: 400 sq ft	Empty: 12,313lb AUW: 18,799lb	Max speed: 311 mph at 18,000ft Service ceiling: 26,000ft Range: 3,000 miles	4×20mm cannon; 3,000lb underwing stores	2
North American XB-70A Valkyrie	6×31,000lb st A/B General Electric YJ93-GE-3 turbojet	Span: 105ft 0in Length: 189ft 0in Height: 30ft 0in Wing area: 6,297 sq ft	AUW: 525,000lb	Max speed: 1,980 mph at 70—80,000ft (Mach 3) Range: 7,500 miles	None	2
Cessna T-41A Mescalero	1×150 hp Lycoming O-320-E2D flat-four	Span: 35ft 10in Length: 26ft 11in Height: 8ft 9½in Wing area: 176 sq ft	Empty: 1,285lb AUW: 2,300lb	Max speed: 139 mph at S/L Service ceiling: 13,100ft Range: 615 miles	None	2
Lockheed C-141A StarLifter	4×21,000lb st Pratt & Whitney TF33-P-7 turbofan	Span: 159ft 11in Length: 145ft 0in Height: 39ft 3in Wing area: 3,228 sq ft	Empty: 133,773lb AUW: 318,000lb	Max speed: 571 mph at 25,000ft Range 4,080 miles	None	4
Lockheed C-141B StarLifter	4×21,000lb st Pratt & Whitney TF33-P-7 turbofan	Span: 159ft 11in Length: 168ft 3½in Height: 39ft 3in Wing area: 3,228 sq ft	AUW: 344,900lb Max payload: 89,152lb	Max speed: 569 mph at 25,000ft Range: 3,200 miles with max payload	None	4

Type	Powerplant	Dimensions	Weights	Performance	Armament	Crew
Sikorsky HH-53C	2×3,925 shp General Electric T64-GE-7 turboshaft	Rotor dia: 72ft 3in Length: 88ft 3in Height: 24ft 11in	Empty: 23,569lb AUW: 42,000lb	Max speed: 196 mph at S/L Service ceiling: 20,400ft Range: 540 miles	None	3+37 troops or 24 stretchers and 4 attendants
Lockheed SR-71A	2×32,500lb st Pratt & Whitney JT11D-20B turbojet	Span: 55ft 7in Length: 107ft 5in Height: 18ft 6in Wing area: 1,800 sq ft	Empty: 60,000lb AUW: 170,000lb	Max speed: 2,000 mph+ at 78,740ft Operational ceiling: 80,000ft+ Endurance: 1hr 30min at Mach 3	None	2
Cessna O-2A	2×210 hp Continental IO-360-C flat-six	Span: 38ft 2in Length: 29ft 9in Height: 9ft 4in Wing area: 201 sq ft	Empty: 2,650lb AUW: 4,630lb	Max speed: 199 mph at 5,500ft Service ceiling: 18,000ft Range: 780 miles	4×underwing pylons	2
Cessna A-37B Dragonfly	2×2,850lb st General Electric J85-GE-17A turbojet	Span: 35ft 10½in Length: 28ft 3¼in Height: 8ft 10½in Wing area: 184 sq ft	Empty: 6,211lb AUW: 14,000lb	Max speed: 507 mph at 16,000ft Service ceiling: 41,765ft Range: 460 miles with max payload	1×7.62mm Minigun; 2×870lb pylons; 2×600lb pylons	2
General Dynamics F-111F	2×25,000lb st A/B Pratt & Whitney TF30-P-100 turbofan	Span: 63ft 0in (extended) Length: 73ft 6in Height: 17ft 1½in	Empty: 47,175lb AUW: 100,000lb	Max speed: Mach 2.5 Service ceiling: 59,000ft Range: 2,925 miles	1×M61 cannon; 2×750lb bombs; 4×wing attachment points	2
General Dynamics FB-111A	2×20,350lb st A/B Pratt & Whitney TF30-P-7 turbofan	Span: 70ft 0in (extended) Length: 73ft 6in Height: 17ft 1½in	AUW: 100,000lb	Max speed: 1,650 mph Range: 4,000 miles	31,500lb bombs or 6×nuclear bombs or SRAM missiles	2
Rockwell International OV-10A Bronco	2×715 ehp Garrett AiResearch T76-G-416/417 turboprop	Span: 40ft 0in Length: 41ft 7in Height: 15ft 2in Wing area: 291 sq ft	Empty: 6,893lb AUW: 14,444lb	Max speed: 281 mph at S/L Combat radius: 228 miles	4×600lb weapon attachment points; 1×1,200lb weapon attachment point	2
McDonnell Douglas C-9A Nightingale	2×14,500lb st Pratt & Whitney JT8D-9 turbofan	Span: 93ft 5in Length: 119ft 3½in Height: 27ft 6in Wing area: 1,001 sq ft	Empty: 57,190lb AUW: 121,000lb	Max speed: 575 mph Range: 1,923 miles	None	2+30-40 stretchers
Vought A-7D Corsair II	1×14,500lb st Allison TF41-A-1 turbofan	Span: 38ft 9in Length: 46ft 1½in Height: 16ft 0¾in Wing area: 375 sq ft	Empty: 19,111lb AUW: 42,000lb	Max speed: 691 mph at S/L Range: 2,281 miles	15,000lb stores on 6 underwing and 2 fuselage stations	2
Lockheed C-5A Galaxy	4×41,000lb st General Electric TF39-GE-1 turbofan	Span: 222ft 8½in Length: 247ft 10in Height: 65ft 1½in Wing area: 6,200 sq ft	Empty: 337,937lb AUW: 769,000lb Design payload: 220,967lb	Max speed: 571 mph at 25,000ft Service ceiling: 34,000ft Range: 6,529 miles with 112,600lb payload	None	5+up to 345 troops
Northrop F-5E Tiger II	2×5,000lb st A/B General Electric J85-GE-21A turbojet	Span: 26ft 8in Length: 48ft 2in Height: 13ft 4in Wing area: 186 sq ft	Empty: 9,683lb AUW: 24,664lb	Max speed: Mach 1.64 at 36,000ft Service ceiling: 50,800ft Combat radius: 656 miles	2×AIM-9 AAM; 2×20mm M39A2 cannon; up to 7,000lb mixed ordnance	2
Boeing T-43A	2×14,500lb Pratt & Whitney JT8D-9 turbofan	Span: 93ft 0in Length: 100ft 0in Height: 37ft 0in Wing area: 980 sq ft	Empty: 27,310lb AUW: 115,500lb	Max speed: 586 mph at 23,500ft Range: 2,995 miles Endurance: 6hr	None	2+18 students
McDonnell Douglas F-15A Eagle	2×25,000lb st A/B Pratt & Whitney F100-PW-100 turbofan	Span: 42ft 9¾in Length: 63ft 9in Height: 18ft 5½in Wing area: 608 sq ft	AUW: 56,000lb	Max speed: Mach 2.5 Absolute ceiling: 100,000ft Ferry range: 2,878 miles	4×AIM-9L Sidewinder; 4×AIM-7F Sparrow; 1×20mm M61A1 cannon	1
Boeing E-4B	4×52,500lb st General Electric F103-GE-100 turbofan	Span: 195ft 8in Length: 231ft 4in Height: 63ft 5in Wing area: 5,500 sq ft	AUW: 800,000lb	Max speed: 608 mph at 30,000ft Endurance: 12hr	None	7

Type	Powerplant	Dimensions	Weights	Performance	Armament	Crew
Rockwell International B-1	4×30,000lb st A/B General Electric YF101-GE-100 turbofan	Span: 136ft 8½in Length: 150ft 2½in Height: 33ft 7¼in Wing area: 1,950 sq ft	AUW: 389,800lb	Max speed: 1,450 mph at 50,000ft (Mach 2.2) Range: 6,000 miles	Max weapon load: 115,000lb	4
Beech C-12	2×750 shp Pratt & Whitney of Canada PT6A-38 turboprop	Span: 54ft 6in Length: 43ft 9in Height: 14ft 0in Wing area: 303 sq ft	Empty: 7,437lb AUW: 12,500lb	Max speed: 333 mph at 15,000ft Service ceiling: 31,000ft Range: 1,709 miles at 25,000ft	None	2 +6 passengers
Fairchild Republic A-10A Thunderbolt II	2×9,065lb st General Electric TF34-GE-100 turbofan	Span: 57ft 6in Length: 53ft 4in Height: 14ft 8in Wing area: 506 sq ft	Empty: 20,796lb AUW: 50,000lb	Max speed: 423 mph at S/L Operational radius: 288 miles	1×30mm GAU-8/A cannon; 4×pylons for up to 16,000lb max external load	1
Boeing E-3A Sentry	4×21,000lb st Pratt & Whitney TF33-PW-100 turbofan	Span: 145ft 9in Length: 152ft 11in Height: 42ft 5in Wing area: 3,050 sq ft	AUW: 325,000lb	Max speed: 530 mph Service ceiling: 29,000ft Endurance: 6hr	None	17
General Dynamics F-16A	1×25,000lb st A/B Pratt & Whitney F100-PW-100(3) turbofan	Span: 31ft 0in Length: 47ft 7¾in Height: 16ft 5¼in Wing area: 300 sq ft	Empty: 14,567lb AUW: 22,785lb	Max speed: Mach 2+ at 40,000ft Service ceiling: 50,000ft+ Combat radius: 575 miles	1×20mm M61A1 cannon; 2×IR missiles; 4×wing hardpoints	1
McDonnell Douglas KC-10A Extender	3×52,500lb st General Electric CF6-50C1 turbofan	Span: 165ft 4½in Length: 181ft 7in Height: 58ft 1in Wing area: 3,958 sq ft	Empty: 239,747lb AUW: 590,000lb	Max range: 3,800 miles	None	3

Photograph Credits

Index

A

A-1 Skyraider 177, 219
A-3 Falcon, Curtiss 35, 209
A-7D Corsair II, Vought 191, 220
A-8 Shrike, Curtiss 47, 210
A-10, Curtiss 47
A-10 Thunderbolt II, Fairchild Republic 199-200, 220
A-11, Consolidated 58, 210
A-11, Lockheed 184-185
A-12, Curtiss 47, 210
A-17 Nomad, Northrop 56-57, 210
A-24 Dauntless, Douglas 90, 212
A-26, Douglas 90, 215
A-29, Lockheed 98, 213
A-31, Vultee 102
A-35 Vengeance, Vultee 102, 213

A-37 Dragonfly, Cessna 187, 220
AC-119K Stinger, Fairchild 216
AT-6 Texan, North American 59, 211
AT-7, Beech 94
AT-8, Cessna 100
AT-10, Beech 97, 213
AT-11 Kansan, Beech 94
AT-17, Cessna 100
AT-18, Lockheed 98
Aeronca L-3 Grasshopper 96, 213
Airacobra, Bell P-39 76, 213
Airacomet, Bell P-59 117, 215
Airacuda, Bell YFM-1 70, 211
Albatross, Grumman SA-16 129, 216
Ascender, Curtiss XP-55 101, 213

B

B-1, Rockwell 197, 221
B-2 Condor, Curtiss 44, 209
B-3, Keystone 38-39, 209
B-4, Keystone 38-39
B-5, Keystone 38-39
B-6, Keystone 38-39, 209
B-9, Boeing 48-49, 210
B-10, Martin 54-55, 210
B-12, Martin 54-55
B-14, Martin 54-55
B-17 Flying Fortress, Boeing 66-69, 211
B-18 Bolo, Douglas 64-65, 211
B-23 Dragon, Douglas 64-65, 211
B-24 Liberator, Consolidated 78-81, 212

B-25 Mitchell, North American 86, 212
B-26 Marauder, Martin 87, 212
B-26 Invader, Douglas 115
B-29 Superfortress, Boeing 109, 214
B-32 Dominator, Convair 119, 215
B-34 Lexington/Ventura, Lockheed 99, 213
B-36, Convair 127, 216
B-45 Tornado, North American 133, 216
B-47 Stratojet, Boeing 142, 217
B-50 Superfortress, Boeing 128, 216
B-52 Stratofortress, Boeing 150-151, 217

B-57 Canberra, Martin 153, 217
B-58 Hustler, Convair 170, 219
B-66 Destroyer, Douglas 159, 218
BC-1, North American 59, 210
BT-2B, Douglas 208
BT-9, North American 59, 210
BT-13, Vultee 74-75, 212
BT-15 Valiant, Vultee 74-75
Barling NBL-1 27, 208
Beech:
  AT-7 94
  AT-10 97, 213
  AT-11 Kansan 94
  C-12 198, 222
  C-43 Traveler 102, 213
  C-45 94, 213
  T-34 Mentor 147, 217
Bell:
  P-39 Airacobra 76, 212
  P-59 Airacomet 117, 215
  P-63 Kingcobra 109, 214
  XP-77 116, 215
  YFM-1 Airacuda 70, 211
Berliner-Joyce P-16/PB-1 45, 210
Black Widow, Northrop P-61 113, 214
Bobcat, Cessna UC-78 100, 213
Boeing:
  B-9 48-49, 210
  B-17 Flying Fortress 66-69, 211
  B-29 Superfortress 109, 214
  B-47 Stratojet 142-143, 217
  B-50 Superfortress 128, 216
  C-97 Stratofreighter 130
  C-135 160
  E-3A Sentry 201, 221
  E-4 196, 221
  KB-50J 216
  KC-97G 216
  KC-135 Stratotanker 160, 218
  P-26 52-53, 210
  PW-9 32, 208
  T-43A 193, 220
  VC-137 160, 218
  XB-15 85, 211
Bolo, Douglas B-18 64-65, 211
Boston, Douglas 85
Breguet 14 18-19, 207
Bronco, Rockwell OV-10 190, 220

C

C-5 Galaxy, Lockheed 192, 220
C-9A Nightingale, McDonnell
    Douglas 190, 220
C-12, Beech 198, 221
C-21, Douglas 50-51, 210
C-26, Douglas 50-51
C-29, Douglas 61
C-32, Douglas 61
C-33, Douglas 61, 211
C-39, Douglas 61, 211
C-43 Traveler, Beech 102, 213
C-45, Beech 94, 213
C-46 Commando, Curtiss 103
C-47 Skytrain, Douglas 93, 213
C-54 Skymaster, Douglas 101, 213
C-56 Lodestar, Lockheed 84, 212
C-57, Lockheed 84
C-66, Lockheed 84
C-69, Lockheed 120-121, 215
C-82 Packet, Fairchild 124, 215
C-87, Consolidated 78-81, 212
C-97 Stratofreighter, Boeing 130,
    216
C-119 Flying Boxcar,
    Fairchild 148-149, 215
C-121 Constellation,
    Lockheed 120-121, 215
C-123 Provider, Fairchild 148-149,
    217
C-124 Globemaster II, Douglas 136,
    216

C-130 Hercules, Lockheed 154-155,
    218
C-131 Samaritan, Convair 139, 217
C-133 Cargomaster, Douglas 161,
    218
C-135, Boeing 160
C-140 JetStar, Lockheed 173, 219
C-141 StarLifter, Lockheed 181, 219
CH-3, Sikorsky 176, 219
Canberra, Martin B-57 153, 217
Cargomaster, Douglas C-133 161,
    218
Cessna:
  A-37 Dragonfly 187, 220
  AT-8 100
  AT-17 100
  O-2 186, 220
  T-37 161, 218
  T-41 Mescalero 180, 219
  U-3 163, 218
  UC-78 Bobcat 100, 213
Commando, Curtiss C-46 103
Condor, Curtiss B-2 44, 209
Consolidated:
  A-11 58, 210
  B-24 Liberator 78-81, 212
  C-87 78-81, 212
  P-30 58, 210
  PB-2 58
  PT-1 26
  PT-3 26, 208
  PT-11 26
  TW-3 26, 208
Constellation, Lockheed
    C-121 120-121
Convair:
  B-32 Dominator 119, 215
  B-36 127, 216
  B-58 Hustler 170-171, 219
  C-131 Samaritan 139, 217
  F-102 Delta Dagger 156, 218
  F-106 Delta Dart 169, 219
  T-29 139, 216
Corsair II, Vought A-7D 191, 220
Curtiss:
  A-3 Falcon 35, 209
  A-8 Shrike 47, 210
  A-10 47
  A-12 47, 210
  B-2 Condor 44, 209
  C-46 Commando 103
  JN-4 8-9, 207
  JN-6 8-9, 207
  O-1 35, 209
  P-1 Hawk 33, 209
  P-2 Hawk 33
  P-3 Hawk 33, 209
  P-5 Hawk 33
  P-6 Hawk 33, 209
  P-36 Mohawk 71, 211
  P-40 Warhawk 82-83, 212
  PW-8 28, 208
  XP-55 Ascender 101, 213
  /Orenco D 24, 208

D

DB-1, Douglas 64
DB-7, Douglas 85
DH-4, de Havilland 16-17, 207
DWC, Douglas 29, 208
Dauntless, Douglas A-24 90, 212
de Havilland DH-4 16-17, 207
Delta Dagger, Convair F-102 156,
    208
Delta Dart, Convair F-106 169, 209
Destroyer, Douglas B-66 159, 218
Dominator, Convair B-32 119, 215
Douglas:
  A-1 Skyraider 177, 219
  A-20 Havoc 85, 212
  A-24 Dauntless 90, 212
  A-26 115, 215
  B-18 Bolo 64-65, 211

B-23 Dragon 64-65, 211
B-26 Invader 115
B-66 Destroyer 159, 218
BT-2B 208
Boston 95
C-21 50-51, 210
C-32 61
C-33 61, 211
C-39 61, 211
C-47 Skytrain 93, 213
C-54 Skymaster 101, 213
C-74 Globemaster 136
C-124 Globemaster II 136, 216
C-133 Cargomaster 161, 218
DB-7 85
DWC 29, 208
O-2 30-31, 208
O-5 29
O-7 30-31
O-8 30-31
O-9 30-31
O-22 30-31
O-25 30-31, 208
O-31 46
O-32 30-31
O-38 30-31, 208
O-43 46, 210
O-46 46, 210
P-70 85, 212
XB-19 91, 213
XB-42 Mixmaster 114, 214
XB-43 114, 214
YO-31 210
Dragon, Douglas B-23 64-65, 211
Dragonfly, Cessna A-37 187, 220

E

E-1, Standard 14, 207
E-3A Sentry, Boeing 201, 221
E-4, Boeing 196, 221
Eagle, General Motors (Fisher)
    P-75 118, 215
Eagle, McDonnell Douglas
    F-15 194-195, 220
Extender, McDonnell Douglas
    KC-10A 204, 221

F

F-4 Phantom II, McDonnell
    Douglas 174-175, 219
F-5A/B, Northrop 172
F-5E Tiger II, Northrop 192, 220
F-15 Eagle, McDonnell
    Douglas 195, 220
F-16, General Dynamics 202-203,
    221
F-82 Twin Mustang, North
    American 126, 216
F-84 Thunderjet, Republic 130, 216
F-84F Thunderstreak, Republic 146,
    217
F-86 Sabre, North American 134,
    216
F-89 Scorpion, Northrop 137-138,
    216
F-94 Starfire, Lockheed 141, 217
F-100 Super Sabre, North
    American 144-145, 217
F-101 Voodoo, McDonnell 162, 218
F-102 Delta Dagger, Convair 156,
    218
F-104 Starfighter,
    Lockheed 164-165, 218
F-105 Thunderchief,
    Republic 166-167, 219
F-106 Delta Dart, Convair 169, 219
F-107, North American 157, 218
F-111, General Dynamics 188-189,
    220
FB-111, General
    Dynamics 188-189, 220

Fairchild:
  C-92 Packet 124, 215
  C-119 Flying Boxcar 124, 215
  C-123 Provider 148-149, 217
  PT-19 76, 212
  PT-23 76
  /Republic A-10 Thunderbolt II
      199-200, 220
Falcon, Curtiss A-3 35
Flying Boxcar, Fairchild C-119 124,
    215
Flying Fortress, Boeing B-17 66-69,
    211

G

Galaxy, Lockheed C-5 192, 220
General Dynamics:
  F-16 202-203, 221
  F-111 188-189, 220
  FB-111 188-189, 220
  /Martin RB-57 Canberra 153, 217
General Motors (Fisher) P-75
    Eagle 118, 215
Globemaster, Douglas C-74 136
Globemaster II, Douglas C-124 136,
    216
Goblin, McDonnell XF-85 132, 216
Grasshopper, Aeronca L-3 96, 213
Grasshopper, Piper L-4 96, 213
Grasshopper, Taylorcraft L-2 94,
    213

H

H-19, Sikorsky 142, 217
H-21 Workhorse, Piasecki
    (Vertol) 144, 217
H-43 Huskie, Kaman 168, 219
HH-53, Sikorsky 182-183, 220
Havoc, Douglas A-20 85, 212
Hawk, Curtiss P-1 to P-6 33, 212
Hercules, Lockheed C-130 154-155,
    218
Hudson, Lockheed A-29 98, 213
Huff-Daland LB-1 36-37, 209
Huskie, Kaman H-43 168, 219
Hustler, Convair B-58 170, 219

I

Invader, Douglas B-26 115

J

JetStar, Lockheed C-140 173, 219
JN-4, Curtiss 8-9, 207
JN-6, Curtiss 8-9, 207

K

KB-50J, Boeing 216
KC-10A Extender, McDonnell
    Douglas 204, 221
KC-97G, Boeing 216
KC-135 Stratotanker, Boeing 160,
    218
Kaman H-43 Huskie 168, 219
Kansan, Beech AT-11 94
Kaydet, Stearman PT-17 62
Keystone:
  LB-3 to 14 38-39, 209
  B-3 to 6 38-39, 209
Kingcobra, Bell P-63 109, 214

L

L-2 Grasshopper, Taylorcraft 95,
    213
L-3 Grasshopper, Aeronca 96, 213
L-4 Grasshopper, Piper 96, 213
L-5 Sentinel, Stinson 108, 214
LB-1, Huff-Daland 36-37, 209
LB-3 to 14, Keystone 38-39, 209
Lancer, Republic P-43 92, 213
Liberator, Consolidated B-24 78-81,
    212
Lightning, Lockheed P-38 89, 212
Lockheed:
  A-11 184-185

A-29 Hudson   98, 213
AT-18   98
B-34 Lexington/Ventura   99, 213
C-5 Galaxy   192, 220
C-56 Lodestar   84, 212
C-57   84
C-66   84, 212
C-69   120-121, 215
C-121 Constellation   120-121, 215
C-130 Hercules   154-155, 218
C-140 JetStar   173, 219
C-141 StarLifter   181, 219
F-94 Starfire   141, 217
F-104 Starfighter   164-165, 218
P-38 Lightning   89, 212
P-80 Shooting Star   122-123, 215
SR-71 Blackbird   184-185, 220
T-33   122-123, 215
TR-1   158
U-2   158, 218
YF-12A   184-185
Lodestar, Lockheed C-56   84, 212
Loening OA-1   28, 208
LUSAC-11, Packard-Le Pere   18-19, 207

M

MB-1, Martin   21-23, 207
MB-2, Martin   21-23, 208
MB-3, Thomas-Morse   25, 208
Marauder, Martin B-26   87, 212
Martin:
  B-10   54-55, 210
  B-12   54-55
  B-14   54-55
  B-26 Marauder   87, 212
  B-57 Canberra   153, 217
  MB-1   21-23, 207
  MB-2   21-23, 208
Mentor, Beech T-34   147, 217
Mescalero, Cessna T-41   180, 219
Mitchell, North American B-25   86, 212
Mohawk, Curtiss P-36   71, 211
Mustang, North American
  P-51   106-107, 214

Mc

McDonnell:
  F-101 Voodoo   162, 218
  XF-85 Goblin   132, 216
McDonnell Douglas:
  C-9A Nightingale   190, 210
  F-4 Phantom II   174-175, 219
  F-15 Eagle   194-195, 220
  KC-10A Extender   204, 221

N

NBL-1, Barling   27, 208
Nieuport:
  17   11, 207
  21   11
  23   11
  24   11
  27   11
  28   15, 207
Nightingale, McDonnell Douglas
  C-9A   190, 210
Nomad, Northrop A-17   56-57, 210
North American:
  AT-6   59, 211
  B-25 Mitchell   86, 212
  B-45 Tornado   133, 216
  BC-1   59, 210
  BT-9   59, 210
  F-82 Twin Mustang   126, 216
  F-86 Sabre   134, 216
  F-100 Super Sabre   144-145, 217
  F-107   156, 218
  O-47   63, 218
  P-51 Mustang   106-107, 214
  T-28 Trojan   140, 217
  XB-70 Valkyrie   178-179, 219
Northrop:
  A-17 Nomad   56-57, 210

F-5A/B   172
F-5E Tiger II   192, 220
F-89 Scorpion   137-138, 218
P-61 Black Widow   113, 214
T-38 Talon   172, 219
XB-35   125, 215
YB-49   125, 215

O

O-1, Curtiss   35, 209
O-2, Douglas   30-31, 208
O-2, Cessna   186, 220
O-5, Douglas   29
O-7, Douglas   30-31
O-8, Douglas   30-31
O-9, Douglas   30-31
O-11, Curtiss   35
O-19, Thomas-Morse   40, 209
O-22, Douglas   30-31
O-25, Douglas   30-31, 208
O-31, Douglas   46
O-32, Douglas   30-31
O-38, Douglas   30-31, 208
O-39, Curtiss   35
O-43, Douglas   46, 210
O-46, Douglas   46, 210
O-47, North American   63, 211
O-57, Taylorcraft   94
O-58, Aeronca   96
O-59, Piper   96
O-62, Stinson   108
OA-1, Loening   28, 208
OA-3, Douglas   50-51
OA-4, Douglas   50-51
OV-10 Bronco, Rockwell   190-191, 220

P

P-1 Hawk, Curtiss   33, 209
P-2 Hawk, Curtiss   33
P-3 Hawk, Curtiss   33, 209
P-5 Hawk, Curtiss   33
P-6 Hawk, Curtiss   33, 209
P-12, Boeing   41-43, 209
P-16, Berliner-Joyce   45, 210
P-24, Detroit Aircraft   58
P-26, Boeing   52-53, 210
P-30, Consolidated   58, 210
P-35, Republic (Seversky)   60, 211
P-36 Mohawk, Curtiss   71, 211
P-38 Lightning, Lockheed   89, 212
P-39 Airacobra, Bell   76, 212
P-40 Warhawk, Curtiss   82-83, 212
P-43 Lancer, Republic   92, 213
P-47 Thunderbolt,
  Republic   104-105, 214
P-51 Mustang, North
  American   106-107, 214
P-59 Airacomet, Bell   117, 215
P-61 Black Widow, Northrop   113, 214
P-63 Kingcobra, Bell   109, 214
P-70, Douglas   85, 212
P-75 Eagle, General Motors
  (Fisher)   118, 215
P-80 Shooting Star,
  Lockheed   122-123, 215
PB-1, Berliner-Joyce   45, 210
PB-2, Consolidated   58
PT-1, Consolidated   26
PT-3, Consolidated   26, 208
PT-11, Consolidated   26, 208
PT-13, Stearman   62
PT-16, Ryan   72-73, 211
PT-17 Kaydet, Stearman   62, 211
PT-19, Fairchild   76, 212
PT-20, Ryan   72-73
PT-21, Ryan   72-73
PT-22, Ryan   72-73
PT-23, Fairchild   76
PW-8, Curtiss   28, 208
PW-9, Boeing   32, 208
Packard-Le Pere LUSAC-11   18-19, 207
Packet, Fairchild C-82   124, 215

Phantom II, McDonnell Douglas
  F-4   174-175, 219
Piasecki (Vertol) H-21
  Workhorse   144, 217
Piper L-4 Grasshopper   96, 213
Provider, Fairchild C-123   148-149, 217

R

R-4, Sikorsky   112, 214
R-5, Sikorsky   112, 214
R-6, Sikorsky   112, 214
RB-57 Canberra, Martin/General
  Dynamics   153, 217
RF-84 Thunderflash, Republic   152, 217
Republic:
  F-84 Thunderjet   130, 216
  F-84F Thunderstreak   146, 217
  F-105 Thunderchief   166-167, 219
  P-43 Lancer   92, 213
  P-47 Thunderbolt   104-105, 214
  RF-84 Thunderflash   152, 217
  (Seversky) P-35   60, 211
Rockwell:
  B-1   197, 221
  OV-10 Bronco   190, 220
  T-39 Sabreliner   171, 219
Ryan:
  PT-16   72-73, 211
  PT-20   72-73
  PT-21   72-73
  PT-22   72-73
  S-T-A   72-73

S

S-4, Thomas-Morse   10, 207
SA-16 Albatross, Grumman   129, 216
SR-71 Blackbird,
  Lockheed   184-185, 220
Sabre, North American F-86   134, 216
Sabreliner, Rockwell T-39   171
Samaritan, Convair C-131   139, 217
Scorpion, Northrop F-89   137-138, 216
Sentinel, Stinson L-5   108, 214
Sentry, Boeing E-3A   207
Seversky P-35   60, 211
Shrike, Curtiss A-8   47, 210
Sikorsky:
  CH-3   176, 219
  H-19   142, 217
  HH-53   182, 220
  R-4   112, 214
  R-5   112, 214
  R-6   112, 214
Skytrain, Douglas C-47   93, 213
Skymaster, Douglas C-54   101, 213
Skyraider, Douglas A-1   177, 219
Sopwith 1½-Strutter   20, 207
SPAD:
  VII   12-13, 207
  XIII   12-13, 207
Standard E-1   14, 207
Starfighter, Lockheed
  F-104   164-165, 218
Starfire, Lockheed F-94   141, 217
StarLifter, Lockheed C-141   181, 219
Stearman:
  PT-13   62
  PT-17   62, 211
Stinson L-5 Sentinel   108, 214
Stratofortress, Boeing
  B-52   150-151, 217
Stratofreighter, Boeing C-97   130
Stratojet, Boeing B-47   142-143, 217
Stratotanker, Boeing KC-135   160, 218
Superfortress, Boeing B-29   109, 214
Superfortress, Boeing B-50   128
Super Sabre, North American
  F-100   144-145, 217

T

T-6 Texan, North American   59
T-28 Trojan, North American   140, 216
T-29, Convair   139, 216
T-33, Lockheed   122-123, 215
T-34 Mentor, Beech   147, 217
T-37, Cessna   161, 218
T-38 Talon, Northrop   172, 219
T-39 Sabreliner, Rockwell   171, 219
T-41 Mescalero, Cessna   180, 219
T-43A, Boeing   193, 220
TW-3, Consolidated   208
Talon, Northrop T-38   172, 219
Taylorcraft L-2 Grasshopper   94, 213
Texan, North American T-6   59
Thomas-Morse:
  MB-3   25, 208
  O-19   40, 209
  S-4   10, 207
Thunderbolt, Republic
  P-47   104-105, 214
Thunderbolt II, Fairchild Republic
  A-10   199-200, 220
Thunderchief, Republic
  F-105   166-167, 219
Thunderflash, Republic RF-84   152, 217
Thunderjet, Republic F-84   130, 216
Thunderstreak, Republic F-84F   146, 217
Tiger II, Northrop F-5E   192, 220
Tornado, North American B-45   133, 216
Traveler, Beech C-43   102, 213
Trojan, North American T-28   140, 218
Twin Mustang, North American
  F-82   126, 216

U

U-2, Lockheed   158, 218
U-3, Cessna   163, 218
UC-78 Bobcat, Cessna   100, 213

V

VC-137, Boeing   160, 218
Valiant, Vultee BT-13   74-75, 212
Valkyrie, North American
  XB-70   178-179, 219
Vengeance, Vultee A-35   102, 213
Ventura, Lockheed   99
Voodoo, McDonnell F-101   162, 218
Vought A-7D Corsair II   191, 220
Vultee:
  A-31   102
  A-35 Vengeance   102, 213
  BT-13   74-75, 212
  BT-15 Valiant   74-75

W

Warhawk, Curtiss P-40   82-83, 212
Warning Star, Lockheed
  EC-121   120-121, 215
Workhorse, Piasecki (Vertol)
  H-21   144, 217

X

XB-15, Boeing   66, 211
XB-19, Douglas   91, 213
XB-35, Northrop   125, 215
XB-42 Mixmaster, Douglas   114, 214
XB-43, Douglas   114, 214
XB-70 Valkyrie, North
  American   178-179, 219
XF-85 Goblin, McDonnell   132, 216
XP-55 Ascender, Curtiss   101, 213
XP-77, Bell   116, 215

Y

YB-49, Northrop   125, 215
YF-12, Lockheed   184-185
YFM-1 Airacuda, Bell   70, 211